SPEECH COMMUNICATION READER

Marcus L. Ambrester
Faye D. Julian

The University of Tennessee

Waveland Press, Inc.
Prospect Heights, Illinois

For information about this book, write or call:

Waveland Press, Inc.
P.O. Box 400
Prospect Heights, Illinois 60070
(312) 634-0081

Contents

Section II

Preface

Human beings communicate verbally and nonverbally in a variety of ways and in a number of situations. Conversations, interviews, committee meetings, public speeches, television newscasting and private meditation have one thing in common: *speech communication*. It is our purpose to introduce the beginning student to this multidimensional field.

This collection of readings is intended to supplement class lectures on the theory and practice of speech communication. The selections represent various perspectives and approaches to the field. They are intended to stimulate personal thought and class discussion. The exclusion of various forms of speech communication (e.g., organizational, intercultural, and mass communication) in no way suggests that these are not worthy topics for consideration. Rather, we have tried to present a body of material that seems manageable in the span of a quarter or semester.

Section one offers definitions and explanations of human communication in general and speech communication in particular. The purpose of this section is to acquaint the student with the breadth of speech communication as a field of study, to present communication concepts, and to examine the components of the speech communication process—verbal communication, nonverbal communication, and listening.

The second section is divided into four speech communication experiences: intrapersonal communication (with oneself), interpersonal communication (with another person or persons), group communication, and public speaking. This last section on public speaking comes closest to a "how-to" division. Materials on preparing a beginning speech are followed by examples of speechmaking.

The selections in this reader are merely a sampling of the wealth of materials available in speech communication. They have proved to be stimulative to students in our introductory speech communication classes, and we feel they afford opportunity for discussion and disagreement. We have found the symposium to be an exciting participatory class exercise, and we have also used demonstration debates and speeches to illustrate some of the selections. The inclusion of poetry is a means of artistically representing some of the ideas we wish to underscore.

We are indebted to our students in the introductory speech communication classes at the University of Tennessee for their comments on
the selections in this book. We are grateful to our colleagues in the
department of speech and theatre for their encouragement, and we especially wish to thank Norma Cook for her helpful suggestions on
revision.

We wish to thank the personnel at Waveland Press, particularly Neil
Rowe, for their interest. For granting us permission to reprint articles
and poems, we would like to thank the authors and copyright holders
who made this book possible. Our special thanks to the Aluminum
Company of America, the Sperry Corporation, Ann Leslie Moore, Paul
Soper, and Blanche Weinberg.

MLA
FDJ

Section I

Explaining Speech Communication

Introduction

How does one explain a phenomenon as complex as speech communication? Sandburg would probably reply, "Very carefully." Some theorists use models, others examples, to illustrate the activity we know as speech communication. Both words (*speech* and *communication*) are familiar to you; each has been in your vocabulary for many years. So you probably already know what the term means; no explanation is necessary. But indulge us a bit as we point out some of the unique aspects of this very ordinary activity.

Two distinguishing characteristics of the human animal are an ability to speak and a propensity to use (and misuse) symbols. The speech act is considered a key to the thinking capacity of humans — an indication of a highly developed nervous system and brain. The physiological processes involved in speech production have other functions, but humans developed verbal codes by adapting the breathing apparatus, resonators, vocal folds, lips, tongue, teeth, hard palate, soft palate for purposes other than the ones they ordinarily served (e.g., breathing, chewing, etc.).

Speech is more than the production of sound. It is the unique human ability to transform sound into symbol. We are the only animals possessed by a fully developed language — that is, a symbol system that is both practical and poetic. Kenneth Burke, leading persuasionist and theorist, says that to be human is to possess and be possessed by language. As one of our defining characteristics, language does not stand for some human state. It becomes that state.[1] Brown and Van Riper vividly describe the significance of this act:

> Speech is the most unique and the most universal of human functions, yet, because it is so commonplace, so natural, so easy, few of us appreciate its enormous power and potential. It is our supreme tool, but like the ape who employs a flute to scratch itself, we have not yet learned

[1]Kenneth Burke, *Permanence and Change*. Los Altos, California: Hermes Publications, 1954.

1

all the uses for this greatest of human inventions. Only a handful of us ever learn to use this tool for more than the most primitive of its functions; to that handful we give the fruits of the earth and our worship. Consider how barren our histories of civilization would be had our great men never learned to talk.[2]

Perhaps now Sandburg's admonition to the little girl is a bit more understandable. When she speaks greetings, or tells jokes, or prays, she is using a potent instrument. She also has other instruments at her disposal which are potentially more powerful than the words or speech she employs. In fact, she possesses another language, another symbol system, and it is nonverbal. The ability to communicate with gestures, body stance, touch, space, clothing, and even silence has become fascinating study for both the expert and the layperson.

The modern field of speech communication deals with all aspects of human communicative behavior. We might explain speech communication, then, as an exchange of symbols, which may be verbal or nonverbal. When we exchange these symbols (or communicate), we are trying to establish a common bond. That is, we try to share information, feelings, ideas. In modern parlance, we try to relate. We send symbols, or messages, and hope they arrive at their destination in the manner we intended. Theorists have reduced this process to a simple objective linear operation which stresses the constituent elements of sender, receiver, message, and channel.

However, speech communication involves more than identification of its parts. DeVito says that human communication is "a means of achieving mutual understanding, a means for relating to each other on a more meaningful level, a means of *communion*."[3] This sharing and participation, the intimate rapport, are parts of the psychological perspective of human communication.

There is also a sociological basis for speech communication: the human need to belong. According to psychologist William Schutz, our most basic needs as humans are inclusion, control, and affection.[4] All three of these are rooted in our capabilities as communicators.

An examination of the varied approaches (e.g., physiological, psychological, sociological) provides no common denominator to simplify the process of human communication, for each scholar in each discipline views the concept from his/her particular and peculiar vantage point. That perspective might not be shared by all members of the given field much less by colleagues in other fields.

[2]Charles Brown, and Charles Van Riper. *Speech and Man.* Englewood Cliffs, N.J.: Prentice-Hall, 1966, pp. 1-2.
[3]Joseph DeVito, *Communication: Concepts and Processes.* Englewood Cliffs, N.J.: Prentice-Hall, 1971, p. v.
[4]William C. Schutz, *The Interpersonal Underworld.* Palo Alto, California: Science and Behavior Books, 1966.

If there is any common ground for a meeting of minds concerning speech communication, it must be a concern for humanity and a humanistic approach to its study. An understanding of our past and our potential is bound up with our understanding of communication — its subject matter, its relationship to various disciplines, its place in the humanities, its components and codes.

To explain this symbolic interaction known as speech communication is not easy; to attempt it is perhaps foolhardy but also exciting. We are indeed fortunate that there have been attempts which are provocative and enlightening, comforting and disquieting. It is through the act of communication that we discover, test, express, and stimulate meaning. This unique process, in its production, purposes, and consequences, sets us apart from other animals and allows us to be like Sandburg's little girl, "whatever we wish to be."

Little Girl, Be Careful What You Say

Carl Sandburg

Little girl, be careful what you say
when you make talk with words, words—
for words are made of syllables
and syllables, child, are made of air—
and air is so thin—air is the breath of God—
finer than water or moonlight,
finer than spider-webs in the moon,
finer than water-flowing in the morning:
    and words are strong, too,
    stronger than rocks or steel
stronger than potatoes, corn, fish, cattle,
and soft, too, soft as little pigeon-eggs,
soft as the music of hummingbird wings.
    So, little girl, when you speak greetings,
when you tell jokes, make wishes or prayers,
    be careful, be careless, be careful,
    be what you wish to be.

As part of a project to classify educational subject matter, members of the Speech Communication Association formulated a taxonomy of speech communication. The difficulty involved in this classification is indicative of the "growing pains" speech communication has experienced in recent years.

Defining Speech Communication

James H. McBath and Robert C. Jeffrey

Almost from the beginning of organized speech communication study members of the profession have sought agreement on conceptual constructs of the field. We have witnessed countless efforts to define "communication" or "rhetoric" or "persuasion." We shall doubtless see more. Recent presidents of our national association have announced their quest for "the central core" of speech communication study. We applaud all such efforts, past and future, as they are ways of stimulating the introspective analyses that are essential to discipline-building.

But at the same time that speech communication scholars have assiduously sought to explain themselves to each other, remarkably little of the explanation has been understood or accepted outside the profession. It is still possible, for example, for the HEGIS[1] Taxonomy to compress the field of speech communication into "speech, debate, and forensic science" within the discipline division of Letters or for the Carnegie Council on Policy Studies in Higher Education to include a

---

[1]Higher Education General Information Survey. This is the national taxonomy used for gathering and reporting statistical information related to enrollments, employment, earned degrees, and other data about higher education.

This selection is reprinted from *Communication Education*, Volume 27, September 1978. Dr. McBath is Professor and Chairman of Speech Communication at the University of Southern California. Dr. Jeffrey is Professor and Chairman of Speech Communication at the University of Texas at Austin. They recently served on the Communication Subject Matter Committee, an advisory body to Educational Management Services and the National Center for Education Statistics.

listing called "dramatics and speech" under the "Fine Arts" category. It is not an overstatement to observe that national public or private agencies rarely employ a description of speech communication and its constituent areas that are acceptable to any more than a fraction of our profession. Many taxonomies simply ignore the field.

The National Taxonomy Project

During the past several years, a sizeable national effort has been directed toward the development of a classification system for educational subject matter. The project affects all fields of study, with its most pronounced influence on newer academic areas and those whose parameters and content have been imperfectly understood. Speech communication clearly will be among those fields that will benefit from sharpened, official awareness of educational substance.

The aim of this article is to identify the motivating purposes of the educational classification project and to discuss the processes by which the project was accomplished. The discussion will deal with two dimensions: first, the omnibus project, including guidelines and constraints affecting the classification process, and then the activities and decisions that relate particularly to speech communication.

In July, 1975, Educational Management Services (EMS) of Minneapolis, Minnesota, was awared a contract by the National Center for Education Statistics (NCES)[2] to develop *A Classification of Educational Subject Matter*. The fundamental purpose of the document is to provide a classification of educational subject matter that currently exists from pre-elementary through post-doctoral studies. It updates subject matter elements as they are presently classified in local, state, and federal reporting documents. It seeks to enhance subject matter data record maintenance and reporting at all levels.

The document is not an inventory of instructional programs; it is a hierarchical array of the knowledge presently known to exist in American education. The document does not propose to serve as a framework for the organization of educational institutions or for academic departments or divisions.

Listed below are the twenty-two basic subject matter areas of the classification:

01 — Agriculture and Renewable Natural Resources

02 — Architecture and Environmental Design

03 — Arts, Visual and Performing

04 — Business

05 — Communication

---

[2]Established in 1965, NCES is charged with developing comprehensive statistics about the state of education in the United States. It is assigned to the office of the Assistant Secretary for Education.

06 — Computer Science and Data Processing

07 — Education

08 — Engineering and Engineering Technology

09 — Health Care and Health Sciences

10 — Home Economics

11 — Industrial Arts, Trades, and Technology

12 — Language, Linguistics, and Literature

13 — Law

14 — Libraries and Museums

15 — Life Sciences and Physical Sciences

16 — Mathematical Sciences

17 — Military Sciences

18 — Philosophy, Religion, and Theology

19 — Physical Education, Health Education, and Leisure

20 — Psychology

21 — Public Administration and Social Services

22 — Social Sciences and Social Studies

The lack of a commonly accepted taxonomy has handicapped agencies responsible for gathering material for educational information. Where classification documents did exist, their applicability often was limited to particular sectors or levels of education. But as students move across educational settings, either vertically through graduation and advancement, or laterally through change in educational objectives, it is essential to have comparable data relating to the courses or subject matter completed. Moreover, if it is required to determine the extent to which a particular subject matter is provided across the spectrum of education from kindergarten to postgraduate, the task can only be done if the descriptions, definitions, and hierarchical relationships between educational levels or settings are compatible.

The rationale for a new classification system for educational subject matter was based on considerations that included the following: (1) A uniform classification of subject material will facilitate the tracing of student progress through a lifelong educational continuum. (2) A uniform classification of subject matter, unencumbered by territorial descriptions, will facilitate student entry, transfer, exit, or re-entry into various educational settings. (3) A uniform classification will promote rapport among people having different interests and needs related to subject matter and instructural programs. (4) Standardized terminology will expedite communications about subject matter and related data among federal, state, and local governmental agencies; colleges and universities; religious institutions; business, industry, and labor; adult education organizations; and others involved in administering, operating, evaluating, and funding educational programs. (5) A uniform classification of subject matter can serve as a reference document. (6) A uniform classification of subject matter might assist legislators, educators, and the public to think in terms of program and subject matter categories as well as in terms of institutional characteristics.

Developing the Taxonomy

Assisting EMS in the development of the *Classification* was a twenty-member National Planning Council which advised on the project approach, the content and format of the document, and the numerical coding and classification structure. The National Planning Council was selected in 1975 from nominations submitted by educational associations whose members represented various levels of education; types of educational institutions; and/or educational agencies, consortia, or coordinating bodies.

Also involved in the development process were twenty-one Ad Hoc Subject Matter Committees whose members advised on the content of the document, its structure, and the definitions for the subject matter entries. Nominations for membership on the Ad Hoc Committees were sought from educational associations whose members were affiliated with specific subject matter areas. Recommendations were then sent to NCES for selection. In addition, NCES established a committee in Washington made up of people within the Center as well as from other federal agencies involved with educational data collection and reporting.

The document was produced in three drafts prior to submission in final form to NCES. The first draft was produced following an extensive review by EMS staff of the literature and of existing systems for classifying educational data. Federal and state classification documents and reporting forms were perused as were those of UNESCO, regional accrediting bodies, private agencies, and professional societies.

After the first draft was prepared, the Council and the Committees met to discuss the draft and to suggest revisions. Following review and emendations, EMS prepared a second draft eight months after the first. Again the document was submitted for review, and again the National Planning Council and the Ad Hoc Subject Matter Committees were called into session. The second review led to the production of a third draft which was mailed out six months after the second. The document then underwent review and modification by the National Planning Council and the Ad Hoc Subject Matter Committees.

A final copy of the *Classification of Educational Subject Matter* was submitted to NCES in July, 1977. Following a national field test, the document was released for use throughout the American educational community in July of 1978.

The Ad Hoc Subject Matter Committees were called into session two or three at a time. Thus meetings of the Communication Committee were concurrent with those of the Language, Linguistics, and Literature Committee. There was opportunity for joint meetings when questions of subject matter placement arose (e.g., language behavior, communication skills, etc.).

Committee members were asked first to examine the substance and form of the draft material prepared by EMS. If elements were missing, they were to be introduced by the committee. If the draft contained inappropriate or outdated elements, they were reconsidered, either to be discarded or considered elsewhere in the document.

Potential conflicts with other subject matter areas were identified early. If an element were considered an application of another subject matter element, it was attached to the one from which it had its genesis. For example, Business Statistics was classified under Mathematical Sciences rather than under Business. Economic History was, however, classified under Economics rather than under History. Parliamentary Procedure was placed under Speech Communication rather than under Law. If a subject matter element were thought to consist of two equal parts of different elements, it could be reported under the section called Multiple Subject Matter (Interdisciplinary).

If two committees laid claim to a subject matter element, it was treated in one of two ways. If the element were acknowledged to have its genesis in one subject matter area but considered essential to the composition of another, it was listed in both areas, defined in its genetic category, and cross-referenced to the other area. In the second instance, the element was listed under both contesting areas (e.g., Film as Art and Film as Communication).

The primary procedural objective of the project was to obtain declared consensus from representatives of all levels and types of education. It was acknowledged from the start that total agreement on content and definitions was not likely. For example, even the project itself, which classified subject matter into discrete categories, caused concern among several educators. When dealing with the substance of one's academic department, division, or school, some participants preferred to have aggregated together those elements with which they were associated or over which they exercised jurisdiction.

The integrity of subject areas was tested through application of several criteria. The first criterion was *maturity*. The subject matter elements had to have been in use long enough to be commonly understood and accepted throughout the educational community to which they were appropriate. New areas of knowledge were included if they were presently recognized by all members of the committee. Esoteric descriptions, sometimes self-serving attempts to retitle venerable subject-matter elements, were rejected.

A second criterion was that of *universality*, which suggested that the subject matter element be found throughout a broad range of educational settings. This would exclude, for example, limited offerings in a highly restricted program to which minimal resources would be devoted. Universality could apply in several ways. Certain subject matter could be found throughout the nation at specific levels or within special types of institutions as is the case with Law. On the other hand, subject matter may be generally found throughout many types of institutions, but within a restricted geographic area as with Forest Biology or Seismology.

The criterion of *magnitude* was also considered. Magnitude could be ascertained from numbers of students enrolled, number of classes taught, amount of resources consumed, or any other characteristic of size of number. At the same time, an indication of great magnitude would not of itself dictate the way in which subject matter would be handled. Even though a course may be taken by virtually all elementary and secondary students, it might still be subsumed under a broader designation.

The program vs. subject matter distinction proved to be troublesome to many of the Ad Hoc Committee members. A major reason for concern is that most of the current reporting relates to instructional programs. For the purposes of this project, an instructional program was defined as a plan of one or more courses or combination of courses and experiences that are designed to accomplish a predetermined objective or set of allied objectives such as qualification for advanced study, qualification for an occupation or range of occupations, or solely to increase knowledge or understanding. By definition, instructional programs relate to educational outcomes.

Instructional programs were differentiated from subject matter, which represents the substance of knowledge. Instructional programs, by contrast, represent the *form* or *style* by which knowledge is transmitted and received. Instructional programs can be defined in terms of the subject matter of which they are composed, but they are also structured around other experiences such as internships, practicums, and field study.

In identifying subject matter elements, Ad Hoc Committees used instructional programs as a reference point. Members were encouraged to specify what a person needed to know to successfully complete an instructional program or to qualify for a vocation or profession. It was interesting to contemplate that a sculptor may need the same knowledge of welding and may take the same welding courses as a body and fender repairman.

Even when the distinction between programs and subject matter was made, committee members sometimes were reluctant to release subject matter elements to other committees. There was a tendency to keep all program related elements in the same subject matter area. An instructional program in Nursing is a good example of the concern facing the

Committee members. To describe a program in Nursing according to its subject matter composition would quite likely require the aggregation of elements from the subject matter areas of Communication; Language, Linguistics, and Literature; Mathematical Sciences, Life Sciences and Physical Sciences; Social Sciences; and Health Care and Health Sciences. Specific courses typically are drawn from departments of Speech Communication, English, Mathematics, Biology, Physical Education, and Psychology.

Speech Communication Participation

The two speech communication representatives served on a 7-member Communication Committee whose concerns embraced the broad range of communication-related knowledge. Communication was defined as "subject matter concerned with the transmission, reception, and evaluation of messages." The main fields of communication study were determined to include the following:

> Advertising
> Communication Technology
> Film as Communication
> Innovative Communication
> International Communication
> Journalism
> Print Media
> Professional Practices in Communication
> Public Relations
> Radio
> Speech Communication
> Special Communication
> Television

The Communication Committee probably exercised greater latitude than did other committees since previous taxonomies often were sketchy or inaccurate (or both) in their treatment of communication fields. Committee members perhaps felt a stronger need to consult with acadmic colleagues than did members of fields that were better defined.

The first communication draft was mailed to about ninety SCA members, including officers, interest group leaders, members of key boards and committees, journal editors, and major textbook writers. Nearly all of the group responded, some with brief notes and others with detailed critiques. Many of the letters suggested that the initial draft had been discussed at department meetings. These suggestions formed the basis for a second draft that was mailed in August, 1976, to those who had responded to earlier calls for assistance plus others who had been recommended to provide expert opinion on particular issues. Also in August the Association for Communication Administration distributed the current version to its members for reaction and comment. Another meeting of the Communication Committee followed in September in Minneapolis. Again the subject areas and definitions were tested by other committee members and by EMS staff and, periodically, by representatives of the Language, Linguistics, and Literature Committee that was meeting concurrently.

The fourth generation of categories and definitions was printed in the December, 1976, issue of SPECTRA, eliciting reactions from persons who had not responded previously and from others who had been contributing critics from the beginning. The SCA representatives, Jeffrey and McBath, then met for a two-day session to weigh all recommendations in preparing the fifth and final version of the speech communication document for submission to EMS.

Our basic task was to represent fairly the consensus *ca.* 1977 on speech communication subject matter. For the most part, experts in subject areas as well as teachers were in greater agreement on the substance of a subject than on the language employed to describe it. The experts divided on subtle points of definition and relationship, much as rival textbooks tend to define key terms in slightly different ways. The evolution of one category over a two-year period may illustrate the process of development for the other categories as well. During the initial committee meeting in Minneapolis in early 1976, a category called "Speech Communication Instruction" was defined as "the study of knowledge and skills designed to develop student competencies in oral communication." During the following months, experts in speech communication education offered a variety of alternative definitions. For example:

— The study of the uses of speech communication in instruction and the development of student competence in speaking and listening.
— The study of the applications of speech communication in educational contexts, including the development of student competence in oral communication.
— The study of speech communication in instructional and educational contexts, its uses, applications, and strategies for individual development.
— The study of speech communication in teaching-learning contexts.
— The study of the interaction of educational theory and communication theory in the speech communication classroom.

The definition that will appear in the final classification document is: *The study of speech communication in pedagogical contexts.* It will include the sub-categories of Communication Development, Oral Communication Skills, and Instructional Communication.

When scholars had to confront and reconcile each other's

definitions, there typically was progress toward agreement. A useful outcome of the taxonomy project would be its fostering a common nomenclature and terminology for speech communication. Occasionally contributed were pet definitions, tautologies, or catchy titles from the home catalog. Since it would be unkind to provide a specific example, the point may be illustrated with an apocryphal submission: "Public address is the study of the heartpounding eloquence of yesteryear." Or again, "Organizational communication is the study of communication in organizations."

The most frequent negative comments stemmed from misunderstandings of the nature of the taxonomy or from incomplete understanding of its scope. In the former case, we were advised that the classification had ignored certain courses that had long appeared in the speech communication curriculum. We replied that the classification rule caused us to focus on subject matter rather than departmental courses or programs. In the second instance, it was pointed out that we had omitted some one area of speech communication study (e.g., theatre, communicative disorders, or language behavior). The areas, of course, were not omitted from the classification; they were placed under the first order categories in which the knowledge has its genesis. Thus, Theatre appears under Visual and Performing Arts, Communicative Disorders under Health Care and Health Sciences, and Language Behavior under Language, Linguistics, and Literature.

In summary, the project to develop A *Classification of Educational Subject Matter* sought to satisfy the need for a national data recording and reporting structure. In order to ensure responsiveness to the needs of the entire educational community, individuals from all levels and sectors were invited to participate in the construction of the document. The field of speech communication has had an unparalleled opportunity to define itself in terms acceptable to the professional community. Publication of the document can have profound consequences for the field. The finished document will serve as the only comprehensive array of knowledge as it is currently presented in American education, pre-elementary through post-graduate. The Speech Communication Taxonomy is as follows:

SPEECH COMMUNICATION

The study of the nature, processes, and effects of human symbolic interaction.

Code Systems

The study of the uses of verbal and nonverbal symbols and signs in human communication.

Intercultural Communication

The study of communication among individuals of different cultural backgrounds.

Interpersonal Communication

The study of communicative interaction occurring in person-to-person and small group situations.

— Conflict Management

The study of the role of communication in the creation and control of conflict.

Organizational Communication

The study of interrelated behaviors, technologies, and systems functioning within an organization.

Oral Interpretation

The study of literature through performance involving the development of skilled verbal and nonverbal expression based on critical analysis of written texts.

— Aesthetics of Literature in Performance

The study of the philosophy of art as it applies to and enhances the performance and evaluation of literature.

— Criticism of Literature in Performance

The study of the analysis and evaluation of literary texts in performance.

— Group Performance

The study of modes of adaptation and oral presentation of a literary text by two or more persons including performances utilizing music, sound, dance, and other paralinguistic effects.

— Oral Tradition

The study of the performance of various forms of verbal art in non-literate and literate societies.

Pragmatic Communication

The study and practice of communication, object of which is to influence or facilitate decision making.

— Argumentation

The study of the processes involved in the development of ideas through reasoned discourse.

— Debate and Forensics

The study of the application of forms of argument to test ideas or reach decisions.

— Discussion and Conference

The study of the principles and procedures employed in problem-solving and decision-making groups.

— Parliamentary Procedure

The study of codes and rules for the conduct of meetings or organizations in a democratic society, including, but not limited to, legislative bodies.

— Persuasion

The study of the principles and strategies of communication that are intended to modify attitudes and actions.

Public Address

The study of speakers and speeches, including the historical and social context of platforms, campaigns, and movements.

Rhetorical and Communication Theory

The study of the principles that account for human communicative experiences and behavior.

— Rhetorical Criticism
  The study of the application of theoretical and evaluative principles to communicative experiences and behavior.

Speech Communication Education

The study of speech communication in pedagogical contexts.

— Communication Development
  The study of the acquistion and use of speech communication skills by normal children.
— Oral Communication Skills
  The study of strategies for improving individual competencies in speaking and listening.
— Instructional Communication
  The study of communicative factors involved in the teaching-learning process.

Speech and Hearing Science

The study of the physiological and acoustical correlates of speech and hearing behavior.

— Biological Aspects of Speech and Hearing
  The study of the anatomy and physiology of speech and hearing mechanisms.
— Phonological and Phonetic Aspects of Speech and Hearing
  The study of the production and perception of verbal and nonverbal human sounds.
— Physical Aspects of Speech and Hearing
  The study of acoustic characteristics of motor speech production and of auditory perception.

Other Speech Communication

Defining Speech Communication

1. In what ways does the article demonstrate that defining the areas of speech communication is an arduous process?
2. Elaborate on the definition of speech communication. What is meant by "human symbolic interaction"?
3. How can one justify the study of nonverbal communication in a discipline entitled *speech* communication?
4. List some additional subject matter under the last category (Other Speech Communication).

*Stephen W. King's definition of speech communi-
cation is analogical. King defines speech communication in relation to its four similarities to
social influence.*

A Frame of Reference

Stephen W. King

Communication and social influence are intimately interrelated. One researcher concluded, for example, that "to study influence one must first study communication. For influence cannot occur without some form of communication" (Walter, 1963, p. 24). Similarly, "if one theme underlies all systems of communication, it is social influence" (Mortensen, 1972, p. 357). But just as the concepts of "love," "democracy," and "honorable peace," are easy to discuss at cocktail parties and in introductions to books but are often difficult to apply to reality, the concept of "communication" must be defined if its relationship to social influence is to be explored.

A Definition of Communication

Rather than survey all the definitions that have been proposed and try to select one from this definition delicatessen, we will stipulate a definition of communication that identifies the conditions necessary for an act of communication to be said to have occurred. That is, communication will be characterized rather than defined in the strictest sense.

The most fundamental characteristic of communication is *the assignation of meaning to behavior*. Communication, therefore, can be said to have occurred whenever one individual perceives another's behavior and attaches significance or meaning to his perception. Communication has occurred when you see another person direct an obscene gesture your way. Communication has occurred when for six consecutive years you don't receive a Christmas card from a "friend."

Communication has occurred when someone laughs at a joke you told. The next section will explore the points of similarity between social influence and communication.

Characteristics of Social Influence and Communication

Social influence and communication are both characterized by a number of fundamental attributes. Indeed, these processes share many of the same characteristics. Both processes are transactional in nature, both are inevitable results of social situations, both are receiver phenomena, and both are context-bound. Recognizing the importance of these shared characteristics is crucial to your understanding of social influence and communication.

Both Are Transactional Processes. A process point of view argues that neither social influence nor communication "has *a* beginning, *an* end, a fixed sequence of events. It is not static, at rest. It is moving. The ingredients within the process interact; each affects all the others" (Berlo, 1960, p. 24). The idea of process *"implies a continuous interaction of an indefinitely large number of variables with a concomitant, continuous change in the values taken by these variables"* (Miller, 1966, p. 33). If one attempts to examine a single element of a process (e.g., the organization of a message or the structure of a group exercising social influence), the isolation of that element distorts the nature of the on-going process and limits the information available about the element because it is out of its natural, changing environment. Most complex social phenomena are processes. The attraction you feel for your best friend, for example, cannot be analyzed in temporally discrete terms — it was, is, and will be continually evolving. It cannot even be asserted that your feeling "began" when you met the person, because the psychological frame of reference you use in evaluating people was the result of much prior experience.

All processes are difficult to explain. The necessary linearity of language usage (one word after another) virtually precludes accurate description of a process. Furthermore, in a real sense, process cannot be scientifically observed. That is, observation is necessarily limited to temporally successive observations (one can only observe aspects of the environment serially), thus severely restricting the study of events of process. Not only is the discussion and observation of process difficult, theorizing about a process is limited, for the most part, to focusing attention on an equilibrium state (Coleman, 1963, p. 68). That is, since it is virtually impossible to describe an on-going process, theory must "stop" the process to describe it. But just as the impossibility of achieving absolute zero has not substantially slowed the advance of physics, the process nature of communication and social influence does not preclude discussion, research, and theorizing about these processes. However, in the study of social influence and communication, those attempts at description, research, and theorizing that incorporate the process notion are the most fruitful.

Given this description of process, it is evident that both social influence and communication are processes. Both communication and social influence defy linear description. What is stimulus and what is response, who is sender and who is receiver, and what is cause and what is effect—all are judgments based on an arbitrary freezing of the system. A different stopping point could and generally does produce a quite different picture of the phenomenon: a still-life picture or representation of a process is simply inadequate. Take the case in which still-life pictures were used to describe a troubled marriage. The marriage, characterized by the husband's passive withdrawal and the wife's nagging criticism, was viewed in quite different ways by the partners. The wife saw her nagging as a reaction to her husband's withdrawal. On the other hand, the husband viewed his withdrawal as a defense against his wife's nagging. Who caused what? Each partner was stopping the on-going communication process to make a cause-effect conclusion that favored his/her innocence. In so doing, each distorted the actual process of communication.

The process viewpoint just presented contends that each participant in social interaction communicates with and affects the other and is affected by numerous continually changing forces. But it is clear that both participants are continually participating in this interaction. It is not accurate, therefore, to view such interaction as an on-off, let's-take-turns exchange. Rather, "all persons are engaged in sending (encoding) and receiving (decoding) messages simultaneously. Each person is constantly *sharing* in the encoding and decoding process, and each person is *affecting* the other" (Wenburg and Wilmot, 1973, p. 5). Communication and social influence are both characterized by *continually active interaction*. What you do, (yawn, laugh, show interest, etc.) for example, while the other person is talking affects the interaction as much as when you are speaking.

Both are Inevitable. Few individuals avoid the minimum social situation. Indeed, man continually seeks at least this minimal condition of human interaction in which one individual is within the perceptual field of another. Once this minimal social situation obtains, two processes are inevitable—communication and social influence (Watzlawick, Beavin, and Jackson, 1967).

Behavior has no opposite. One cannot think of an antonym to behavior, with the possible exception of death. Thus, if one is alive, "one cannot not behave." Furthermore, all behavior has potential message value. That is, behavior has the potential of having others attach significance or meaning to it. Thus, if all behavior *can* communicate and man cannot avoid behaving, "one cannot not communicate." What, for example, could you do in response to your fiance's question "Do you love me?" that would not have meaning attached to it? Obviously, anything you said would have importance. What if you ignored the question? What if you laughed? Cried? Ran away? Hit her? Indeed, one cannot not communicate, as much as you might want to on occasion.

Not all behavior *does* communicate, but man must operate as if it did. Simply, the sender cannot control the behavior to which a receiver will attach meaning. An accidental burp in public, for example, may not have been heard or might have been heard and ignored, but most of us blush a little because it is possible that it might have communicated something about us. Unfortunately, we can't control whether it does, in fact, communicate or not. Therefore, since all behavior has the potential of communicating, and the determination of those behaviors which do communicate rests solely with the receiver, the sender must accept the possibility that all of his behavior is communicating. For example, the fact that you may have an unusual "tic" or eye twitch is probably of little import to most, but a psychiatrist will probably attach great significance to such a quirk. This fact of social interaction puts man in a position similar to that of the advertising executive who once remarked that he knew that 50 percent of his advertising was ineffective, but since he didn't know which 50 percent it was, he was forced to continue running all of it. In sum, man simply cannot "turn off" communication as he can a water faucet.

If communication is usually inevitable, so is influence. "To say that influence occurs is to insist that some necessary effects, outcomes, or consequences function as defining attributes of communication" (Mortensen, 1972, p. 357). Even if communication does not result in gross behavioral change or drastic opinion modification, the perception of behavior and assignment of meaning to that behavior "has an accumulative impact on the meaning of *whatever* is said and done" (Mortensen, 1972, p. 358). Meaning is learned through experiences with the symbol, and each experience with symbolic behavior refines the meaning of that symbol. Thus, whether subtle or drastic, communication cannot avoid changing the state of the receiving organism: one cannot not influence. What, for example, would you think if you walked into a lecture hall and all of the students were sound asleep? Wouldn't you conclude that the lecture was boring and then either leave or join the crowd and take a nap? What if all the students were on the edge of their seats in concentrated attention? Wouldn't you probably stay and see what was so interesting? Is there any behavior of that audience that wouldn't have meaning for you and at least partially determine (influence) your behavior?

When man enters a minimal social situation and attempts to understand the situation by attaching meaning or some interpretation to the objects of his social environment, communication and social influence are inevitable.

Both are Receiver Phenomena. For communication and social influence to occur, the receiver must be affected. *The receiver* assigns meaning to behavior. *The receiver* changes. Alternatively, one could assert that neither communication nor social influence is a sender phenomenon; try as one will, neither communication nor social influence will occur without another individual.* These concepts differ, it should be noted, from concepts such as "love," "hate," or "envy." One can love, hate, or envy another without the object of one's emotion being aware of the emotion. Furthermore, the fact that the object of one's emotion is unaware of its existence in no way diminishes the reality of the feeling. Social influence and communication, on the other hand, take place *in* the receiver.

If you saw one of your professors downtown, for instance, and said "Hi" to him and he failed to respond, you might well conclude that he ignored you on purpose. Your anger at this rebuff might result in your skipping that professor's class for a week. Now both the meaning assigned to the behavior and the ultimate influence of the social slight were due to and took place within you. The communication ("He hates me") and the influence (skipping class) occurred in the receiver. This example illustrates two additional characteristics of social influence and communication which will determine the way each process is viewed. First, the intention of the communicator, or influencer, is irrelevant to the determination of the existence of the process.** Communication has occurred, whether or not one intends to communicate with another, if the receiver attaches meaning to the communicator's behavior. Though probably unintentionally, your professor communicated with and influenced you. Second, in neither communication nor social influence is the receiver a passive respondent; rather, he is actively involved. The receiver does not merely react to the behavior in his perceptual field as an amoeba does to light; he activates his entire person in the process of interpretation. In so doing, the meaning ultimately attached to a perception and any resultant change in internal state are as much a result of the individual himself as is the environment which initiated the need for interpretation. That is, one's psychological environment is, functionally, only that which he created. To digress for a moment, if you were predisposed to like that particular professor in the first place, you might have interpreted the professor's behavior as reflecting the fact that he didn't hear you say "hi." If that meaning was assigned to the behavior, you probably would not have been influenced to skip class. Behavior does not carry inherent communicative meaning or necessary influence; both are the products of an active perceiver.

*Of course, we do communicate with ourselves—*intrapersonal* communication. In this case, however, an individual is functioning as both source and receiver.

**The intention of the sender does become relevant, however, in the determination of success, the correspondence between the desired and the achieved outcomes.

Both are Context-Bound. Neither communication nor social influence can exist independent of context. Just as one cannot give a speech without content (despite the apparent attempts by some politicians to do just that), social influence must occur someplace. Researchers and theorists in both communication and social influence have recognized this characteristic of social interaction. Referring to the process of persuasion, Fotheringham (1966) remarked, "Contextual factors, rather than the message, often become the major determinants of response" (p. 46). Brockreide (1970) noted that the rhetorical act is the interrelationship of "interpersonal, attitudinal, and situational factors" (p. 26). Eskola (1961), in a study of social influence, asserted that "the fact that x exerts influence on y in a situation z can be expressed through the three-termed sentential function xyz (x influences y in situation z). Influence itself (V_{xyz}) is consequently a function of three factors" (p. 22).

What happens when the context is changed? Isn't is probable that a sergeant would get a different reaction from a private to the command "Do 30 push-ups!" when they were both on duty than when they were both in a tavern in town? Is telling "a little white lie" the same at a cocktail party as it is in a courtroom? Would you prefer to solicit funds for cancer research by going door to door in your neighborhood or by making your "pitch" to visitors to a cancer research and treatment facility? Obviously, context affects the processes of social influence and communication.

There are at least two readily identifiable contexts—the physical context (those objectively verifiable factors such as room color, furniture arrangement, temperature, etc.) and the functional context (the perception and interpretation of the physical context plus the psychological, sociological, and cultural environment that each individual brought to the immediate situation). As will be demonstrated throughout this book, not only is it possible for both types of contexts to alter the processes of communication and social influence, but often the context can almost totally account for observed behavior. Understanding when the context, either physical or functional, inhibits, complements, or obviates the processes of communication and social influence is one of the major goals of this book.

Communication and Social Influence: Isomorphic Processes

To this point we have arrived at the following conclusions:

1. Social influence cannot occur without communication.
2. Social influence is the inevitable result of communication.
3. Communication is the process of assigning meaning to behavior.
4. Social influence is the process by which the behavior of one or more individuals induces change in the state of another individual or group of individuals.

5. Both social influence and communication:
   a) are transactional processes.
   b) are inevitable in social situations
   c) are receiver phenomena.
   d) are context-bound processes.

Are these processes really one process masquerading as two separate, independent processes? Are they functionally equivalent? Has academia been duplicating efforts by studying the car on one hand and the automobile on the other? Or, is one process a subset of the other, as a terrier is a subset of the class of dogs? Does one process focus on means and the other on ends? Obviously, the answers to these questions are crucial to further investigation.

The concept of social influence includes all instances in which the behavior of one person induces changes in the state of another person. To do so, however, the behavior of the first individual must be attended to and have meaning attached to it by another, which is the minimal condition of communication. Therefore, all social influence involves communication. For example, earlier in this chapter Clyde was influenced by four confederates of an experimenter, but only because those four behaved in a way that meant something to Clyde—they said "C." Could the other four have influenced Clyde without doing something Clyde wouldn't interpret or attach meaning to? Probably not.

Similarly, as communication inevitably results in the alteration of the state of the individual perceiver, all communication involves social influence. Even if it is only the addition to a person's experience with a symbol, all communication influences. Thus, just as a consideration of dominance involves the consideration of submissiveness, and vice versa, *the processes of communication and social influence are isomorphic, or equivalent.* They are inseparable aspects of an undifferentiated social process.

Questions:

1. What is the basis for King's argument that social influence cannot occur without communication?
2. What is the nature of the influence of communication in the following social situations:
   a. in a college classroom
   b. at the dinner table in your home
   c. in your bedroom as you dress for the day
   d. at a political rally

   e. in your car at a drive-in theatre
      (1) with your mother
      (2) with your girl/boyfriend
      (3) with someone you personally dislike
      (4) with your younger sister and her boyfriend
3. In what ways would you like to change your communication "style" in social situations?

Confronted with the question, "What is speech communication?", many in the discipline find themselves lacking an appropriate response. In his article, Marlier suggests a strategy for answering the question. In addition, he calls for more cross-disciplinary research.

What Is Speech Communication, Anyway?

John T. Marlier

The Problem of Disciplinary Identity

Virtually everyone involved in the discipline of speech communication is, at some time, approached by either a stranger or a colleague from another discipline and asked to explain, in twenty-five words or less, just what speech communication is, anyway. Some of these interrogators are sincerely motivated and genuinely curious about what we in speech communication do and how our work relates to that of scholars in other disciplines. For others, the question serves as a conversational entree which provides the questioner with the opportunity to explain to us what we do and to more or less forcefully suggest that we have no legitimate disciplinary identity and ought, therefore, to disband and allow the other, more established departments on campus to divvy-up our budget allocations as a way of promoting more legitimate academic enterprise. Whichever type is represented, if the questioner approaches three members of our discipline, three different and more or less inconsistent responses are likely to be obtained.

As a result, these colleagues from other disciplines frequently conclude, with varying degrees of reluctance, that we really do not know what we are about and that we therefore cannot realistically expect

This selection is reprinted with permission from *Communication Education*, Volume 29, September 1980.
John T. Marlier is Assistant Professor of Speech Communication at Northeastern University.

academicians from other disciplines to figure out how our work might relate to theirs. Consequently, many of our academic colleagues remain unaware both of the possible benefits of incorporating our pedagogical offerings into their curricula and of the potential for synergy in cross-disciplinary research efforts involving researchers in speech communication.

We in speech communication are too often perceived as being content to view speech communication as a disunified field rather than as a discipline with an agreed-upon focus which unites us. Unfortunately, this perception of our academic self-concept is also too often an accurate one.

It should, perhaps, be noted that to argue for acceptance of an agreed-upon focal point around which our disciplinary identity is established is *not* equivalent to arguing for homogenization of our research methodologies, fields of specialization, or theoretical perspectives. Psychology and sociology, for example, have disciplinary identities. With regard to methodologies, psychologists and sociologists employ a great variety. Fields of specialization also vary widely in these disciplines, and the competition between conceptual schema and theoretical perspectives in these (or any other) disciplines is the source of their vitality and development. Any healthy discipline, in fact, will exhibit diversity in all of these areas.

What speech communication has lacked, that other disciplines have and which is the basis for their disciplinary identity, is a general agreement, both within and outside the discipline, as to the *kinds of questions* which are properly addressed by the practitioners of those disciplines.

The purpose of this essay is to delineate a kind of question which is properly addressed by a practitioner in the discipline of speech communication. Agreement as to this focal point within the discipline and advertisement of this agreement to academicians outside the discipline would facilitate the realization of the potential synergy of our cross-disciplinary pedagogical and research efforts, especially the latter. Before defining this focal point, however, it will be helpful to delineate some of the problems associated with the currently common perception of speech communication as a disunified field.

Relationships with Other Disciplines

When speech communication courses have been included in the curricula of other departments, the inclusion has typically been the result of (1) a general recognition both within and outside the discipline that oral competency is a universally needed life skill and (2) internal agreement within a particular speech communication department that their basic courses should develop a student's oral communication competency. Many of our curricular offerings (and our research efforts), however, deal with non-oral communicative phenomena. Consequently, the recognition that some of our courses develop necessary oral communication competency has not let to a generally recognized disciplinary identity.

Cross-disciplinary research efforts involving cooperation between researchers from other disciplines and researchers in speech communication, when they have occurred, have often been associated with perceptions on the part of the researchers from other fields that their collaborators are closet colleagues. Many speech communication scholars specialize in the study of communicative phenomena within specific contexts. These specialists often utilize concepts, research methodologies, and jargon borrowed from another discipline which studies what happens in some particular context. Consequently, such specialists are seen by colleagues from that other discipline (and, too often, by themselves as well) as misplaced political scientists (or sociologists, or psychologists, etc.). Cross-disciplinary research efforts, therefore, have frequently served to reinforce the image of speech communication as a disunified field rather than to stimulate an awareness on the part of colleagues from other disciplines that a specialized understanding of the process of communication, built upon conceptual schema and research methodologies appropriate to the examination of that process across contexts, is a valuable addition to any contextually specific research effort in which the subject being examined exhibits changes over time stimulated by, and accomplished through, communication.

Speech communication scholars who specialize in the study of communicative phenomena in particular contexts, therefore, have inadvertently promoted the misconception that what a speech communication scholar brings to a collaborative research effort is a specialized knowledge *within* a collaborator's discipline rather than a separate but valuable scholarly perspective.

Relationships within the Discipline

Researchers in speech communication with exclusive special interests in areas defined by the context in which communication occurs, who borrow conceptual frameworks, research methods, and jargon from other disciplines which study those contexts, have also inadvertently contributed to problems within our discipline. Some departments of speech communication have come to resemble Towers of Babel, in which there are minimal interchanges among researchers studying similar communicative phenomena. The political communication specialist studying image making, the organizational communication researcher studying leadership styles, the specialist in educational communication examining the means by which a teacher establishes classroom control, and the specialist in interpersonal communication studying power in interpersonal relationships might all inform each other's work more than they have. To the extent that they have depended upon other disciplines for their concepts and methodologies, however, and to the extent to which they have been defensive of their own perspectives, the integration of existing knowledge and the accumulation of widely useful new knowledge of the communication process has been impeded. To the extent that this integration and accumulation has been impeded, the insights and fresh perspectives which a speech communication researcher brings to a collaborative effort with a researcher from another discipline, beyond those available within that other discipline, have been limited. The potential synergy of cross-disciplinary research has been, therefore, largely unrealized.

A Synergy Facilitating View of Speech Communication

The potential synergy of cross-disciplinary research efforts involving speech communication is high, and the fresh insights and perspectives which a speech communication scholar might bring to such an effort are numerous. To understand why this is so, however, it is necessary to make another effort at defining speech communication and its relationship to other disciplines.

Speech communication is not only a distinct discipline; it is also a distinct kind of discipline. When the field of natural philosophy was split into the myriad parts which we recognize today as distinct and financially competitive academic disciplines, the division was made largely in terms of which scholars were studying what happened in similar contexts. Natural, or hard, scientists, for example, study what happens in the natural world apart from man. Sociologists study what happens when man congregates. Political scientists study what happens when people attempt to govern themselves. In each case, the central question being addressed by a particular discipline is "What is happening?" within the content area or context which defines that discipline. Speech communication, on the other hand, is a discipline concerned with the study of a dynamic process which occurs in every social context. The general question which we properly address is not "What is happening?" in a particular context, but rather "How are things happening?" in every social context.

The line of disciplinary demarcation, then, is a simple albeit slippery one. Speech communication is a discipline which studies the dynamic interactive process through which changes are wrought in the social world. As such, it overlaps portions (but only portions) of many other disciplines. Its identity derives from its focus on process rather than content, and its strength derives from its cross-contextual generality.

Researchers in speech communication, therefore, are (or should be) specialized generalists. They are specialists in that they apply a set of conceptual tools and research methodologies which (regardless of whether they are humanistic or empirical) are informed by an awareness of the similarities and differences in *how* things happen across content areas or contexts and are designed to address a limited number of specialized questions within any one context. They are generalists in that they should feel at home addressing the question of *how* things happen in a wide range of contexts and content areas.

Researchers from other disciplines argue, of course, that their disciplines include not only the study of *what* is happening in their content areas, but also of *how* it is happening. In fact, virtually every discipline contains an area of specialization concerned with just such questions. But while there may be specialized scholars in other disciplines who concentrate on answering questions of how things happen, their study is confined to the content areas and contexts of that discipline. Their understanding of process is, therefore, uninformed by either an in-depth knowledge of the similarities and differences in the ways things happen across content areas and contexts or by knowledge of the various methodologies which have been developed specifically to address such questions in other contexts. These scholars could, therefore, benefit from collaboration with researchers in speech communication.

Some scholars *within* the field of speech communication, too, object to the idea of specialized generalization, but for different reasons. To suggest that researchers in our field should be specialized generalists, and thereby broaden their understanding of the similarities and differences in the communication process across content areas and contexts, appears at first glance to amount to suggesting that one should not do research in speech communication unless one is prepared to become omniscient. Obviously, examination of the communication process in any given context requires in-depth knowledge of the elements contained in that context and of the manifestations of variables which influence the communication process in that context. To expect a speech communication researcher to develop the requisite level of contextually specific knowledge to be able to conduct research in more than one or two content defined contexts would be unrealistic.

Specialized generalization, in other words, is not feasible for any individual researcher working alone, which is precisely why the researcher in speech communication should be constantly seeking collaborators in other disciplines with whom he or she can conduct research. Researchers in other fields *have* the specialized and in-depth knowledge of *what* is happening in those areas, which we need to enable us to address the question of *how* it is happening. But if we concentrate on the development of integrated, cross-contextual, and in-depth knowledge of *how* things happen, then we also bring to the collaborative effort resources which our collaborators could not otherwise obtain.

The potential for synergistic cooperation between scholars in the speech communication discipline and scholars in other disciplines, then, is great but largely unrealized. This potential is especially evident in the area of cross-disciplinary research. A major reason for the lack of realization of this potential is a common misconception, both within and outside our discipline, that speech communication lacks a central focus around which our disciplinary identity could be established. More widespread acceptance of a concern with process (with attempting to address questions as to *how* things happen across social contexts), as the focal point around which the disciplinary identity of speech communication *has* been established, would facilitate the realization of this potential.

Questions:

1. For speech communication scholars, what are the inherent problems regarding disciplinary identity?
2. What problems have arisen from the association of speech communication scholars with scholars in other disciplines?
3. What is the difference in a field and a discipline?
4. What is synergy?
5. Explain "specialized generalization." Is it a valid concept? Is it an oxymoron?

The study of spoken language is a necessity for the liberally educated person. Proficiency in spoken language provides the basis for enlightened choice, according to Dance.

Speech Communication as a Liberal Arts Discipline

Frank E.X. Dance

In its essence the argument for the academic viability and necessity of programs in the discipline of speech communication is simple and direct. The argument has four propositions:

Proposition 1: Human language is necessary, although insufficient, for the liberal education of human beings.

Proposition 2: Spoken language is the natural and primary manifestation of human language, from which written language is derived.

Proposition 3: Speech communication is the academic discipline that historically and presently has the study and practice of spoken language as its primary subject matter.

Proposition 4: Academic training and experience in speech communication result in improved understanding of and more effective use of spoken language.

The remainder of this essay shall treat each of these four propositions in turn.

Human language consists of words and of the syntactic arrangement of those words. Human words are symbols. Symbols are distinguished from signs in that symbols are arbitrary and are free from any necessary pair-wise association with the symbol's referent: e.g., a highly variable, carnivorous, domesticated mammal, probably de-

This selection is reprinted with permission from *Communication Education*, Volume 29, September 1980. Frank E.X. Dance is Professor of Speech Communication at the University of Denver.

scended from the common wolf, may, depending on the specific cultural manifestation of human language being used, be called "dog," or "chien," or "canus," or "perro," or any of a number of other arbitrary names. The human word/symbol facilitates a moving away, a decentering, from a rooting in infant egocentricity and a freedom from bondage to a specific time and/or place. Animals other than humans seem bound to the internal constraints of their being, whereas a human being, through the symbol, can step outside of him/herself, can step away from a specific time or place. This ability to move away from the immediacy of self, of moment, or of place is prerequisite to the development of a point of view, an overview, that fosters choice. If one is bound to a single point of self, of place, or of time, there is no way in which a choice can be made. However, if one has the ability to conceive of and to hold in memory and in vision points outside of oneself (points in other places or in other times), then the capacity for choice is fostered and mandated.

Thus, the symbol allows for choice. Choice is necessary for freedom. Intentional choice is the instrument of freedom, the instrument and the sign of liberation and of being liberated. The education which prepares a person to make wise choices in the pursuit of individual and social goals is a liberating, or liberal, education. Liberal education prepares one for the informed fulfillment of what seems to be an internal human imperative — the progressive acquisition of autonomy. Human beings, the more humanly they behave, demand ever-increasing control over their own individual and social destinies, ever-increasing autonomy and freedom from dependency. Individuals and groups of individuals have, across the ages, devoted themselves to loosening whatever constraints shackled their free expression of choice whether those constraints be of environment or of government. The success of a program of liberal education is reflected in the quality of an individual's choices across the life span. The understanding of human word/symbols, of human language, illuminates the understanding of such human intentional choice. The liberal arts thus must be concerned with the development and argumentation of the individual's capacity to use human language, to use symbols with respect for their power and with discrimination as to their ends, to use symbols knowingly and freely. The use of natural human language in general and then the use of derived human language, such as mathematics, philosophy, chemistry, history et al., constitute the liberal arts which allow the individual to gain ever-widening control over symbols and their specific applications. Technology can multiply human mobility in space and in time; the fine arts can expand human risk-taking proclivities by calling our attention to the implications of our technologically based opportunities, but the liberal arts have the primary responsibility for preparing human beings to make the informed choices which arise from technology and art.

The development of spoken language is the natural source, or familial pre-requisite, for an individual understanding of the meaning and power of the symbol, whether an individual's symbol or a social symbol. The development of spoken language, and the later development of spoken language's visual/motor derivatives (reading and writing), is an indispensible prior condition for all liberal educational experiences on any formal educational level. Human beings are born vocalizing and grow into spoken language. Human infants are born to engage in spoken language, that jointure of genetically determined speech with a specific, culturally determined language which allows a child to speak English, Dutch, Thai, or any one or combination of the thousands of cultural languages of the past and of the present. Human language is, in its natural origin, spoken, although many cultures have developed visual/motor representations, written forms of the originally spoken languages. Since spoken language underlies all other forms of human language, the more we understand about spoken language, and the more proficient we become in the use of spoken language, then the more understanding and control we should have in our pursuit of enlightened, intentional choice. The fact that human language is spoken, in its original state, is nontrivial to our understanding of human language in all of its manifestations. The fact that human language is originally and at root spoken is essential to our understanding of the effects of human language upon all human thought and human behavior.

Human beings always have appreciated the role played by spoken language in the achievement of individual and social human goals. The study of spoken language is one of the oldest of organized human studies, having an oral history before the evolution of the written form of spoken language. Even with the important advent of writing, the study of spoken language maintained a significant place in both informal and formal education. Spoken language, as a field of study, has had different disciplinary labels at different historical times. For the greatest portion of recorded human history (from ancient Greece to the second third of the nineteenth century), the study of spoken language was known as rhetoric and figured as one of the original liberal arts. From the middle 1800s to the present, the disciplinary label has undergone a number of transformations—from rhetoric to speech and now to speech communication. Each of these disciplinary foci (rhetoric, speech, and speech communication) has had as its main concern the study of spoken language and the improvement of the use of spoken language. Whereas the discipline of speech communication draws upon materials from numerous sources (a natural event since spoken language so permeates human behavior in all of human behavior's numerous manifestations), the study of spoken language itself has always been, and is now, the discipline's primary concern. Although sometimes taken to be eclectic, the discipline in reality is the study of a subject, i.e., spoken language, which has significant intellectual substance in its own right. Whatever the specific speech communication course, the discipline's focus on spoken language remains as a root constant. When speech communication, as a discipline, deals with the skills of spoken language, the treatment of those skills springs from avowed and stated theoretical bases. The life of the mind finds its source in the development of spoken language. It is an extraordinarily important reality that human beings share their thoughts through spoken language. It is even more important to understand that human thoughts are inextricably intertwined with human language. The field of speech communication studies the relationship between spoken language and human thought and then treats the manner in which human beings use spoken language to share their thoughts and their emotions. Speech communication courses may center upon either or both concerns.

At present the field of speech communication includes departments, programs, concentrations, and courses at all levels of formal education. Within these offerings one may find such familiar topics as argumentation, rhetoric, persuasion, and public speaking. Somewhat less familiar to many, yet still having a history and tradition, are courses in the spoken interpretation of literature, problem solving, conflict resolution, semantics, spoken language acquisition and behavior, and organizational speech communication. There are also courses dealing with topics such as animal communication and nonverbal communication, courses which study such topics as a means of examining what is unique to human communication. As in any discipline, researchers, scholars, and teachers have particularistic interests, all of which have as their goal the shedding of light upon human communication, communication which rests upon spoken language. In some departments, and in some courses, the spoken language base may become obscured—but this does not deny its presence. Students of speech communication have testified across the ages as to how their study of this discipline has aided their personal and professional lives. Rhetoricians, debaters, public speakers, persuaders, interpreters, conciliators, diplomats, teachers, scholars, and researchers who have studied spoken language, under the rubric of rhetoric or speech or speech communication, have testified as to how their study and practice have aided their pursuit of individual and social goals. Concentrated study of how spoken language interacts with thought assists the student both in conceptualization and in expression. Study of the techniques of public speaking helps the student to develop mental agility as well as spoken facility. Argumentation and debate, when studied both as theory and as practice, exalts acuity of thought as well as the presentation and defense of cases. The study of literary texts as a means of teasing out their meaning so as to provide the best spoken expression develops an interpretive skill that enhances the understanding of student both as speaker and as listener. The study of per-suasion helps the student to analyze the sources of conflict as well as some means for the resolution of honest differences. The utilization of the phenomenological method and the phenomenological stance for the study of spoken language, when joined with traditional methdological approaches, helps to uncover the basic processes of human communication. An understanding of the functions of spoken language aids the student in developing uniquely human social linkages, the development of higher mental processes, and the use of spoken language as a regulator of human behavior.

Enough! The ethical use of human language is essential to the liberal education of a human being. The understanding and acquisition of spoken language is the initial formative stage in the development of human language. Speech communication is the academic discipline having an historical and current commitment to the study of spoken language. Academic experiences and training in speech communication augment our understanding and use of spoken language.

The student who is denied study and experience in speech communication and in its subject matter of spoken language, is essentially denied the essence of a liberal education. Speech communication, the study of spoken language, is one of the foundations of a liberal education and is a basic requirement of all programs which intend to produce a liberally educated human and humane being.

Questions:

1. How does Dance distinguish between a sign and a symbol?
2. How does a symbol allow choice?
3. What is the subject matter of the discipline, according to Dance? Do you agree or disagree with him? Why?
4. What meaning does the term liberal arts hold for you? How important are liberal arts to your education?
5. In what ways can training in speech communication improve the quality of your life after you leave the university?

The axioms presented in this selection have become the bases of existing interpersonal communication theory. The distinction between digital and analogic communication sets up the progression of the next articles on verbal and nonverbal language.

Some Tentative Axioms of Communication

Paul Watzlawick, Janet Beavin, and Don Jackson

The Impossibility of Not Communicating

First of all, there is a property of behavior that could hardly be more basic and is, therefore, often overlooked: behavior has no opposite. In other words, there is no such thing as nonbehavior or, to put it even more simply: one cannot *not* behave. Now, if it is accepted that all behavior in an interactional situation[1] has message value, i.e., is communication, it follows that no matter how one may try, one cannot *not* communicate. Activity or inactivity, words or silence all have message value: they influence others and these others, in turn, cannot *not* respond to these communications and are thus themselves communicating. It should be clearly understood that the mere absence of talking or of taking notice of each other is no exception to what has just been asserted. The man at a crowded lunch counter who looks straight ahead, or the airplane passenger who sits with his eyes closed, are both communicating that they do not want to speak to anybody or be spoken to, and their neighbors usually "get the message" and respond

[1]It might be added that, even alone, it is possible to have dialogues in fantasy, with one's hallucinations (15), or with life (s. 8.3). Perhaps such internal "communication" follows some of the same rules which govern interpersonal communication; such as unobservable phenomena, however, are outside the scope of our meaning of the term.

appropriately by leaving them alone. This, obviously, is just as much an interchange of communication as an animated discussion.[2]

Neither can we say that "communication" only takes place when it is intentional, conscious, or successful, that is, when mutual understanding occurs. Whether message sent equals message received is an important but different order of analysis, as it must rest ultimately on evaluations of specific, introspective, subject-reported data, which we choose to neglect for the exposition of a behavioral-theory of communication. On the question of misunderstanding, our concern, given certain formal properties of communication, is with the development of related pathologies, aside from, indeed in spite of, the motivations or intentions of the communicants.

In the foregoing, the term "communication" has been used in two ways: as the generic title of our study, and as a loosely defined unit of behavior. Let us now be more precise. We will, of course, continue to refer to the pragmatic aspect of the theory of human communication simply as "communication." For the various units of communication (behavior), we have sought to select terms which are already generally understood. A single communicational unit will be called a *message* or, where there is no possibility of confusion, a communication. A series of messages exchanged between persons will be called *interaction*. (For those who crave more precise quantification, we can only say that the sequence we refer to by the term "interaction" is greater than one message but not infinite.)

Further, in regard to even the simplest possible unit, it will be obvious that once we accept all behavior as communication, we will not be dealing with a monophonic message unit, but rather with a fluid and multifaceted compound of many behavioral modes—verbal, tonal, postural, contextual, etc.—all of which qualify the meaning of all the others. The various elements of this compound (considered as a whole) are capable of highly varied and complex permutations ranging from the congruent to the incongruent and paradoxical. The pragmatic

---

[2]Very interesting research in this field has been carried out by Luft (98), who studied what he calls "social stimulus deprivation." He brought two strangers together in a room, made them sit across from each other and instructed them "not to talk or communicate in any way." Subsequent interviews revealed the highly stressful nature of this situation. To quote the author:

> ...he has before him the other unique individual with his ongoing, though muted, behavior. At this point, it is postulated, that true interpersonal testing takes place, and only part of this testing may be done consciously. For example, how does the other subject respond to him and to the small non-verbal cues which he sends out? Is there an attempt at understanding his enquiring glance, or is it coldly ignored? Does the other subject display postural cues of tension, indicating some distress at confronting him? Does he grow increasingly comfortable, indicating some kind of acceptance, or will the other treat him as if he were a thing, which did not exist? These and many other kinds of readily discernible behavior appear to take place....

effect of these combinations in interpersonal situations will be our interest herein.

The impossibility of not communicating is a phenomenon of more than theoretical interest. It is, for instance, part and parcel of the schizophrenic "dilemma." If schizophrenic behavior is observed with etiological considerations in abeyance, it appears that the schizophrenic tries *not to communicate*. But since even nonsense, silence, withdrawal, immobility (postural silence), or any other form of denial is itself a communication, the schizophrenic is faced with the impossible task of denying that he is communicating and at the same time denying that his denial is a communication. The realization of this basic dilemma in schizophrenia is a key to a good many aspects of schizophrenic communication that would otherwise remain obscure. Since any communication, as we shall see, implies commitment and thereby defines the sender's view of his relationship with the receiver, it can be hypothesized that the schizophrenic behaves as if he would avoid commitment by not communicating. Whether this is his purpose, in the causal sense, is of course impossible of proof; that this is the effect of schizophrenic behavior will be taken up in greater detail in s. 3.2.

To summarize, a metacommunicational axiom of the pragmatics of communication can be postulated: *one cannot not communicate.*

The Content and Relationship Levels of Communication

Another axiom was hinted at in the foregoing when it was suggested that any communication implies a commitment and thereby defines the relationship. This is another way of saying that a communication not only conveys information, but that at the same time it imposes behavior. Following Bateson (132, pp. 179-81), these two operations have come to be known as the "report" and the "command" aspects, respectively, of any communication. Bateson exemplifies these two aspects by means of a physiological analogy: let A, B, and C be a linear chain of neurons. Then the firing of neuron B is both a "report" that neuron A has fired and a "command" for neuron C to fire.

The report aspect of a message conveys information and is, therefore, synonymous in human communication with the *content* of the message. It may be about anything that is communicable regardless of whether the particular information is true or false, valid, invalid, or undecidable. The command aspect, on the other hand, refers to what sort of a message it is to be taken as, and therefore, ultimately to the *relationship* between the communicants. All such relationship statements are about one or several of the following assertions: "This is how I see myself...this is how I see you...this is how I see you seeing me..." and so forth in theoretically infinite regress. Thus, for instance, the messages "It is important to release the clutch gradually and

smoothly" and "Just let the clutch go, it'll ruin the transmission in no
time" have approximately the same information content (report
aspect), but they obviously define very different relationships. To avoid
any misunderstanding about the foregoing, we want to make it clear
that relationships are only rarely defined deliberately or with full
awareness. In fact, it seems that the more spontaneous and "healthy"
a relationship, the more the relationship aspect of communication
recedes into the background. Conversely, "sick" relationships are
characterized by a constant struggle about the nature of the relationship, with the content aspect of communication becoming less and less
important.

It is quite interesting that before behavioral scientists began to
wonder about these aspects of human communication, computer
engineers had come across the same problem in their work. It became
clear to them that when communicating with an artificial organism,
their communications had to have both report and command aspects.
For instance, if a computer is to multiply two figures, it must be fed this
information (the two figures) and information about this information:
the command "multiply them."

Now, what is important for our consideration is the relation existing
between the content (report) and the relationship (command) aspects of
communication. In essence it has already been defined in the preceding
paragraph when it was mentioned that a computer needs *information*
(data) and *information about this information* (instructions). Clearly,
then, the instructions are of a higher logical type than the data; they
are *metainformation* since they are information *about* information, and
any confusion between the two would lead to a meaningless result.

If we now return to human communication, we see that the same
relation exists between the report and the command aspects: the
former conveys the "data" of the communication, the latter how this
communication is to be taken. "This is an order" or "I am only joking"
are verbal examples of such communications about communication.
The relationship can also be expressed nonverbally by shouting or
smiling or in a number of other ways. And the relationship may be
clearly understood from the context in which the communication takes
place, e.g., between uniformed soldiers, or in a circus ring.

The reader will have noticed that the relationship aspect of a communication, being a communication about a communication, is, of
course, identical with the concept of metacommunication elaborated in
the first chapter, where it was limited to the conceptual framework
and to the language the communication analyst must employ when communicating about communication. Now it can be seen that not only he
but everyone is faced with this problem. The ability to metacommuni-
cate appropriately is not only the *conditio sine qua non* of successful
communication, but is intimately linked with the enormous problem of
awareness of self and others. This point will be explained in greater

detail in s. 3.3. For the moment, and by way of illustration, we merely want to show that messages can be constructed, especially in written communication, which offer highly ambiguous metacommunicational clues. As Cherry (34, p. 120) points out, the sentence "Do you think that one will do?" can have a variety of meanings, according to which word is to be stressed—an indication that written language usually does not supply. Another example would be a sign in a restaurant reading, "Customers who think our waiters are rude should see the manager," which, at least in theory, can be understood in two entirely different ways. Ambiguities of this kind are not the only possible complications arising out of the level structure of all communication; consider, for instance, a notice that reads "Disregard This Sign." As we shall see in the chapter on paradoxical communication, confusions or contaminations between these levels—communication and meta-communication—may lead to impasses identical in structure to those of the famous paradoxes in logic.

For the time being let us merely summarize the foregoing into another axiom of our tentative calculus: *Every communication has a content and a relationship aspect such that the latter classifies the former and is therefore a metacommunication.*[3]

Symmetrical and Complementary Interaction

In 1935 Bateson (6) reported on an interactional phenomenon which he observed in the Iatmul tribe in New Guinea and which in his book *Naven* (10), published a year later, he dealt with in greater detail. He called this phenomenon *schismogenesis* and defined it as *a process of differentiation in the norms of individual behavior resulting from cumulative interaction between individuals.* In 1939 Richardson (125) applied this concept to his analyses of war and foreign politics; since 1952 Bateson and others have demonstrated its usefulness in the field of psychiatric research (Cf. 157, pp. 7-17; also 143). This concept, which, as we can see, has a heuristic value beyond the confines of any one discipline, was elaborated by Bateson in *Naven* as follows:

> When our discipline is defined in terms of the reactions of an individual to the reactions of other individuals, it is at once apparent that we must regard the relationship between two individuals as liable to alter from time to time, even without disturbance from outside. We have to consider, not only A's reactions to B's behaviour, but we must go on to consider how these affect B's later behaviour and the effect of this on A.

[3]We have chosen, somewhat arbitrarily, to say that the relationship classifies, or subsumes, the content aspect, although it is equally accurate in logical analysis to say that the class is defined by its members and therefore the content aspect can be said to define the relationship aspect. Since our primary interest is not information exchange but the pragmatics of communication, we will use the former approach.

It is at once apparent that many systems of relationship, either between individuals or groups of individuals, contain a tendency towards progressive change. If, for example, one of the patterns of cultural behaviour, considered appropriate in individual A, is culturally labelled as an assertive pattern, while B is expected to reply to this with what is culturally regarded as submission, it is likely that this submission will encourage a further assertion, and that this assertion will demand still further submission. We have thus a potentially progressive state of affairs, and unless other factors are present to restrain the excesses of assertive and submissive behavior, A must necessarily become more and more assertive, while B will become more and more submissive; and this progressive change will occur whether A and B are separate individuals or members of complementary groups.

Progressive changes of this sort we may describe as *complementary* schismogenesis. But there is another pattern of relationships between individuals or groups of individuals which equally contains the germs of progressive change. If, for example, we find boasting as the cultural pattern of behaviour in one group, and that the other group replies to this with boasting, a competitive situation may develop in which boasting leads to more boasting, and so on. This type of progressive change we may call *symmetrical* schismogenesis (10, pp. 176-77)

The two patterns just described have come to be used without reference to the schismogenetic process and are now usually referred to simply as symmetrical and complementary interaction. They can be described as relationships based on either equality or difference. In the first case the partners tend to mirror each other's behavior, and thus their interaction can be termed *symmetrical.* Weakness or strength, goodness or badness, are not relevant here, for equality can be maintained in any of these areas. In the second case one partner's behavior complements that of the other, forming a different sort of behavioral Gestalt, and is called *complementary.* Symmetrical interaction, then, is characterized by equality and the minimization of difference, while complementary interaction is based on the maximization of difference.

There are two different positions in a complementary relationship. One partner occupies what has been variously described as the superior, primary, or "one-up" position, and the other the corresponding inferior, secondary, or "one-down" position. These terms are quite useful as long as they are not equated with "good" or "bad," "strong" or "weak." A complementary relationship may be set by the social or cultural context (as in the cases of mother and infant, doctor and patient, or teacher and student), or it may be the idiosyncratic relationship style of a particular dyad. In either case, it is important to emphasize the interlocking nature of the relationship, in which dissimilar but fitted behaviors evoke each other. One partner does not impose a complementary relationship on the other, but rather each behaves in a manner which presupposes, while at the same time providing reasons for, the behavior of the other: their definitions of the relationship (s.2.3) fit.

A third type of relationship has been suggested—"metacomplementary," in which A lets or forces B to be in charge of him; by the same reasoning, we could also add "pseudosymmetry," in which A lets or forces B to be symmetrical. This potentially infinite regress can, however, be avoided by recalling the distinction made earlier (s. 1.4) between the observation of behavioral redundancies and their inferred explanations, in the form of mythologies; that is, we are interested in *how* the pair behave without being distracted by why (they believe) they so conduct themselves. If, though, the individuals involved avail themselves of the multiple levels of communication (s. 2.22) in order to express different patterns on different levels, paradoxical results of significant pragmatic importance may arise (s. 5.41; 6.42, ex. 3; 7-5, ex. 2d).

The potential pathologies (escalation in symmetry and rigidity in complementarity) of these modes of communication will be dealt with in the next chapter. For the present, we can state simply our last tentative axiom: *All communicational interchanges are either symmetrical or complementary, depending on whether they are based on equality or difference.*

Summary

Regarding the above axioms in general, some qualifications should be re-emphasized. First, it should be clear that they are put forth tentatively, rather informally defined and certainly more preliminary than exhaustive. Second, they are, among themselves, quite heterogeneous in that they draw from widely ranging observations on communication phenomena. They are unified not by their origins but by their *pragmatic* importance, which in turn rests not so much by their *pragmatic* importance, which in turn rests nos so much on their particulars as on their *interpersonal* (rather than monadic) reference. Birdwhistell has even gone so far as to suggest that

> an individual does not communicate; he engages in or becomes part of communication. He may move, or make noises...but he does not communicate. In a parallel fashion, he may see, he may hear, smell, taste, or feel—but he does not communicate. In other words, he does not originate communication; he participates in it. Communication as a system, then, is not to be understood on a simple model of action and reaction, however complexly stated. As a system, it is to be comprehended on the transactional level. (28, p. 104)

Thus, the impossibility of not communicating makes all two-or-more-person situations *interpersonal*, communicative ones; the relationship aspect of such communication further specifies this same point. The pragmatic, interpersonal importance of the digital and analogic modes lies not only in its hypothesized isomorphism with content and relationship, but in the inevitable and significant ambiguity which both sender and receiver face in problems of translation from the one mode to the other. The description of problems of punctuation rests precisely on the underlying metamorphosis of the classic action-reaction model. Finally, the symmetry-complementarity paradigm comes perhaps closest to the mathematical concept of *function*, the individuals' positions merely being variables with an infinity of possible values whose meaning is not absolute but rather emerges only in relation to each other.

Questions:

1. Does the idea that you are always communicating make you apprehensive about your communication?

2. In what ways are the contents of a message affected by the relationship between the communicants? Conversely, how is the relationship between the communicants affected by the contents of the message?

3. Why is it difficult to define relationships with full awareness? How might the content of the message serve to mask the actual relationship?

4. What are the differences in anaological and digital communication?

Human beings are the only animals possessed by a fully developed language. Dance reports on experiments with chimpanzees which suggest that only humans can learn typically human forms of communication.

The Rhetorical Primate

Frank E.X. Dance

Throughout history the human race has shown a fascination for communicating with other animals. Darwin's *On the Origin of Species* gave additional impetus to the interest in cross-species communication. In fact, for some, the last barrier to an acceptance of a Darwinian evolutionary position is the barrier presented by what is alleged to be the species specificity of human communication (14).

Currently there are several attempts to induce a form of human language in other primates. Extensive experiments are being conducted by five major research teams, all working with chimpanzees. Each team, having reviewed the work done by the Kellogs in the thirties and the Hayeses in the fifties, has concluded explicitly or implicitly that the oral/aural channel of human speech communication is either physically impossible for chimpanzees to master, or not essential for defining human linguistic performance. Starting with those assumptions, each of the teams has constructed different descriptions of human speech communication and has established different behavioral criteria for the chimpanzees to fulfill.

Three of the teams — those headed by Allen and Beatrice Gardner (8) in Reno, Nevada, by their former graduate student, Roger Fouts (7), in Norman, Oklahoma, and, more recently, by Herbert Terrace (15) in New York City — are using American Sign Language (ASL or Ameslan) as their non-spoken language substitute. ASL was chosen because it is already accepted as a language among the American deaf. The two

Reprinted from "The Rhetorical Primate" by Frank E.X. Dance in the *Journal of Communication* (Volume 27, Number 2), pages 12-16.

other teams, lead by David Premack (12) and Duane Rumbaugh (13), have created their own idiosyncratic languages which they believe maintain the essence of human language without the factor of speech. Premack has based his on the functional operations language users are capable of performing; Rumbaugh has emphasized strict adherence to a rule-governed grammar or syntax (as opposed to richness of vocabulary used in the three ASL studies) which he considers to be the essence of human language.

These endeavors are valuable for what they may be able to tell us about chimpanzee cognition, about some possible techniques for assisting the mentally retarded or mentally disturbed to reach their highest potential in human communication, and about new techniques for deaf education. But if the ultimate purpose is to teach a form of human language to non-human primates, then the work falls far short of that goal.

The difficulty is definitional. If human communication is that form of communication unique to humans, which is the fusion of genetic speech ability with culturally determined language, rather than simply anything in the repertoire of communication used by human beings, then the five research teams have eliminated human communication from their experiments.

Their research can be evaluated in the following way. (1) Those behaviors said to result from the presence of a form of human language in the chimpanzees may be satisfactorily explained as the results of mechanisms simpler than human communication. (2) Given that the oral-aural modality is central to human communication, the chimpanzees either have failed to acquire the ability of speech or have not been expected to acquire a true form of human language.

The research indicates that chimpanzees can learn complex, rule-governed behavioral routines.

Rule-governed behavior (according to the combination of Parsimony, Occam's Razor, and Morgan's Canon[1]) does not require intentionality or semantic purpose on the part of the chimpanzee. This behavior (for the experimenter but not necessarily for the chimpanzee) posits knowledge, understanding, and compliance with either prescriptive or constitutive rules. The research also indicates that the chimpanzees

---

[1]The Principle of Parsimony states that the simplest satisfactory explanation for a phenomenon is to be preferred over a more complex explanation. "Occam's razor" is the name given to a principle established by a Franciscan friar, William of Occam (or Ockham) in the early fourteenth century. The statement has been variously related as "Don't multiply miracles without necessity," and "Entities must not be unnecessarily multiplied." Morgan's Canon was stated by Lloyd Morgan in the early twentieth century: "In no case may we interpret an action as the outcome of the exercise of a higher psychical faculty, if it can be interpreted as the outcome of the exercise of one which stands lower in the psychological scale."

show some cognitive capabilities that they had not previously been known to possess.

However, the presence or absence of some degree of cognitive ability is not the determining factor in the acquisition of human language. It is rather a question of the quality or kind of cognitive abilities. The cognitive capacities and rule-governed behavior so far evidenced may comfortably be accounted for by the presence of perceptual rather than conceptual thought in the chimpanzees. As Adler writes of the differences between perceptual and conceptual thought:

> ...Animal thinking is confined to the perceptual present, whereas human thinking transcends the immediate environment and extends not only to objects in the remote past and the remote future but also to objects that have no temporal locus whatever (1).

The chimpanzee's behaviors do not necessarily indicate the presence of conceptual thought (4). And the process of isolating and defining such higher mental processes involves the presence of speech communication. Thus we are led to an essentially circular argument.

There are those who level accusations of anthropocentrism to this line of reasoning.

Indeed, anthropocentrism riddles the whole question of trying to teach a non-human primate a form of human language. Since language, in its fundamentally spoken manifestation as well as in its written and gestural derivatives, traditionally has been held as being unique to human beings, language is thus essentially anthropocentric. Obviously then, anthropocentrism is an intrinsic aspect of any form of human language and must be projected in all efforts to teach a form of human language to non-human primates. The only way of doing away with the anthropocentrism is by doing away with the *human* part of human communication and this may be exactly what the experimenters have done by trying to eliminate the oral-aural modality.

But have they really eliminated it? Premack's plastic tokens only derive meaning from their place within Premack's total linguistic system, which in turn derives from his own speech communication. The selections from American Sign Language used by the Gardners and Fouts are in turn derived from a total linguistic heritage with its roots inextricably deep in the oral traditions.

The experimenters' dilemma is that insofar as the experimental language systems have anything in common with human communication, the animals have been incapable of doing anything but imitating them; insofar as the experimental language systems are free of the essential commonality with uniquely human language, thus far they prove nothing in terms of non-human primate ability to acquire human language in any form. From the contrast we can draw two opposite conclusions: (1) the speech or oral-aural mode is unimportant, or

(2) the speech mode is all-important and is species-specific.

The first conclusion seems difficult to accept. The fact that all written languages and all symbol systems derive from spoken languages testifies to the force of the spoken word in the genesis of language. At the same time that fact does not suggest that derivative systems such as writing and gesture cannot exist in modalities other than the spoken. What it does suggest is that there is a hierarchy in the development of these modes which, once conceptualization has taken place, smoothes out into an apparent equality of potential for all types of modes. As Luria states:

> As special forms of speech activity, writing and reading differ essentially from spoken speech both in their genesis and psychophysiological structure and in their functional properties. Whereas spoken speech is formed in the early stages of the child's development in the course of direct association with other people, written speech does not appear until much later and is the result of special training. In contrast to spoken speech, which usually proceeds automatically and without the conscious analysis of its phonetic composition, from the very beginning written speech is a voluntary organized activity with the conscious analysis of its constituent sounds (10).

Contemporary research indicates that the human infant's nervous system is peculiarly and uniquely attuned to sounds within the spectrum of human adult speech and that human infants are also uniquely adapted to the perception and processing of the speech code (5, 9, 11).

The conceptual intentionality which results from speech communication also seems to be absent in chimpanzee behavior.

Intent, as used in this context, refers to the ability of the individual, upon reflection, to report his goals for his own behavior. When you can say to someone, "What did you intend to say in that situation?" and he can give a response sketching what he had hoped to accomplish, then that response mirrors his intent. It seems that as we move from lower mental processes to higher mental processes, we can note a corresponding increase of intentionality in the communication process. The intent becomes ever more accessible to awareness until it finally results in self-consciousness (4).

Obviously, the movement from external speech communication to inner speech communication is absent; and the seemingly unique functions of speech communication (namely the linking of the individual with his environment, the development of higher mental processes, and the regulation of human behavior) are also missing with the non-human primate (4, 6, 16).

References

1. Adler, Mortimer J. *The Difference of Man and the Difference It Makes.* New York: Holt, Rinehart and Winston, 1967.

2. Dance, Frank E.X. "Speech Communication as the Sign of Mankind." In *The Great Ideas of Today, 1975.* Chicago: Encyclopedia Brittanica, 1975.

3. Dance, Frank E.X. and Carl E. Larson. *Speech Communication: Concepts and Behavior.* New York: Holt, Rinehart, and Winston, 1972, pp. 11-12.

4. Dance, Frank E.X. and Carl E. Larson. "The Mentation Function: Regulating Human Behavior." In *The Functions of Human Communication: A Theoretical Approach.* New York: Holt, Rinehart, and Winston, in press.

5. Eimas, P.D. "Linguistic Processing of Speech by Young Infants." In Richard L. Schiefelbusch and L.L. Lloyd (Eds.) *Language Perspectives: Acquisition, Retardation, and Intervention.* Baltimore: University Park Press, 1974, pp. 55-73.

6. Fodor, J.A., T.G. Bever, and M.F. Garrett. *The Psychology of Language.* New York: McGraw-Hill, 1974.

7. Fouts, Roger S. "Acquisition and Testing of Gestural Signs in Four Young Chimpanzees." *Science* 180, June 1973, pp. 978-980.

8. Gardner, R. Allen and Beatrice T. Gardner. "Two-Way Communication with an Infant Chimpanzee." In A. Schrier and F. Stollnitz (Eds.) *Behavior of Nonhuman Primates.* New York: Gardner and Gardner, 1970, pp. 117-184.

9. Liberman, A.M., F.S. Cooper, D. Shankweiler, and M. Studdert-Kennedy. "Perception of the Speech Code." *Psychological Review* 74, 1967, pp. 431-461.

10. Luria, Alexander R. *Higher Cortical Functions in Man.* New York: Basic Books, 1966, p. 408.

11. Morse, P.A. "Infant Speech Perception: A Preliminary Model and Review of the Literature." In Richard L. Schiefelbusch and L.L. Lloyd (Eds.) *Language Perspectives: Acquisition, Retardation, and Intervention.* Baltimore: University Park Press, 1974, pp. 19-53.

12. Premack, David. "A Functional Analysis of Language." *Journal of the Experimental Analysis of Behavior* 14, July 1970, pp. 107-125.

13. Rumbaugh, Duane M. "Lana [chimpanzee] Learning Language: A Progress Report." *Brain and Language* 1, 1974, pp. 205-212.

14. "Symposium on the Species-Specificity of Language." In *The Great Ideas Today, 1975.* Chicago: Encyclopedia Brittanica, 1975.

15. Terrace, Herbert S. and T.G. Bever. "Linguistic and Cognitive Development of the Chimpanzee." Research proposal submitted to the National Science Foundation, 1975.

16. Vygotsky, Lev S. *Thought and Language,* Cambridge: MIT Press/Wiley, 1962.

Questions:

1. How do writing and reading differ from spoken language as speech activity?

2. In what ways do "rule-governed behavioral routines" differ from symbol usage?

3. Do you believe that the charge of anthropocentrism is valid? Is the oral-aural modality essential to the process of symbolization?

4. Recount stories you have heard about animal communication that challenge the premise in this article.

*Weinberg discusses some of the problems asso-
ciated with the arbitrary assignment of meanings
to language. One means of breaking the language
barrier, he says, is the use of "phatic communion."*

Some Limitations of Language

Harry L. Weinberg

Irving J. Lee often likened language to a tool, perhaps man's most important one, more useful than fire, the wheel, or atomic energy. It is most likely that none of these, most certainly not the latter, could ever have been put to use by a non-symbol-using creature. But, like any tool, language has its limitations. There are certain things we cannot do with it, and the attempt to make it do what it cannot do often leads to trouble.

In expanding upon this, Lee compared language with a fish net. The very small fish escape from the web; the very large ones cannot be encircled. In the case of language, the small fry are the infinite details of the material world; no matter how fine we weave the mesh, an infinity escape. We can never describe completely even the simplest bit of matter. We can never exhaust what could be said about a single grain of sand. For convenience, and by utter necessity, we concentrate on a large number (though relatively few) of the characteristics of grains of sand, noting those similarities important to us at the moment and neglecting differences which seem to make no difference for our generalizations. In this way we come to talk about "properties" of sand. These are the fish — descriptions and inferences — for which the net of language is most suited.

But there is something very peculiar about the catch: it is nonexistent. It is as though the fish had slipped from their skins and what we

The late Harry L. Weinberg was professor of speech at Temple University. This article is from "Some Limitations of Language," *Levels of Knowing and Existence* by Harry L. Weinberg (Harper and Row, Publishers, 1959) pp. 34-47. Copyright © 1959, by Harry L. Weinberg. Reprinted by permission of Blanche Weinberg.

have left is lifeless and unchanging, a dull and hazy replica of the ones that got away. For words are *about things*: they are *not* the things themselves. The world of things is constantly changing; it "is" bright, hard, soft, green, rosy, acrid, black, burnt, rubbery, loud, sharp, velvety, bitter, hot, freezing, silent, flowing, massive, ephemeral, wispy, granitic. Or rather, these are the names we use for the way it seems to us. Above all, it appears "real"; it is not words. Whatever we call a thing, whatever we say it is, it is not. For whatever we *say* is words, and words are words and not things. The words are maps, and the map is not the territory. The map is static; the territory constantly flows. Words are always about the past or the unborn future, never about the living present. The present is ever too quick for them; by the time the words are out, it is gone. When we forget this, we tend to act as if words were things, and because they are so much more easily manipulated and molded to our desires, there is the danger of building maps that fit no known territory and the greater danger of not caring whether or not they do. We then tend more and more to live in the past and the future and we lose the present, the sense of nowness, the feeling of the immediacy, mystery, and flow of the sensory world; we drift into the gray, dead world of words.

The Queerness of Thingness: What Is Red Like, "Really"?

The nonverbal quality of the sensory world—the world of thingness—is the large fish which escapes the net of language. If you were asked to describe the color "red" to a man blind from birth, you would very quickly discover that this is an absolute impossibility. No matter what you said, you could never convey to him the sensation you experience when you see a color called red. The same observation applies to smells, tastes, sounds—any sensory perceptions. They are literally unspeakable, as are all feelings and emotions. During his lectures, Alfred Korzybski would ask the members of the audience to pinch themselves, to concentrate on the feeling, and then try to describe the pain. It does no good to say sharp, dull, or prickly, for then you have to describe these words, *ad infinitum.* Incidentally, it might interest the reader to know that it is quite difficult to get some people, especially the more sophisticated intellectuals, to perform this little experiment. It is silly, childish, and obvious. They "know" words are not things. But to really know it on all levels of abstraction, one must actually do and experience this nonverbal act. If not, then one is acting as if his words were the actual sensations.

All that words—descriptions and labels—can do is evoke sensations and feelings which the reader or listener has already experienced. They can never transmit new experience. If one has never experienced what is described, one is absolutely incapable of experiencing it through description alone. No woman can make me feel what it is like to give birth to a child. I may infer it is similar to a bad case of cramps, but I will never know, no matter what she says. Since I know that a toothache differs in "quality" from a headache, and that a burn does not feel like bruised skin, it is a reasonable inference on my part that birth pains are different in some respects from anything I have ever experienced or ever will.

This poses an interesting question. If you feel a pain in your jaw and say, "I have a toothache," have you made an inferential or factual statement? Certainly it has been made after observation, but what about verification by accepted standards? What is the accepted standard for sensations, feelings, emotions? It can only be the person experiencing them. Only you can feel your pain and the experience itself represents the verification. Your statement is a factual one for you and inferential for everyone else. We can only guess that you are reporting the "truth" about your feelings.

The limitations of language go even further. I have no way of knowing what "red" looks like even to another sighted person. He cannot tell me; I cannot check. I can only infer that what he experiences is similar to what I experience. It cannot be identical because our nervous systems are different, and an experience is a product of both what is "out there" and the way the organism reacts to it. But in order to get on with the business of living together and reaching some kind of agreement, we are forced to assume a similarity in response. The danger lies in our forgetting that this similarity is only a convenient inference. There may be important differences in what different people perceive in the "same" situation or in what one individual perceives at different moments. Hundreds of experiments designed by psychologists, physiologists, and others demonstrate this dependence of perception upon both the structure of the stimulus and the structure and state of the responding organ.

Let us take a simple example. Eat a lump of sugar and concentrate on the taste. Then take another and another. After a few lumps, the sweetness changes. It may become cloying or its sweetness may be diminished. What has happened? Has the sugar changed its taste? If you say no, you have become satiated, but the sweetness of the sugar is the same, why do you assume that the first taste of sugar is the "real" taste, and that after six lumps it is less "real"?

Or place a piece of red paper on a gray background. Place another piece of the same paper on a bright green background. Compare the two and you will find that the pieces of red paper look different. Which is the "real" color? It won't do to say that the real color is that of the red paper by itself. It is never by itself; there is always a background. Which is the right background? One is as arbitrary as the other.

We could go on and on with this. How about the color-blind man who presumably sees only a shade of gray when he looks at your red sheet? Who is seeing the correct, the "real" color? If you say you are because your range of color perception is greater than his, consider these facts: The majority of people cannot see ultraviolet light. If we filter out light in the range of the visible spectrum, red to violet, in an ultraviolet lamp, the average person would see nothing and would say that the lamp is not lit. However, it has been discovered that a few people do see a fraction of the ultraviolet range. This means that they see a color they cannot describe to us if we are one of the majority who cannot see ultraviolet light, and we cannot imagine what the color is like. It is no good to say it is like violet; that would be like saying green must be like yellow because it follows it in the spectrum. If you have seen yellow but never green, you cannot imagine, on the basis of yellow, what green is like.

Now, since there is, normally, ultraviolet light in daylight, it will be reflected from the "red" sheet of paper, so that the person who can see ultraviolet light will see a different shade of "red," that is, red and ultraviolet. Which is the "real" color of "red," his or ours?

We met this problem before when we tried to find the "real" height of the table, which upon analysis we found to be a meaningless, unanswerable question. A similar solution can be found in this case by tracing the sequence of events. Light waves (shower of particles?), reflected from the paper to our eyes, are electromagnetic waves and have no color. These waves hit our eyes and give rise to a series of complex psychophysical responses, resulting in the sensation red, gray, or some other color. Two things should be noted here. First, the electromagnetic (light) waves have no qualities (no color, sounds, smells) and their existence is inferred. Second, when a response is aroused in an organism, that response is in terms of some sensation like red, gray, and so forth. The particular quality of the response depends upon the structure and condition of the organ and the organism. Given a different organism, a different sensation arises in response to the "same" electromagnetic waves. Thus, the light *waves* produce this sensation of *light* in the organism, but one is not the other.

Incidentally, by distinguishing between sound waves and sound, we can speedily dispatch that old riddle concerning the tree that falls in the forest when no one is about. Does it make a sound? The answer is no! We infer that the tree produces sound waves, a reasonable inference based on past factual data on falling objects. But sound is sensation produced in and by an organism as a result of being stimulated by sound waves (which are not sound) and until such an organism is present, the tree makes no sound. If a man is present when the tree falls, it is a factual statement for him to say, "I hear a sound," provided he is not deaf. But any statement I make about his hearing it is purely inferential.

What Is a Quality: To-Me-Ness

In asking what is the "real" color of a piece of paper, we imply that color is *in* the paper, that it exists independently of the responding organism. But since the color, or any quality for that matter, is a product of both the observer and the observed, in order to make language fit these facts as discovered by science, we must change the question to, "What color does it appear to me at this moment?" In this way, the structure of the language fits the structure of reality. By adding "to me at this time," we imply in our language a universe characterized by constant change, one whose qualities are given it, projected upon it, by a responding organism. By omitting these words, we imply a simple, absolute, static world where the organism is simply a mirror, largely a distorting one, of an ideal world whose qualities are independent of and unchanged by the observer.

This may not matter much when talking about color, taste, or sound, but when we are evaluating the realm of the social it makes quite a difference whether one says "Johnny is bad" or "Johnny appears bad to me now." If he *is* bad, he has badness in him; it is a part of him, and he is always bad in everything he does and will appear that way to every "normal" observer. When we add "to me now," we imply there is a possibility that he may not appear that way to everyone else. We are more prepared to consider other evaluations of his behavior, on the possibility that they may be more accurate than our own. Actually, if I tell you Johnny is bad, I tell you very little about him other than that I probably dislike him if I dislike those I label bad. If I say that he appears bad to me, I invte the obvious questions, "What kind of behavior do you call bad? What did Johnny do?" If I then describe what he did, we might discover that you do not consider such behavior bad; rather, to you, it may show that Johnny is independent and self-reliant. To Mr. X, this behavior may mean Johnny is trying to hide his insecurity and lack of parental affection. Who is right? All may be partly right and partly wrong, but at least the situation can be discussed on a much more objective, descriptive level. The probability of agreement and of more appropriate behavior with respect to Johnny is much greater. When we say *and mean*, "It appears this way to me," we invite checking, discussion, reevaluation. When we say, "It is," we cut off further investigation. It is the contention of the general semanticist that the constant, conscious use of the "to me" will help make proper evaluation more likely, for language structure influences thought, behavior, and feelings. Constant talking in absolute terms produces a feeling of the "rightness" of such patterns of evaluation, and this emotional barrier is most difficult to crack in attempting to change behavior. It stifles questioning the appropriateness of patterns of evaluation and talking both by the speaker himself and by others, and is one of the foundation stones in man's grimmest prison—prejudice.

Cracking the Language Barrier: Phatic Communion

Because feelings, sensations, and emotions cannot be transmitted by language, but only evoked in the listener, and because of our great need to find out how others feel and to communicate our own feelings to them, we spend much time trying to crack this sound barrier. A writer uses hundreds of examples, descriptions, image-evoking words, hoping they will be similar enough to past experiences of the reader to provoke his memory and recreate a similar nonverbal reaction in him. For this reason it may take an entire novel or play to make a simple point. One of the themes of the play *Death Takes a Holiday* is that love is stronger than the fear of death. Why doesn't the author simply make the statement and call it quits? Obviously because it doesn't work; we don't "feel" this by reading one sentence. It takes the writer with his shotgun loaded with pellets of description to wing the emotions of the reader.

Another technique we use in our attempt to overcome this linguistic barrier, interestingly enough, involves the use of nonsymbolic language, the language of sound as such. This is the language of lovers and infants and animals, and we all use it in addition to symbolic language. Bronislaw Malinowski called it "phatic communion."

When Fido growls and bares his teeth, he is letting us and other animals know that he is angry. When the baby howls and bares his gums, he communicates to us his unhappiness. And Fido and the baby are equally adept at reading our feelings by the tone of our voice totally apart from the verbal meanings of the words used. All of us gather our impressions of a person's sincerity, for example, by the inflections of his voice, not by any protestation by him.

Not only do sounds serve to convey expressions of feelings, but also the general musculature of the body plays a part in this type of communication. The good poker player "reads" the faces (the tiny movements of the muscles around the eyes and mouth) of the other players to see if they are bluffing or suppressing excitement. Indeed, there is evidence to suggest that the very young infant is frighteningly adept at picking up the "true" feelings of his mother toward him, which she herself may have repressed. Thus, if she unconsciously rejects him and, feeling guilty, talks fondly or rather, uses fond language, he will feel this rejection by "reading" the inflections in her voice and the tensions in her muscles.

When Sense is Nonsense

Much social talk is in the same category. It is our attempt to escape the desperate loneliness that is, in a sense, our lot. No one can know how we feel, what we see; nor we, they. Each is a solitude. No logic or analysis or theorizing is nearly as effective in softening this aloneness as phatic communion. Misevaluation enters when we expect them to. It has been stated that a bore is a man who, when you greet him with, "How are you?" tells you. You are not really asking about his health but saying, "Let's be friends." If you are fixing a flat tire on a hot day and a passerby asks, "Got a flat?", he is asking you to be friendly. If you take his words literally, you are likely to become angry and say, "Any damn fool can see I have."

It is often a temptation to snicker or feel very superior to the logically absurd "itsy bitsy boo" talk of lovers. But if we remember that it is the sound, not the literal meaning that conveys the affection in this case, then any attempt to talk "sense" in this kind of situation is itself a form of nonsense. Consequently the general semanticist does not demand that we talk sense all the time. All he asks is that we distinguish between situations that call for big talk and those that do better with small talk, and not confuse the two or try to pass off one as the other. Small talk is the oil in social machinery. Big talk—logic, theorizing, factual statements—will help solve the problems; small talk eases the way.

Most commonly both types of communication occur simultaneously and in varying degrees, which serves to complicate mutual understanding and gives the lie to the assertion that facts speak for themselves. Meaning occurs on all levels of abstraction, and differs in character at each level. At the feeling level it is a diffuse, deep, primitive, alogical meaning expressed in the scream of anguish, the coo of affection, the snarl of hatred, the *tra la la* of the poet.

Questions:

1. How does Weinberg's concept that reality exists in the perceiver rather than in the object affect your view of the communication process?

2. Two schools of philosophy have argued for years over an abstract dilemma epitomized in the question, "When I leave the room, does the desk in the room cease to exist?" The school of philosophy characterized as "skeptic" argues that the desk ceases to exist while the "empiricist" school contends that the desk continues its existence.

   a. What is the purpose of this abstract argument?

   b. Does this dilemma exist in nature, or is it strictly language based?

   c. How does this dilemma demonstrate some of the limitations of language?

   d. How could Weinberg's general semantics perspective help resolve this philosophical dilemma?

3. Weinberg compares language to a tool and a fish net. What comparisons can you think of?

Reading nonverbal cues is a game we all play. Though in its relative infancy as a field of scientific inquiry, nonverbal communication has a code and symbol system complete with rules. The principles of this fledgling science are discussed along with some of the differences in verbal and nonverbal communication.

Nonverbal Communication

William D. Brooks

Every message is put into a code. The codes to which we direct most of our attention are the spoken and written codes—verbal communication. Actually, verbal signals carry only a small part of the information that people exchange in everyday interaction. It has been estimated that in face-to-face communication no more than 35 percent of the social meaning is carried in the verbal message.[1] Still, we sometimes slip into the error of thinking that *all* communication must be verbal. Another code does exist, however—the nonverbal code, a relatively little studied but much used vehicle of communication. It includes the full range of human communication: tone of voice, gestures, posture, movement, and other signals that we call nonverbal communication. Many of the meanings generated in human encounters are elicited by touch, glance, vocal nuance, gesture, or facial expression. A good deal of this nonverbal communication goes on around us and is important because we make decisions based on it and relate to each other through it. From nonverbal communication cues we make decisions to argue or agree, to laugh or blush, to relax or resist, to continue or end conversation. Many, and sometimes most, of the criti-

---

[1]Randall Harrison, "Nonverbal Communication: Exploration into Time, Space, Action, and Object," in *Dimensions in Communication*, eds. J.H. Campbell and H.W. Hepler (Belmont, Calif.: Wadsworth Publishing Co., 1965), p. 161.

From Brooks, William D., *Speech Communication* 3rd Ed. © 1974, 1978. Wm. C. Brown Company Publishers, Dubuque, Iowa. Reprinted by permission.

cal meanings in communication are transferred through the nonverbal codes. Although we do not always realize that we are sending and receiving messages nonverbally, the influence of nonverbal communication is always present in face-to-face communication situations. We gesture with our hands, raise our eyebrows, meet someone else's eyes and look away, and shift positions in a chair. Although the actions may seem random, researchers have discovered in recent years that there is a system to them. Messages come across not only in words but also in body language, and such nonverbal messages often get there faster than do the verbal messages.

Every culture has its own body language, its own nonverbal code. The difference that may exist between cultures was at one time dramatically illustrated in the public baths in Japan. Japanese girls traditionally express their approval of male guests with shy and subdued laughter. This behavior unnerved and unmanned many male tourists from Europe and America. In order to overcome the cultural differences in meaning, Geisha girls had to be trained to reserve their giggles for Oriental men. A German talks and moves in German, while a Frenchman talks and moves in French. One's sex, ethnic background, and social class all influence his body language. Research has also shown that persons who are truly bilingual are also bilingual in body language. Politicians with a bicultural constituency are fortunate ·if they are truly bilingual, for they can campaign to each culture in the verbal and nonverbal languages of that culture. New York's famous mayor Fiorello La Guardia is said to have been able to campaign in English, Italian, and Yiddish. When films of his speeches are run without sound, it is not difficult to identify from his nonverbal communication the language he is speaking.

Many verbal expressions attest to the importance of nonverbal communication. We say "actions speak louder than words," or "one picture is worth a thousand words." Yet in speech we have placed great emphasis on verbal communication while giving little attention to nonverbal communication. The result is that some speakers too often display great skills in using words in interpersonal and public communication, but little understanding of, or a real feel for, the total phenomenon of communication itself. In this chapter we will describe the types of nonverbal communication, compare nonverbal communication with verbal communication, and identify some tentative principles of nonverbal communication.

Types of Nonverbal Communication

Nonverbal communication, as we will discuss it in this chapter, falls into eight categories: paralanguage (vocal nonverbal communication), sign language, gestures and body action, object language, tactile communication, space, time, and silence.

Paralanguage

We have recognized for a long time that there is information included in the manner in which words are spoken — that is, that there are clear messages in the tone of the voice, in the emphasis or inflections given certain words, and in the pauses inserted in the sentence. We know from experience that a simple "Yes" may express defiance, resignation, acknowledgment, interest, enthusiasm, or agreement, depending on tone and emphasis. Most of us, at one time or many times, have remarked, "It wasn't *what* he said but *how he said it* that made me angry!" We were referring to the nonverbal vocal phenomena — intonation, emphasis, stress, and so forth. These vocal phenomena, often referred to as *paralanguage,* consist of vocal modifiers, vocal differentiators, vocal identifiers, and a general category called voice quality.

One type of phenomena in paralanguage is vocal qualifiers. *Vocal qualifiers* are usually thought of as *tones of voice.* Increasing loudness or increasing softness is one type of vocal qualifier. The part of the utterance bearing the increasing loudness or softness may be a single syllable, word, sentence, or a group of sentences. Increasing loudness often expresses anger, hostility, or alarm. If you listen to persons in the midst of a heated argument, you will often notice that the loudness of the speaking voice increases. Playwrights and fiction writers, as they have recorded man's behavior in literature, have included "shouting at each other" in their descriptions of hostile arguments and angry exchanges. On the other hand, increasing softness is often used to express disappointment. Loudness or softness is seldom used alone as a qualifier of the verbal message, but each is used along with other techniques (pitch, voice quality, and rate) to convey the message of anger or disappointment.

Loudness or softness may be used to give emphasis to certain words — to make a particular word stand out from the others. In infinite and subtle ways, loudness (increasing or decreasing) can be used to add vocal cues to verbal messages.

A second set of vocal qualifiers is *pitch: raised pitch* or *lowered pitch.* A raised pitch often accompanies loudness and can be used to communicate alarm, annoyance, and anxiety. The whining, high-pitched voice may tell a story of tenseness, fear, and anxiety that is as revealing as the verbal message itself; or the relaxed, low-pitched voice may communicate calm and relaxation.

We use pitch to indicate declarative messages and messages that are questions. In fact, by using certain pitch patterns or inflections, we can utter a statement constructed declaratively ("That was a *basketball game?*") as a question. Such is the capacity of pitch to qualify the meanings of verbal messages.

A third pair of vocal qualifiers — the *spread register* and the *squeezed register* — refers to the spreading or compressing (lengthening and shortening) of the time interval between the pitches as one speaks. *Spread register* is heard when you call to a person across the street. You will tend to draw out the saying of the person's name over a longer period of time ("Hey, Jim—my") *Squeezed register* is the opposite of spread register in that the intervals between the pitches are shortened to give a monotone effect. You can hear the difference between spread register and squeezed register by listening to Jimmy's mother call to him from across the street and then, at a later time, listening to her say his name while scolding him when he is near her.

Rasp or *openness* is the fourth set of vocal qualifiers. Rasping is determined by the amount of muscular tension in the larynx. The strained or rasping quality is associated with tenseness. Openness, characterized by a hollowness or booming acoustic characteristic (and said to be associated with a lack of sincerity, signaling that the speaker is of superordinate status, purporting to have the answers to one's problems), is often used by clergymen, politicians, and undertakers.[2] Between the extremes of hollowness and coarse raspiness is a wide range of characteristics of this phenomenon that are used to modify verbal messages.

Drawling or *clipping*, the fifth set of verbal qualifiers, has to do with the individual syllables. With clipping, the syllable is chopped off or shortened, but with drawling, the syllable is elongated and drawn out as if found in the stereotyped cowboy drawl.

Tempo, increased or decreased, is the last vocal qualifier to be discussed. Increased tempo or rate of speaking sometimes (especially as it is associated with other vocal qualifiers) indicates annoyance; at other times it may indicate anxiety; and it is sometimes associated with energy and intelligence. An extremely slow tempo often signals uncertainty.

Many psychiatrists and others skilled in communication rely heavily on the information in nonverbal messages. Through experience they have come to have confidence in the validity of the information received from vocal qualifiers.

Among the most commonly used *vocal differentiators* are *crying*, *laughing*, and *breaking*. These types of communication are used according to the rules of each culture. In America, for example, women have more freedom to use crying to communicate than do men; while in Persia men are allowed to cry and, in fact, are expected to weep to convey certain messages. Laughing and crying may mean quite different things in different cultures. Custom may dictate who can cry and who cannot cry, how much they can cry, and what things can be meant by crying.

Breaking refers to speaking in a broken, halting voice, or to some rigid and intermittent interruption of speaking. The nervous giggle, for

[2]Robert E. Pittenger and Henry Lee Smith, Jr., "A Basis for Some Contributions of Linguistics to Psychiatry," *Psychiatry*, 20 (1957): 61-78.

example, is considered to be a form of breaking. The quavering voice of emotion is another example of breaking. In our culture, breaking in any form communicates insecurity and loss of control. Laughing, crying, breaking — any one of these vocal differentiators — could be applied to the same verbal message at different times and, under different circumstances, to create totally different messages.

This set of phenomena included in paralanguage consists of "un-huh" and "ah-hah" that mean *yes,* and "huh-uh" and "ah!ah!" that mean *no.*

A fourth set of phenomena, not yet researched fully so as to describe them systematically as has been done for vocal qualifiers, vocal differentiators, and vocal identifiers, is the set called voice quality. Although specific elements have not yet been identified and shown to be predictively related to given meanings, we do know that meanings are conveyed and understood by others through voice quality. Anxiety, calm, hostility, and other similar emotional states have been identified with voice quality as a general characteristic of a particular emotional state. Psychiatrists, medical doctors, counselors, and teachers who are skilled in and sensitive to nonverbal communication messages make use of voice quality in interpreting messages.

Although each type of vocal communication has been discussed separately, it would be a mistake to think in terms of each operating separately and individually to communicate nonverbal messages. In practice, these phenomena are combined with each other in many different ways. Hence, people who do more than just react to nonverbal messages unintentionally — that is, people who attempt to purposefully receive, interpret, and understand nonverbal messages — focus on the *general* or *multiple nonverbal factors* rather than first on one specific factor and then on a second, and so forth. Loudness, high pitch, rate, hollowness, and crying are more meaningful considered together than is any one of these when considered by itself.

Sign Language

Sign language includes all those forms of codification in which words, numbers, and punctuation have been supplanted by gestures. Examples range from the simple gesture of the hitchhiker to the complete sign language of the deaf. Other features of sign language, as well as posture, facial expressions, and body movements, are called action language and will be discussed as a third category of nonverbal communication.

Sign language gestures are believed to have been used by primitive man long before oral systems of language were developed. Sign languages were developed in various cultures throughout the world. There is evidence that some seven hundred thousand distinct and meaningful gestures can be and have been used by communicating man.[3] The North American Indians, for example, were especially adept at sign language; the Cheyennes had at least seven thousand symbols in their language. One advantage of the use of sign languages by the Indians was that any tribe could communicate at least roughly with any other tribe. One disadvantage, reported by Thomas in reference to the Bushmen, is that it is possible to have so many visual signals — and to rely only on them — that it is difficult to communicate in the dark.[4] Although the American culture does not rely heavily on sign language, there is considerable use of sign language in our communication.

Action language

Action language includes all gestures, posture, facial expressions, and movements that are *not* used exclusively as substitutes for words. Walking, for example, serves the function of giving one mobility, but it may also communicate. Similarly, eating can be action language. Eating rapidly, for example, can communicate something about the person's hunger, upbringing, or emotional state.

It is useful to divide language into two categories: (1) expressive actions that are unintentional, and (2) purposive actions that are intentional. The former are often subliminal, while the latter are overt and identifiable by either the listener or the talker. Expressive actions are constantly adaptive, responding to feelings and needs of the moment, while overt actions are purposely communicative and instrumental. Expressive actions result in the message that is "given off," while purposive actions result in a given message. These two categories are not absolute; they do overlap at times. Some expressive actions are noticeable, and some communicative gestures become so habitual that we use them almost unconsciously. It is not uncommon for a person to develop over a period of time certain habituated movements and gestures that are used regardless of whether they have any connection with the verbal message or not. Most public officials and entertainers have their idiosyncratic, habituated gestures, and these are often used by comedians who impersonate well-known public figures. For example, Perry Como is impersonated by pulling on the ear, as are Bing Crosby and Carol Burnett; and Richard Nixon is impersonated by rolling the eyes and holding both hands over the head, with the fingers in double V's.

As overt, intentional actions, gestures are used to locate, to describe, to emphasize, and even to express abstract concepts. As expressive, unintentional action, gestures, facial expression, posture, and movement reveal the personality and emotional states. We can observe in the musculature twitching, blotching, dilated pupils, rising

[3]Mario Pei, *The Story of Language* (New York: J.B. Lippincott Co., 1949), p. 13.
[4]W.I. Thomas, *Source Book for Social Origins* (Chicago, University of Chicago Press, 1909), p. 706.

hair, and so forth, the fear, nervousness, anger, joy, and other emotional states of the individual. We may not observe the individual cues, but rather we probably will observe the total visible pattern. We perceive the visual meaning as a configuration and interpret it almost instantly.

There is little doubt that we differ in our ability to send messages in the action language channel—both intentional and unintentional messages. Some people are more expressive than others in their visible behavior, and some people are more reserved and concealing in their visible behavior than are other people.

We also vary greatly in our ability to receive and interpret nonverbal messages. Some people are keenly sensitive and accurate in understanding or reading the nonverbal signs, while other persons plunge ahead, ignoring the nonverbal messages.

Coleman found that people vary in their ability to send visual cues and in their ability to interpret them. Not only is there a difference from person to person, but there appears to be a difference between men and women in their ability to use nonverbal communication. Generally speaking, women seem to be better than men in sending nonverbal messages, but men seem to be better than women in interpreting nonverbal messages.[5] Through the eyes, facial expression, gestures and movement much meaning can be conveyed. The human body is a versatile instrument for expressing a wide range of ideas and feelings. One of the most potent elements in body language is eye behavior. Americans are careful about how and when they meet one another's eyes. In normal conversation, they allow each *eye contact* to last only about a second, then one or both will look away. If they maintain eye contact longer than that, emotions are heightened and the relationship takes on new dimensions. Hence, we avoid this except in appropriate circumstances. It should not be surprising that baseball pitchers, mothers, confidence men, and girl friends are capable of conveying much while saying little, since they are not reluctant to maintain eye contact.

Various types of human encounters have been filmed in order to study the use of action language. As a result of such studies, we have discovered that gestures and all action language are better studied in specific social contexts and in relationship to all other nonverbal communication cues if they are to be understood accurately. We have to learn to attend to gestures, body positions and movement, facial expressions, tonal qualities of the voice—in short, all of the nonverbal messages. It is easy, as adults, to focus all our attention on the verbal and to forget the nonverbal, but it is as we attend to all messages that we catch the more accurate meaning.

[5]James C. Coleman, "Facial Expressions of Emotion," *Psychological Monographs* 63 (1949): 1-36.

The most readily observed of all gestures or action language are facial expressions. We focus on the face more often than on any other part of the body. Especially, we focus on the eyes. Avoidance of eye contact, in fact, is often interpreted in our culture as indicative of efforts to escape, of hiding, and of dislike. In some cultures, however, eye contact is to be avoided, especially a woman establishing eye contact with a man. In America, prolonged eye contact usually indicates interest and liking. Julius Fast, in his book *Body Language* relates the story of how one of his soldier friends picked up five girls within thirty minutes. His friend simply used nonverbal communication, particularly eye contact. Fast writes, "Walking along the street, he would catch a prospect's eye, hold it a bit longer than was necessary, and lift one eyebrow. If the girl faltered in her stride, stopped to look at her compact, to fix her stockings, or window-shop down the street, it was one of a number of return signals that meant, 'I am aware of you and possibly interested. Let's pursue this further.'" Of course the nonverbal cues used by men and women today may be different from those Fast identified in describing his friend's success, but the same type of communication does occur.

Eye contact is also sought more when speaking than when listening. And aversion to eye contact, rightly or not, is often associated with discomfort or guilt. We say the person is "shifty-eyed."

Another type of action language is how one walks. Pace, length of stride, and walking posture vary with the emotional state and the personality of the individual. Our personalities are so much reflected in our manner of walking that it is not difficult to identify those people you know well by hearing their walk. You can probably think of persons you know whose walking is uniquely an identification of that person. Happy, goal-oriented, achievement-motivated persons often have a light, rapid walk; while dejected, tired, and unmotivated persons often shuffle along with heavy feet and drooping shoulders.

Another interesting thing about walking as action language is that the leader among a group of walkers "sets the pace." Pace setting seems to be associated with power, control, and status. Moreover, in every society (man and animal), the leaders set the pace. This principle has been used by the FBI, Kremlinologists, and others to successfully identify the leaders among the Mafia and other groups under surveillance.[6]

Through our actions, we communicate inner feelings and attitudes. Openness, approachability, and acceptance are communicated nonverbally just as are closedness, withdrawal, and defensiveness. Nierenberg and Calero report from observed negotiation situations a significantly higher frequency of agreement among men whose coats

[6]Gerard I. Nierenberg and Henry Calero, *How to Read a Person Like a Book* (New York: Pocket Books, Inc., 1973), p. 38.

are unbuttoned than among those whose coats are buttoned. Hands open, arms open, legs uncrossed, and coats unbuttoned seem to go with the positive relationship of acceptance and openness; while folded arms, hidden hands, crossed legs, and buttoned coats go with defensiveness and negative attitudes.[7] The story is told of a new bride who was trying to identify family members from nonfamily guests at a reception. She was advised that members of the family wore their coats unbuttoned or took them off. Using that sign only, she correctly identified eight of ten, and of the two she missed, one was an old friend of the family who had attended all family functions (unbuttoned coat) and a distant relative who was a loner and seldom attended such family functions (coat buttoned).[8]

If you have attended a baseball game and the team manager has rushed out to argue with the umpire, you have probably observed a classic demonstration of closedness. Usually, the umpire crosses his arms, and may even turn his back, in stubborn defensiveness that says, "I'm closed to negotiation!" According to Darwin, crossed arms are indicative of defensiveness almost throughout the world. It is probably a good way for you to cause people to be "turned off" by you.

There are gestures and actions that are associated by salesmen, teachers, executives, and lawyers with evaluating, thinking, or preparedness for action. These include sitting on the edge of the chair, leaning forward, supporting the head or chin with one hand to the cheek (as portrayed by Rodin's *The Thinker*), and tilting the head to one side. Darwin noticed that animals as well as men tilt their head to one side upon being attracted to something they hear. Also, stroking the chin or pulling the beard is said to be associated with considering and decision making.

Can action tell you when a person is lying or being secretive? There are those who answer yes. They say the best indicator is incongruity among nonverbal messages (smiles, but clasps hands nervously; crosses legs and points the feet toward the door) or between a verbal message and a nonverbal message. Nose touching, nose rubbing, rubbing the eye, crossing the legs, covering the mouth with the hands — these, also, are said to be suggestive of strong rejection.

There are nonverbal signals for reassurance and reinforcement. When we want our ideas accepted and confirmed, we often emit signals that are calls for such reassurance. Our anxiety and lack of confidence is revealed through hand clenching, cuticle picking, pen or pencil chewing, nail biting. Or a woman may bring her hand to her throat or feel or play with her necklace. All may indicate anxiety and worry over being accepted.

Frustration, which is different from anxiety over being accepted or

[7]*Ibid.*, p. 46.
[8]*Ibid.*, p. 47.

rejected, may be revealed by rubbing the back of the neck, running fingers through the hair, hand wringing, and short breathing.

Fear or uptightness may be shown by rapid movements, rapid speech, selecting the chair farthest away, crossing the arms or legs, unceasing shifting of the body, turning the body away from the other communicator, turning so as to point toward the door, clearing the throat, suddenly expelling air "Whew!"), and cigarette smoking. It has been found that it is not the lighting and smoking of cigarettes that indicate fear or tension. In fact, smokers usually light up after the threat has passed — after the tension subsides. Rather, it is the putting out of the cigarette or letting it burn without smoking it that indicates uptightness.

When one wants to interrupt, the most commonly used gestures are ear pulling and putting the index fingers on the lips. The index finger — the pointing finger — is also used in another way. If you have had the experience of having someone jab you with his finger and say, "Know what I mean?" you know how the pointed finger is symbolic of a bayonet or weapon. Little wonder that it indicates aggressiveness and dominance. Some persons have refined the gesture by using their eyeglasses in the same way. If you want someone to become hostile toward you, wave your pointed finger in his or her face. It may seem natural to use this gesture when we are communicating forcefully, but we really ought to be aware of the danger of arousing antagonism in others. I have always wondered just how successful the armed forces advertisement picturing Uncle Sam, with pointing finger, saying "I want You!" really was.

Whether it is the locked ankles (I'm not giving anything away!); the tapping of fingers, doodling, toe-tapping, or ball-point pen clicking (I'm bored and impatient!); the smoothing and arranging of hair, smoothing of the dress balancing a shoe half on and half off, or the gesture of touching the breast (courtship and flirtation); or the erect posture, shoulders back, and "steepling" gesture (confidence) — action language is rich in the communication of intended and unintended messages. If we could develop skill in reading action language consciously — in verifying their meanings in a given encounter — we could possibly prevent some of the communication breakdowns and misunderstandings we experience day after day. We might also learn more about our own action language and the effect we have on others through our nonverbal communication.

Object Language

Object language comprises the display of material things — art objects, clothes, the decoration of a room, hair style, implements, machines, and the human body. Engagement and wedding rings are examples of objects of communication, as is the American flag, a peace decal, and the sports-letter jacket. It is well known that the clothing one wears and its style and condition tell something about the person. We make inferences from the shine of the shoes, the cut of the hair, and other material things that reveal one's social sensitivity, associations, preferences, and values. Personal apparel seems to be a major source of information. Clothing, jewelry, cosmetics — these represent deliberate choices and are guides to personality. How one dresses, for example, shows sexual attraction and sexual interest, group identification, status, identification of role, and expression of self-concept. Compton's study is one of several that has found close relationship between selection of clothing and expression of one's self, particularly between selection of clothing and personality and status.[9] Similarly the effect of wearing glasses has been shown to produce favorable judgments of intelligence and industriousness.[10]

Tactile Communication

Tactile Communication is communication by touch, the earliest and most elementary mode of communication of the human organism. Tactual sensitivity is the most primitive sensory process in most lower organisms. Many subhuman organisms orient themselves to the world by their feelers or antennae. They literally *feel* their way through life. Tactile communication is also the primary mode of orientation to the world in organisms living underground, in fish, and probably in many reptiles.

Tactile communication is of special significance to human beings. It is the first form of communication experienced by the infant, and it is known that these early tactile experiences are crucial in the later development of symbolic recognition and response. The infant's need for tactile contacts — nuzzling, cuddling, patting, feeling — and his quick response to and acceptance of tactile messages are well-known facts. Parental care and love through infancy and childhood are largely matters of tactile communication — tactual contacts that comfort, reassure, express acceptance, give encouragement, and build confidence in the child. Moreover, the kind of and duration of early tactile experiences wherein the infant or child can send and receive messages have an effect on early personality development.

Sometimes a small child will transfer tactile communication to objects other than his mother. A baby may become attached to the feel of a specific blanket (as is the case with the comic character, Linus), a soft cuddly animal, or a toy and begin to enjoy these textures and tactile contacts. Denial or deprivation of early tactile experiences may impair future learning such as speech, cognition, and symbolic recognition, as well as limit the individual's capacity for more mature tac-

[9]N. Compton, "Personal Attributes of Color and Design Preferences in Clothing Fabrics," *Journal of Psychology* 54 (1962): 191-95.
[10]G. Thornton, "The Effect of Wearing Glasses Upon Judgments of Personality Traits of Persons Seen Briefly," *Journal of Applied Psychology* 28 (1944): 203-7.

tile communication; for through early tactile experiences the infant begins to communicate, then gradually enlarges his communication as he develops capacities for other sensory perception and other forms of response. The foundation for these other forms of communication, both verbal and nonverbal, is tactile communication.

We need to note a second developmental stage in tactile communication because it too is related to subsequent adult tactile communication. This is the stage when the child learns that there are curtailments and prohibitions connected with tactile communication. He learns to define some things (property, sacred places, forbidden objects, persons, and so forth) as untouchables except under certain conditions (when one has permission, has performed certain rituals, has made a purchase, and so forth). Sometimes the child's naive use of tactile communication is prohibited by strong and painful punishment. The process of *socializing* the child according to the rules of tactile communication may vary from successful to unsuccessful, that is, it may be accompanied by fears and strong inhibitions. Not only does it vary within cultures from person to person but it also varies from culture to culture. Nevertheless, tactile communication experiences of the infant and the child are directly related to the effectiveness of adult interpersonal communication. Through the early tactile experiences of baby and mother, child and parents, child and others, the first patterns of interpersonal relations are established, and they will affect subsequent interpersonal relation patterns. These early tactile experiences are related to the individual's confidence in the world and trust in people.

For adults, tactile communication is a potent form of nonverbal communication. Tactile communication has at least four distinguishing characteristics: (1) tactile experience is ordinarily limited to two persons; (2) tactile experience is immediate and transitory, operating only as long as contact is maintained; (3) tactile communication is reciprocal in the sense that who or what a person touches also touches him; and (4) tactile communication takes place on the level of signals (direct stimulation through the sense of touch) rather than through symbolic mediation. Tactile experiences, as emotional and attitudinal messages and responses, are powerful, clear, and capable of an amazing variety of transformations in human communication. Through the touch of a hand one can feel fear, coldness, and anxiety, or love, warmth, and security. Tactile communication plays a pervasive role in human communication.

Space

Does Dad have his own chair in your home? Is the kitchen Mom's? Anthropologist Edward T. Hall has pointed out that cultures establish meanings that are related to distance or space.[11] In the United States,

[11]Edward T. Hall, *The Silent Language* (New York: Doubleday & Co., Inc., 1959), p. 163.

the comfortable and appropriate distance to stand for conversation is about an arm's length. The Brazilian, as he talks with an American, moves in closer; the American is apt to interpret that space violation as pushy, overbearing, or aggressive; and, if the American backs away, the Brazilian is apt to think the American is being standoffish or cold.

The American and the Arab are even less compatible in terms of the space defined as appropriate for conversation. The Arab may stand quite close and look intently into the American's eyes as he talks. This space element and eye-contact behavior may be associated with sexual intimacy by the American, who consequently may find it disturbing in a nonsexual context. Hall believes that the space or distance between persons in communication is related to the nature of the messages. He has identified eight distances that may be indicative of certain types of messages. They include (1) very close (3 to 6 inches)—soft whisper, top secret, or intimate information; (2) close (8 to 12 inches)—audible whisper, very confidential information; (3) near (12 to 20 inches)—soft voice, confidential; (4) neutral (20 to 36 inches)—soft voice, personal information; (5) neutral (4½ to 5 feet)—full voice, nonpersonal; (6) *public* distance (5½ to 8 feet)—full voice; (7) and (8) stretching the limits of distance (up to 100 feet)—hailing and departure distance.[12] The first two distances constitute the intimate zone; numbers three and four are the personal; five and six make up the social zone; and further distances are called the public zone.

The intimate distance in the American culture is used by lovers, husband and wife, children or members of the family, and very close friends. This distance is acceptable for two women talking together in the United States, but it is not acceptable for men at this time in our culture. For men in the Arab culture, intimate distance is acceptable. It is quite acceptable, for example, for two Arab men to stroll along hand in hand as they visit. Generally, we do not want our intimate space boundaries violated by those with whom we are not on intimate relationships. One place in which you can observe people sometimes uptight because of the necessary violation of the intimate zone is a crowded elevator. You can easily observe the many nonverbal messages that people send to each other as they cope with this situation—messages that say, "I'm not doing this intentionally; I have to." "I apologize for being so close to you." or "Get away! There is room enough to permit you to stand farther away." You probably have noticed that when one, two, or three people are in an elevator, they stand at opposite ends of the elevator so as to not invade each other's intimate or personal zones. As the elevator becomes crowded, people pull themselves in and stand stiffly, trying not to touch anyone. If they do touch, they may verbally apologize for it. And if they just have to touch, they usually tense their muscles in the touching area so as to be

[12]*Ibid.*, pp. 163-64.

'cold." To be relaxed and "warm" against a stranger will probably elicit cold and harsh looks or even verbal reprimands.

Even the *personal zone* (1½ to 3 feet) has many restrictions attached to it. It is a normal and acceptable distance for conversation at a party, for many work relationships, for talk with your classmates, and for chatting with close friends on the street, but it assumes a well-established acquaintanceship and a trusting relationship.

The social zone is said to be the distance at which American business is transacted. It is the distance between the housewife and the appliance repairman, the salesman and the customer, the boss and the secretary, and those only casually acquainted at social gatherings.

Public distance is often used for public speaking, for acting (distance between actor and audience), and for certain business situations.

All of these meanings in space relationships vary from culture to culture. The Japanese, for example, do not fear crowding as do many Americans; rather, the Japanese see crowding as a warm and pleasant experience. Arabs, also, enjoy closeness and touching. They do not recognize rules about not coming too close nor resent it.

Birds, animals, and people mark out the territory they stand on as their own personal space. They let others approach, but not too closely. In one experiment, a person deliberately intruded on the personal space of female college students seated at study tables in a library. The intruder sat down right next to any coed sitting alone at a library table. Each of the victims tried to restore an appropriate distance by moving her chair farther away, turning sideways, and by building a barrier of books, purse, and coat. The experimenter then pursued by moving his chair closer to the retreating victim. When all avoidance mechanisms failed, the victims took flight. Only one of the eighty students whose personal space had been invaded asked the experimenter to move over. Personal space, like sex, seems to be one of those things we react to but do not acknowledge in words. The amount of space a person needs is influenced by his personality. Introverts, for example, seem to need more elbow room than extroverts.

Mood is also indicated by space. We put more space between ourselves and those we dislike than between ourselves and those we like. Drawing away can communicate avoidance, rejection, or fear; while drawing closer can communicate acceptance, admiration, and liking. Space speaks.

It is said that each of us has a personal space that we carry around with us. Like a bubble that encloses us, it is our personal territory, our "body buffer zone." Others may not enter it without permission or invitation. Studies by Dr. A.F. Kinzel with federal prisoners indicate that prisoners with histories of violence against other persons have body buffer zones at least four times larger than men without histories of violence. Several of the violent prisoners he studied made reference to their "not being able to stand invasion of their buffer zone." They lashed out violently when such violations occurred. Kinzel and others have raised a question concerning the effect of overcrowding in the cities upon man's behavior. We know that animals have clearly marked territories and personal space needs, and we know from experiments that overcrowding and destruction of their minimal space require- ments cause animals to become hostile, aggressive, and even self- destructive at times. We have yet to determine whether man can adjust satisfactorily to overcrowding or whether he too has certain space requirements for survival psychologically. We do know that we can easily observe people staking out and holding their territories. The person who puts his feet on his desk while you talk with him in *his* office is saying very clearly, "This is my territory!" He may say the same thing by pulling a desk drawer out and putting his foot on it; by throwing his leg over the arm of the chair; by leaning back and placing both hands behind his head; or by standing up after inviting you to be seated. You have probably observed students staking out and holding their space in the library. Barriers and lines of demarcation are built with books, pencils, and coats. Or coats are placed on seats to "hold them." At Purdue, books are dropped on tables in the cafeterias to "hold the tables" while the students wait in lines to get their meal. I recall once this year I went into the Depot, a Purdue cafeteria room, and saw only a half-a-dozen or so tables with people seated at them, but every one of the remaining forty or fifty tables was "taken." It was a room all staked out, with all territories claimed, and yet it was practically empty of people!

It has been discovered that placing physical barriers between persons to insure their territorial space improves morale in certain situations. Protective counters between waitresses and cooks have served such a function. Waist-high or shoulder-high partitions in large offices have had a similar effect. We recognize the integrity of per- sonal space in ways other than through the erection of walls, counters, and partitions, however. The butler or waitress does not listen to the conversations of guests, and the pedestrian avoids staring at the em- bracing couple.

The arrangement of furniture and the distance between chairs utilizes space to communicate certain messages—messages having to do with rules, relationships, and status. It has been discovered, for example, that patients are more at ease with the doctor if the doctor is not behind a desk. At one time it was the practice for executives to communicate from behind their desks, but now one finds easy chairs, sofas, and coffee tables integral parts of the executive furnishings. Now the executive can communicate status, power, and aloofness by staying behind the desk, or he can invite his caller to sit at a table with him or they may sit in two easy chairs—thus communicating informal- ity, warmth, and equality.

Even in the home, furniture arrangement and where people place

themselves via the use of furniture communicates certain relationships. Often, the father will sit at the head of a rectangular dining
table. The mother may sit by her husband or at the opposite end of the
table.

In discussion groups, committee meetings, or other business
meetings, the chairman will generally assume the head-of-the-table
position, and other places around the table may have special status
meanings. For this reason, many of us like to work in discussion groups
in which everyone is seated in a circle. King Arthur made rather
famous the use of a "round table" to indicate the equality of the status
of his knights.

Pay special attention to how professors, deans, and others arrange
and use furniture in their offices. What are they communicating to
you? Do you suppose it is intentional or unintentional nonverbal communication? Is their furniture arranged to keep you at a distance; to
show roles and status? Is the furniture arranged to form primarily a
"work office," a "social office," or a "counseling office"?

The use of furniture and space to communicate status, role, and
power is an interesting phenomenon in nonverbal communication.
Studies have shown, for example, that persons of low status, when
entering the office of a superior, stop just inside the door and talk
across the room to the seated superior; if the person entering the office
walks halfway to the desk of the seated superior, he probably is a
person of higher status; if he walks right up to the desk, he probably
has as much power as the fellow seated at the desk; and if he walks
around behind the desk and stands over the other fellow, he probably
holds a superior position to the person seated at the desk. These
movements are space oriented. They are penetrations into the territory
of the person in whose office they occur.

Offices themselves — by their size, furnishings, and locations — also
indicate power and status levels. The largest offices on the highest
floors, with corner windows, sofas, and carpets, are for the top
personnel. Then come the offices on high floors that are somewhat
smaller and have no corner windows, with probably only one or two
windows on one wall. Finally, there are offices with no windows. And
even lower in status are those offices that are cubicles. Some cubicles
are of higher status than other cubicles, however, as some have
frosted-glass partitions while others have clear-glass partitions,
making them "public." Probably the lowest rank is the single desk that
sets alongside twenty-nine other desks in an open room.

One other facet of using "space-speaks" principles is that of police
interrogation work. Police investigators are advised to keep moving
closer to the person being interrogated and to allow no object — table,
chair, desk, and so forth — to come between themselves and the subject
that will act as a buffer or a shield for the subject. Such an object gives
the subject something to hide behind and bolsters his confidence and

security. Rather, the questioner wants to give the person nothing to hide behind psychologically. One of the detectives in a police communication class I taught this spring told me he holds the subject's knees together tightly with his own knees; and as he finds it necessary, he restrains the fellow by grasping his wrists and holding his arms tightly too. With "no place to go," and his personal and intimate space dominated, the subject often loses his superior confidence and resistance. Not being able to escape physically or nonverbally, he cannot escape the question psychologically, and so the tendency is for the subject to spill out the truth.

Space does speak and it can speak powerfully. We ought to become aware of what we communicate with our own use of space and distance, and with what others about us are saying via their use of space. If we can perfect such skills, our communication will be greatly improved.

Time

As with space, so time is a type of nonverbal communication. Time talks. In America, punctuality communicates respect and tardiness can be an insult. In other cultures, however, being on time is an insult. In America, a late message, whether term paper, business report, or press release, is likely to have undesirable consequences. Tardiness often communicates a low regard for the receiver and for the message. Many persons purposely use air mail only for their letters, believing that it builds credibility and respect by communicating a high regard. Time is used to communicate role relationships and status. The "boss" may walk right into the subordinate's office, while the subordinate knocks before entering the boss's office, or a receptionist or secretary calls the boss to gain entry for the subordinate. Then the subordinate may have to "wait to see the boss." It has been verified in studies made that the lower the status of the visitor, the longer he waits before getting in to see the person upon whom he is calling.

If further evidence is needed to establish the fact that time talks, remember the telephone call you received at a very late hour, 2:30 A.M. for example. You probably felt some sense of urgency and importance, even danger perhaps. It was the element of time that communicated the alarm.

Silence

Silence can be used to communicate. It is not unusual that what is *not* said is as important or more important than what *is* said. Silence can have message value. Silence can influence others. One need not be exceptionally sensitive to silence as a cue to be aware of its clarity and power as a vehicle of communication. Surely most of us have been rebuffed with silence. We have been "told" clearly by someone through his silence, his avoidance of eye contact, and his lack of response that he wished to be left alone, that he did not want to engage in interaction. Or perhaps you have asked someone a question and she has continued to read or do whatever she was doing, without saying a word or responding in any way other than in tight-lipped silence. Such treatment by the "silence-user" is quite insulting and hostility provoking, but there is no question about it communicating. We "get the message" easily. The use of silence to communicate varies from culture to culture as do other forms of nonverbal communication.

In summary, we have identified eight kinds of nonverbal communication — vocal characteristics, sign language, action language, object language, tactile communication, communication by the use of space, time communication, and silence. Any of the codes, singularly or in combination, may be used to modify verbal messages — to reinforce, validate, or complement the verbal message, or to contradict and negate it; or nonverbal communication may be used in its own right, without accompanying verbal messages, to establish bonds and relationships necessary for survival.

Differences Between Verbal and Nonverbal Communication

The two systems, verbal and nonverbal, constitute *different languages* and operate according to different laws. When we talk face-to-face with another person we are sending discrete, digital, verbal symbols while at the same time sending continuous, analogical, nonverbal cues. One of the differences between analogical and digital information, according to neurologists, is that the human nervous system handles the two kinds of cues differently; they travel over different neural pathways in the brain. The analogical information travels over the older portions of the brain — those portions that develop in the infant months and years before words and numbers (digital information) are learned. Digital pathways lie in those parts of the brain that develop late in the child and that developed more slowly in the evolutionary growth of man. Medical science has shown that in cases of brain pathology the newer portions of the brain usually degenerate first, and so it is not unusual for the person to lose his ability to handle verbal symbols while retaining his ability to read visual and other nonverbal cues.

Another difference is that *analogical messages* are received rapidly, while *digital messages* reach us more slowly and are processed more slowly. This means that the message sent by one's body is perceived and reacted to before the meaning of verbal messages are perceived. Hence nonverbal messages often create in us a set that acts as a filter affecting our perception and-reaction to verbal messages.

Yet another difference between digital and analogical messages is that words can and do represent abstractions such as love and hate, but nonverbal messages observed in one's behavior (expressive messages) are more likely to represent nothing but themselves. They are directly related to the feeling of the moment.

Finally, most verbal messages are governed by one's will — are constructed intentionally — while many nonverbal cues are not under one's control. One cannot so easily govern body movements and psycho-physiological responses. The following table further compares verbal and nonverbal communication.

Table 6.1 Verbal and Nonverbal Codification Differences*

Nonverbal Communication	Verbal Communication
Nonverbal communication is based on continuous functions; the hand is continuously involved in movement.	Verbal communication is based on discontinuous functions; sounds or letters have a discrete beginning and ending.
Nonverbal communication is regulated primarily by principles governed by biological necessity.	Verbal communication is governed primarily by arbitrary, man-made principles.
Nonverbal communication influences perception, coordination, and integration, and leads to the acquisition of skills.	Verbal communication influences thinking and leads to the acquisition of information.
Understanding of nonverbal detonation is based upon the participants' emphatic assessment of biological similarity; no explanation is needed for understanding what pain is.	Understanding of verbal detonation is based on prior verbal agreement.
Nonverbal communication uses the old structures of the central and autonomic nervous systems.	Verbal communication uses younger brain structures, particularly the cortex.
Nonverbal communication is learned early in life.	Verbal communication is learned later in life.
Action and objects exist in their own right.	Words do not exist in their own right. They represent arbitrary symbols representing abstractions of events.
Nonverbal communication is emotional to a great extent.	Verbal communication is intellectual to a great extent.
Nonverbal communication represents an intimate language.	Verbal communication represents a distant language.

*It should be recognized that these differences are *not* absolute. There are exceptions and qualifications, but we are interested in calling attention to differences frequently found between verbal and nonverbal communication.

Note: Adapted from Jurgen Ruesch, "Nonverbal Language and Therapy," *Psychiatry* 18 (1955): pp. 323-30. Used by permission.

Because of these differences between nonverbal and verbal communication — because nonverbal communication has several unique characteristics — it is possible to suggest some tentative axioms or principles of nonverbal communication.

Three Principles of Nonverbal Communication

One Cannot *Not* Communicate

All observed behavior has message value. Behavior has no opposite; there is no such thing as nonbehavior. Hence it follows that one cannot avoid communicating. One can avoid communicating verbally, but nonverbal communication cannot be avoided. Even inactivity and silence have message value. The mere absence of talking does not mean that there is no communication. Purposeful silence and avoidance of verbal communication is in itself communication. Sigmund Freud once wrote: "No mortal can keep a secret. If his lips are silent, he chatters with his finger tips; betrayal oozes out of him at every pore." Thus, an individual may appear calm and self-controlled—unaware that signs of tension and anxiety are leaking out in the tapping of his foot or the tenseness of his fingers.

Nonverbal Channels Are Especially Effective in Communicating Feelings, Attitudes, and Relationships

Man communicates verbally to share cognitive information and to transmit knowledge, but he relies heavily on nonverbal communication to share emotions, feelings, and attitudes. In fact, some nonverbal communication (tactile communication, for example) is used almost entirely to communicate noncognitive information. Watzlawick has stated that when relationship is the central concern of communication (superior-subordinate, leader-follower, helper-helped, etc.), verbal language is almost meaningless.[13] In courtship, love, or combat, nonverbal communication is the effective mode. One can, of course, verbally profess love or trust, but it is most meaningfully communicated through the nonverbal codes. The verbal channel has a high potential for carrying semantic information, but the nonverbal channel has a high potential for carrying affective information. The emotional side of the message is very often expressed by the nonverbal elements. When a person is liked or disliked, often it is a case of "not only what he said, but the way he said it."

Through the nonverbal codes (all the types we have identified—vocal, object, action, etc.) we communicate power, trustworthiness, status, affection, hostility, acceptance, and the full range of attitudes and feelings. From the student in conversation with the professor who holds his eyes with hers a little longer than usual to communicate admiration and affection, to the student who narrows his eyes and sharpens his voice as he communicates hostility to the professor, nonverbal communication makes its impact on interpersonal transactions.

---

[13]Paul Watzlawick, Janet Helmick Beavin, and Don D. Jackson, *The Pragmatics of Human Communication* (New York: W.W. Norton & Company, Inc., 1967), p. 63.

Recent studies tend to show that attitudes are communicated non-verbally. Posture, for example, often reflects a person's attitude toward people he is with. One experiment indicates that when men are with other men whom they dislike, they either relax very much or are very rigid, depending on how threatening they perceive the other man to be. Women in this experiment always signaled dislike with a very relaxed posture. Several studies have identified strong relationships between posture (particularly trunk and head positions) and attitudes, as well as between body movement (turning away or toward, moving nearer to or further from, etc.) and attitudes.[14] Four general postural attitudes have been identified—withdrawal, approach, expansion, and contraction. Therapists, psychiatrists, and others sensitive to non-verbal communication use these postures and other non-verbal cues to diagnose and understand persons whom they wish to help.

Not only posture but also expressive gestures, facial expressions, and vocal cues communicate inner states and emotion. Autistic gestures (interlaced fingers, closed fist, finger on the lips, nose rubbing, ear pulling, etc.) have been found to be related to inner conflict states.[15] Other signals such as clearing the throat, closing the eyes, scratching, tapping the fingers or feet are related to attitudes and emotions.

The face (smiles, frowns, etc.) is often used to express affiliation, liking and approval, or disliking and disapproval. Nods of the head may be social reinforcers. A continued exchange of glances may indicate a willingness and desire to be involved in ongoing interaction; while avoidance of eye contact often is an indication of lack of interest and a desire to break away from interaction.[16]

It is apparent to the student of communication that the nonverbal codes are especially effective in communicating affective messages.

Involuntary Nonverbal Messages Often Are of High Validity

When people interact they rarely trust in words alone. They observe the shifting forward, withdrawing, frowning, smiling, speaking in strained or serious tones; the straightening of clothing; the manipula-

[14]See W. James, "A Study of the Expression of Bodily Posture," *Journal of General Psychology* 7 (1932): 405-36; F. Deutsch, "Analysis of Postural Behavior," *Psychoanalytic Quarterly* 16 (1947): 195-213; Howard M. Rosenfeld, "Instrumental Affiliative Functions of Facial and Gestural Expressions," *Journal of Personality and Social Psychology* 4 (1966): 65-72; and R. Taguiri, R.R. Blake, and J.S. Bruner, "Some Determinants of the Perception of Positive and Negative Feelings in Others," *Journal of Abnormal and Social Psychology* 48 (1953): 585-92.

[15]See M. Krout, "An Experimental Attempt to Produce Unconscious Manual Symbolic Movements," *Journal of General Psychology* 51 (1954): 93-120; and S. Feldman, *Mannerisms of Speech and Gesture in Everyday Life* (New York: International Press, 1959).

[16]Ralph Exline, David Gray, and Dorothy Schuette, "Visual Behavior in a Dyad as Affected by Interview Content and Sex of Respondent," *Journal of Personality and Social Psychology* 1 (1925): 201-9.

tion of a cigarette, coffee cup, or pencil. Nonverbal cues are often used to determine the authenticity of verbal messages. Thus the blush or the frown is likely to be taken as more reliable than the accompanying verbal reassurances. When verbal cues and the nonverbal cues tell different stories, the nonverbal story tends to be believed. Words can be chosen with care, but expressive nonverbal cues cannot be chosen; the body is not so easily governed. Further, because we are trained primarily in verbal communication and often disregard nonverbal communication, we are probably far less guarded even in our instrumental nonverbal behavior than in our verbal behavior, and hence we may reveal information nonverbally that we carefully control or censure in our verbal messages.

When we are able to communicate honestly we do not send out contradictory messages. Some of the social games we play, however, force us to send verbal messages that are inconsistent with our true feelings that are revealed through nonverbal cues. We say, "Delighted that you could come," "We had a wonderful time," "Glad to meet you," and so forth, regardless of our feelings. Our real attitudes and emotions are often communicated nonverbally, and when the nonverbal message contradicts the verbal, people tend to believe the nonverbal.[17] It has higher validity. Actions *do* speak louder than words. We rely on the nonverbal cues to gain our *real* impression of others. In one experiment, perfect strangers described their impressions of each other based on observing the visual nonverbal cues (posture, movement, facial expression, clothing, etc.) with no verbal communication. Not only did each believe he could describe the other person after observing him, but an analysis of their descriptions revealed exceptionally high agreement on many factors, including submissiveness, assurance, friendliness, psychological state, and extroversion.[18] The validity of nonverbal messages that express feelings, emotions, and relationships have been demonstrated by a number of scientists.[19] Labarre has noted that successful psychiatrists, artists, anthropologists, and teachers rely on the validity of nonverbal communication:

> Dr. H.S. Sullivan, for example, is known to many of his acute understanding of the postural tonuses of his patients. Another psychiatrist,

[17]Albert Mehrabian, "Orientation Behaviors and Nonverbal Attitude Communication," *Journal of Communication* 17 (December 1967): 331.

[18]R. Barker, "The Social Interrelations of Strangers and Acquaintances," *Sociometry* 5 (1942): 169-79.

[19]See Charles Darwin, *The Expression of the Emotions in Man and Animals* (New York: D. Appleton & Company, 1862; reprint ed., Chicago: University of Chicago Press, 1965); Dr. Duchenne, *Micanisme de la Physionomie Humaine* (folio edition, 1862); Paul Ekman and Wallace V. Friesen, "Nonverbal Behavior in Psychotherapy Research," in *Research on Psychotherapy*, vol. 3, ed. J. Schlien (Washington, D.C.: American Psychological Association, 1967); and Clyde L. Rousey, *Diagnostic Implications of Speech Sounds* (Springfield, Ill.: Charles C. Thomas, Publisher, 1965).

Dr. E.J. Kempf, evidences in copious illustrations of his "Psychopath-ology" a highly cultivated sense of the kinaesthetic language of tonuses in painting and sculpture, and can undoubtedly discover a great deal about a patient merely by glancing at him. The linguist, Dr. Stanley Newman, has a preternatural skill in recognizing psychiatric syn-dromes through the individual styles of tempo, stress, and intonation. The gifted cartoonist, Mr. William Steig, has produced, in The Lonely Ones, highly sophisticated and authentic drawings of the postures and tonuses of schizophrenia, depression, mania, paranoia, hysteria, and in fact the whole gamut of psychiatric syndromes. Among anthropolo-gists, Dr. W.H. Sheldon is peculiarly sensitive and alert to the emo-tional and temperamental significance of constitutional tonuses. I believe that it is by no means entirely an illusion that an experienced teacher can come into a classroom of new students and predict with some accuracy the probable quality of individual scholastic accom-plishment — even as judged by other professors — by distinguishing the unreachable, unteachable, Apperceptions Masse-less sprawl of one student from the edge-of-the-seat, starved avidity and intentness of another. Likewise, an experienced lecturer can become acutely aware of the body language of his listeners and respond to it appropriately until the room fairly dances with communication and counter-com-munication, head noddings, and the tenseness of listeners soon to be prodded into public speech.[20]

In this chapter we have noted that nonverbal communication plays a significant role for us in exchanging meanings with other persons. Hopefully, you will become more aware of the nonverbal messages sent by those with whom you communicate, more aware of your own non-verbal communication with others, and better able to send and receive messages clearly.

We have identified and described eight of the most important kinds of nonverbal messages. They included paralanguage; sign language; action language; object language; tactile, spatial, and time communica-tion; and silence as a means of nonverbal communication. It is helpful to remember that paying attention to several cues from many or all of these sources will allow us to be more accurate in knowing what the person is communicating to us rather than relying on one small movement, a single voice intonation, or a one-time scratching of the nose.

We have emphasized that the nonverbal channels often seem to be especially effective channels for messages having to do with feelings, attitudes, and interpersonal relationships. And we have emphasized that those nonverbal messages that are involuntary may often be of high validity. Because of their validity, they can help receivers to more accurately interpret accompanying verbal messages.

[20]Weston Labarre, "The Cultural Basis of Emotions and Gestures," Journal of Personality 16 (1947): 64, 65.

References

Goffman, Erving. *Relations in Public.* New York: Basic Books, Inc., 1971.
    A popular treatment of public interaction through nonverbal communication.
Hall, Edward T. *The Silent Language.* New York: Doubleday & Co., 1959.
    A popular treatment of the various types of nonverbal communication.
Harrison, R.P. *Beyond Words.* Englewood Cliffs, N.J.: Prentice-Hall, 1974.
    A readable and interesting introduction to nonverbal communication.
Knapp, M.L. *Nonverbal Communication in Human Interaction.* New York: Holt
    Rinehart and Winston, 1972.
    The most complete summary of theory and its supporting research that is
    written for the college student.
Montagu, Ashley. *Touching.* New York: Columbia University Press, 1971.
    An in-depth treatment and review of research of tactile communication.

Questions:

1. In what ways does your nonverbal communication differ from your verbal communication:
    a. when you are angry?
    b. when you are very attracted to someone but want to conceal it?
    c. when you have to be cordial to someone you intensely dislike?
    d. when someone hurts your feelings?
    e. when you are trying to show interest even though you are ex-extremely bored?
    f. when you are interviewing for a job you really want?
    g. when you are lying?
    h. when you are purposely manipulating someone to get them to do something for you?

2. Go back to the article "Some Tentative Axioms of Communication." Does the Brook's article help you understand digital and analogical communication? What other similarities do you find in the two articles?

3. How valid do you consider the idea that about 65% of the social meaning in face-to-face communication is nonverbal?

4. Why should nonverbal communication be included in intercultural communication study?

This article critiques popular books on nonverbal communication and asks if they are manuals of fakery.

"Body Language Taught Here"

Judith A. Hall

A woman plans to tilt her head to one side during her next conversation with a man whom she likes. A man watches his female companion to see if she starts gesticulating palms-upward. A businessman, during a conference with his superior, carefully widens and narrows his eyes with alternate intensity.

The people enacting these odd behaviors probably read one or several of the current popular books on "body language," a catchall phrase that includes facial expressions, body gestures, tone of voice, touch, interpersonal space, and even dress. The head tilt is said to impress a man; in fact, one popular author says "women instinctively understand the significance of this gesture" (10, p. 60). The open palm supposedly indicates an invitation, probably sexual (4, 11). Widening and narrowing the eyes makes someone think you are reacting to him when you are not (11).

During the last ten years a body of serious research on nonverbal communication has emerged, associated with names like Ekman, Birdwhistell, Mehrabian, and Davitz. Many researchers in several fields see nonverbal communication as an important social process. This work has been popularized in the last three or four years by several different authors, and their books and articles have sold millions of copies.

The "body language" books purport to introduce the public to the "fledgling science" of kinesics (4). The most popular are probably *Body Language* by Julius Fast (7), *Body Talk* by Maude Poiret (11), *How to Read a Person Like a Book* by Gerard I. Nierenberg and Henry H.

Reprinted from "Body Language Taught Here" by Judith A. Hall (formerly Judith H. Koivumaki), in the *Journal of Communication* (Volume 25, Number 1), pages 26-30.

Calero (10), *Inside Intuition* by Flora Davis (4), and the chapter called
"Nonverbal Contact" in Leonard Zunin's *Contact: The First Four
Minutes* (12).

These books have slightly different emphases. *Body Talk* is mostly
about sociosexual encounters—cocktail parties and the like. *How to
Read a Person Like a Book* deals mainly with business encounters. *Body
Language* makes a slightly broader and fairer attempt to cover the field
of nonverbal communication. *Inside Intuition* is the best; its author
relates many findings back to their researchers, using footnotes, and
she is often properly tentative, but in the end her desire to write an
appealing book subverts the scholarly nature of the nonverbal communication research she reports. Finally, the chapter in *Contact: The
First Four Minutes* is about first encounters of all sorts, and in it Zunin
liberally ascribes meanings to all manner of gestures and postures
whose meanings are by no means so easy to pin down, without indicating on what authority he ascribes the meanings. He also cites Fast
(7) and Nierenberg and Calero (10) as recommended readings.

*The book-buying public is keen on this literature, judging from sales
figures quoted on the book covers and from the frequency with which
the books can be found in bookstores and drugstores.*

As a scholarly topic, too, nonverbal communication itself has some
attractive features. The topic is relevant in sociology, psychology, psychiatry, ethology, and anthropology. There is no single, correct method-
ology for studying nonverbal communication. One can examine a single
nonverbal act microanalytically, by poring over movie film frame by
frame, or, at the other extreme, one can generalize about nations or
ethnic groups. One can look at nonverbal communication in dyads in
larger groups; one can perform statistical analyses or draw conclusions impressionistically. The *meanings* of nonverbal cues can be
examined—for example, the meanings of different kinds of smiles can
be explored in different cultural settings. Or, people's *skills* at
encoding and decoding nonverbal cues can be studied; this study cuts
across the meanings of individual gestures and seeks to find stable
differences between people in how well or poorly they communicate
nonverbally. Nonverbal skills can be related to other facts about
people, such as their sex, their experiences, their values, or their
personal happiness. One can examine "channels" of nonverbal communication: tone of voice, face cues, body gestures, proxemic (spatial)
behavior, touch, smell, even ESP. In short, nonverbal communication
seems relevant in an enormous range of ways, and there is much
research both good and bad being done on it.

Its appeal also stems from the fact that, on the face of it, anyone who
has eyes and ears (or a nose, or whatever) has the equipment to be an
expert. People carry around with them implicit theories of nonverbal
communication which they test and modify informally; and they would
do so both consciously and unconsciously even if books and articles on

body language had never been written. Our knowledge and use of non-verbal communication are important tools (some would say our key tool) for getting along in a social environment.

Why should such "important" knowledge not be spread around?

The first problem with the present popularization has to do with how accurately the research is represented. Reading just a few pages convinces the informed (and often the uninformed) reader that findings are oversimplified, hypotheses and truisms are stated as facts, and the reader is often in the dark as to whose research is being reported. Because the authors invoke the word *science,* the reputation of more scholarly research stands to suffer.

But even if readers could distinguish between hard findings and mere intuition or anecdote, another, much more serious, criticism would remain. These books exploit our curiosity — indeed, our ignorance — about why relationships succeed and fail, and they feed our apparently insatiable desires to improve our social status, to make it with the opposite sex, and to succeed in business — in short, to exercise social control. These books encourage, quite literally, the exploitation of one person by another.

The reader may not think so at first glance. In the prefaces, first chapters, or ads one may find lofty statements about improving understanding, harmony, and self-fulfilment. But the authors quickly reveal their theme: how to. How to enhance your bargaining position by "psyching out" the competition. A business customer is interested in your product if his pupils dilate (7), or if he sits in a certain posture (10). A potential customer can be put at a disadvantage if you take him to a restaurant and then gradually move your water glass and silverware onto his side of the table; by so doing, you encroach on his territory, making him anxious and defensive (7). To assert dominance or superiority over someone, "all you have to do is physically elevate yourself above him" (10, p. 101). You can also dominate under the guise of communicating intimacy and confidentiality, by speaking softly at a very close distance (this subordinates the other person) (10).

If you are a woman, you can force a young man to interact with you, and he will never know you planned it (7). You can make a fellow student uncomfortable and eventually force him to flee, by sitting too close in a library (7). To act like a boss, just enter the subordinate's office without knocking (7). To attract a man at a party, you should unobtrusively imitate his body signals (11), thus producing what some researchers call interactional synchrony. A man at a party can invade a woman's personal space, "gradually so his quarry won't know what's happening until she's hooked on his appeal" (11, p. 53). You can keep a male boss interested in you, if you are a woman, by displaying carefully timed, underplayed pseudo-sexual gestures; if your boss is of the same sex as yourself you can also learn how to behave so you will not seem like competition (11).

An irony should be noted. One key assumption the popular authors make is that people's unconscious nonverbal cues are "truer" than their conscious or intended cues (such as what they say). One of the authors states outright that body language probably cannot be faked (4). The hypothesis that people cannot always control their nonverbal behavior is also held by many serious researchers, who study the famous "double bind" (2), nonverbal "leakage" (5), lying (6), and the phenomenon called "channel discrepancy" (when two or more mutually contradictory messages are sent simultaneously) (3). The authors of the popular books base their whole case on the assumption that people's "real" feelings are reflected in their nonverbal behavior. However, these books are, in essence, manuals of body language fakery, the very thing assumed to be impossible or at least very difficult to do!

If the current fascination with reading and sending nonverbal cues—whether authentic or faked—had only academic implications, then there would not be cause for alarm. Unfortunately, at least to me, this seems not to be the case. Encounter groups, T-groups, and the like are popular and prevalent. A public high school in New York City offers a course that is oversubscribed each semester called "Body Language," and the teacher uses Fast's book (7) as a text (1). What all this means is that people are learning to apply this supposed "knowledge" of body language in settings that have an air of legitimacy and even a pseudo-scientific aura.

This is not a diatribe against popular books in general. Such a book can be clearly written and faithful to the spirit of the work which it describes. *Inside Intuition* (4) comes closer to this standard than the others.[1] Although accuracy is a major problem, by no means is everything in these particular books untrue or even exaggerated. Whether a particular statement is accurate or not becomes a secondary problem compared to the overwhelming fact that the selection and combination of "data" reported are clearly motivated by a desire to convey an ideology of exploitation—a kind of psychopornography—in which you destroy the other's confidence by taking advantage of his unintended nonverbal messages, and in which you manipulate the other by manufacturing credible cues that are actually fake.

References

1. Anderson, Virginia. Personal communication. April 27, 1964.
2. Bateson, G., D. Jackson, J. Haley, and J. Weakland. "Toward a Theory of Schizophrenia." *Behavioral Science* 1, 1956, pp. 251-264.

---

[1] Some relatively elementary and respectable books on nonverbal communication do exist. Mark Knapp's *Nonverbal Communication in Human Interaction* (9) has been praised by Randall P. Harrison and his associates in a review of the nonverbal communication literature (8).

3. Bugental, D.E., J.W. Kaswan, and L.R. Love. "Perception of Contradictory Meanings Conveyed by Verbal and Nonverbal Channels." *Journal of Personality and Social Psychology* 16, 1970, pp. 647-655.

4. Davis, Flora. *Inside Intuition: What We Know About Nonverbal Communication.* New York: McGraw-Hill, 1973.

5. Ekman, Paul, and Wallace V. Friesen. "Nonverbal Leakage and Clues to Deception." *Psychiatry* 32, 1969, pp. 88-106.

6. Ekman, Paul, and Wallace V. Friesen. "Detecting Deception from the Body or Face," *Journal of Personality and Social Psychology* 29, 1974, pp. 288-298.

7. Fast, Julius. *Body Language.* New York: Pocket Books, 1971.

8. Harrison, Randall P., Akiba A. Cohen, Wayne W. Crouch, B.K.L. Genova, and Mark Steinberg. "The Nonverbal Communication Literature." *Journal of Communication* 22, 1972, pp. 460-476.

9. Knapp, Mark L. *Nonverbal Communication in Human Interaction.* New York: Holt, Rinehart, and Winston, 1972.

10. Nierenberg, Gerard I., and Henry H. Calero. *How to Read a Person Like a Book,* New York: Pocket Books, 1973.

11. Poiret, Maude. *Body Talk: The Science of Kinesics.* New York: Award Books, 1970.

12. Zunin, Leonard. *Contact: The First Four Minutes.* New York: Ballantine Books, 1972.

Questions:

1. List other popular nonverbal books. Do you consider them "psycho-pornography"? Why or why not?

2. Did the popularization of nonverbal communication help or hinder its growth as a legitimate subject area?

3. What other subjects have been treated with similar "manuals of fakery"?

4. On the next page you will see two "concrete poems." How do you think they got that name, and what do you think they mean? Why are they placed after a section dealing with nonverbal communication?

— Mary Ellen Solt

The other half of speaking is listening, but we often wonder if anyone out there really is.

Is Anyone Out There Listening?

In communication, what you say isn't nearly so important as what the other person hears.

Unfortunately, not nearly enough people are listening.

Everybody knows that somebody listening to a joke is not really listening; he is impatiently awaiting his turn to tell a joke of his own. Everybody knows that husbands give half an ear to their wives — and wives respond in kind.

Abraham Kaplan, professor of philosophy at the University of Michigan, calls these one-sided conversations duologues, indicating two separate participants, rather than dialogues, which means an exchange of ideas.

"Duologues take place in schools, churches, cocktail parties, the U.S. Congress and almost everywhere we don't feel free to be wholly human."

The duologue has its unforgiving rules: "You have to give the other person his turn, and you give signals during his turn, like saying "uh huh' or laughing at what he says, to show that he is having his turn. You must also refrain from saying anything that really matters to you as a human being, as it would be regarded as an embarrassing intimacy."

A truly perfect duologue would be two TV sets tuned in and facing each other.

Dialogue, on the other hand, invoves serious listening, insists Professor Kaplan — listening not just to the other, but listening to one-self. "It seems impossible to me," he said, "to teach unless you are listening. You cannot really talk unless you are listening."

We should also recognize that not all communication is done by

Excerpted from March 1969 issue of *The Alcoa News*. Courtesy of Alcoa Aluminum Company of America.

words alone. The fact is we communicate whether we want to or not. Silence often says more than a lengthy comment. And if our words say one thing but our actions say another, the receiver of the communication gets a mixed signal. The message he decides to accept is usually based on his past experience or his "relationship" with the communicator.

The communication of relationship then, it seems to us is the strongest and most effective that we have going. This is so because it has to be honest. It's the kind of communication that ultimately demands "put your money where your mouth is;" "put up or shut up."

A communication of relationship has the potential to nurture a friendship, cement a marriage, build a community, unite a nation and bring peace to the world.

Relationship is that special something that makes a group function as a team.

Unlike even dialogue, communication of relationship will not deceive and cannot be ignored.

Unfortunately, it has an equal potential to destroy these same relationships, because ultimately the communication of relationship communicates truth.

Questions:

1. What percentage of your communication would you classify as duologue and what percentage dialogue? Can you think of some ways you might increase your dialogue percentage?

2. What do you think the authors mean by the phrase "communication of relationship"? Can you think of ways one could improve a relationship through communication?

3. How can silence communicate?

The prospect of being taught to listen seems absurd. We have done it all our lives. But Nichols suggests that we may not be as skilled at this activity as we think we are.

Do We Know How to Listen?

Practical Helps in a Modern Age

Ralph G. Nichols

In 1940 Dr. Harry Goldstein completed a very important research project at Columbia University. It was underwritten by one of our educational foundations, was very carefully drawn, and two very important observations emerged from it. One, he discovered that it is perfectly possible for us to listen to speech at a rate more than three times that at which we normally hear it, without significant loss of comprehension of what we hear. Two, he suggested that America may have overlooked a very important element in her educational system, that of teaching youngsters how to listen.

Shortly after that Richard Hubbell, an important figure in the television industry, produced a new book. In it, he declared without equivocation that 98 per cent of all a man learns in his lifetime he learns through his eyes or through his ears. His book tended to throw a spotlight upon a long-neglected organ we own, our ears.

Together, the declarations of Goldstein and Hubbell put into perspective the highly significant studies of Paul Rankin, of Ohio State University. Rankin was determined to find out what proportion of our waking day we spend in verbal communication. He kept careful log on 65 white-collar folk, much like you and me, at 15-minute intervals for two months on end. Here is what he found: seven out of every ten minutes that you and I are conscious, alive, and awake we are communicating verbally in one of its forms; and our communication time is devoted 9 per cent to writing, 16 per cent to reading, 30 per cent to speaking, and 45 per cent to listening.

Our Upside-down Schools

Quantitatively speaking, American has built her school system upside down. Throughout the twelve years a youngster normally spends in school, some teacher is continually trying to teach him how to write a sentence, in the hope that sometime he will be able to write a full paragraph, and then a complete report. Countless tax dollars and teacher hours of energy go into improving the *least used* channel of communication.

For some reason inexplicable to me, we usually chop off all reading improvement training at the end of the eighth grade, and from that time on the reading done is of an extensive, voluntary, and general character. Then we decry, sometimes, the fact that America is a nation of sixth-grade reading ability. We should not be shocked at that fact, in view of the maximum training received. However, a lot of tax dollars are devoted to improving this *second least-used* channel of communication.

Then we come to something important — speech itself. Thirty percent of our communication time is devoted to it; yet speech training in America is largely an extracurricular activity. In a typical school you will find an all-school play once or twice a year. There may be a debating team with a couple of lawyer's sons on it. There may be an orator, along with an extempore speaker, and that is about the size of it. You will find it very difficult to discover a single high school in America where even one semester of speech training is required of the youngsters going through. Actually much of the speech taught in America today is provided by Dale Carnegie and his cohorts in night classes at a cost of about $125 per student for enrollment. Too expensive, and too late in life, to do many of us much good!

Then we come to listening. Forty-five per cent of our communication time is spent in it. In 1948, when I first became concerned about this field, you could hardly find anyone really concerned about refining his listening ability. I asked my University for a sabbatical leave that year, and spent twelve months doing research related to the characteristics of good and bad listeners. First, I learned that nobody knew much about effective listening. Only three researches which you could call experimental and scientific had been published in 1948 in the field of listening comprehension. By comparison, over 3,000 scientific studies had been published in the parallel learning medium, that of reading comprehension.

Ten Years Makes A Difference

Between 1950 and 1960 a very dramatic page has been turned. Many of our leading universities are now teaching listening, under that label. Today these schools are not only teaching listening — they are doing, at long last, graduate-level research in the field. Today, also, scores of business and industries have instituted their own listening training programs for selected management personnel. Three departments of the Federal Government and a number of units of our military service have followed suit.

Very important to the growing interest in listening training in the public schools has been the steady support given by the National Council of Teachers of English and The Speech Association of America. Under their guidance and help new "language arts guides" are being widely adopted. Typically, these guides give equal emphasis to the four communication skills of reading, writing, speaking, and listening.

Two Central Questions

In view of this rather sudden surge of interest in effective listening, I should like to raise two questions, and very closely pursue answers to them.

Question number one: Is efficient listening a problem? For insight on this issue, let us revert to the classroom for a moment, for the first person to produce important evidence on it was H.E. Jones, a professor at Columbia University. One year he was in charge of the beginning psychology classes there, and frequently lectured to a population of some 476 freshmen.

It seemed to him, when he gave comprehension tests over his lecture content, that the students were not getting very much of what he was trying to say. He hit upon a very novel idea for an experiment. He talked 50 of his colleagues on the faculty at Columbia into cooperating with him. Each professor agreed to prepare and deliver to Jones' students a ten-minute lecture from his own subject-matter area. Each one submitted his lecture excerpt to Jones ahead of time, and Jones painstakingly built an objective test over the contents. Half of the questions in each quiz demanded a recalling of facts, and the other half required the understanding of a principle or two imbedded in the lecture excerpt.

Efficiency Level — 25 per cent

Professor Number 1 came in, gave his little ten-minute lecture, disappeared, and the group was questioned on its content. Number 2 followed. At the end of the fiftieth presentation and the fiftieth quiz, Jones scored the papers and found that freshmen were able to respond correctly to about half the items in each test. Then came the shock. Two months later he reassembled the 476 freshmen and gave them the battery of tests a second time. This time they were able to respond correctly to only 25 per cent of the items in the quizzes. Jones was forced to conclude, reluctantly, that without direct training, university freshmen appear to operate at a 25 per cent level of efficiency when they listen.

I could not believe it could be that bad. I decided to repeat the experiment at the University of Minnesota, and did so. I did not let two months go by before the retest, for I was pretty certain that the curve of forgetting takes a downward swoop long before two months have passed. Yet I got exactly the same statistics: fifty per cent response in the immediate test situation; 25 per cent after two weeks had passed.

Several other universities have run off essentially the same experiment, and all tend to report approximately the same statistics. I think it is accurate and conservative to say that we operate at almost precisely a 25 per cent level of efficiency when listening to a ten-minute talk.

What Can Be Done?

Let us turn to a second major question: Is there anything that can be done about the problem? After all, if you and I listen badly, only 25 per cent efficiently, and can do nothing about it, the future holds a pretty dismal outlook. Fortunately, if we want to become better listeners, or to make our students or employees better listeners, it is a goal perfectly possible to attain.

A few years ago we screened out the 100 worst listeners and the 100 best listeners we could identify in the freshman population on my campus. Standardized listening tests and lecture-comprehension tests were used, and we soon had two widely contrasting groups. These poor suffering 200 freshmen were then subjected to about 20 different kinds of objective tests and measures.

We got scores on their reading, writing, speaking, listening; mechanical aptitude, mathematics aptitude, science aptitude, six different types of personality inventories; each one filled out a lengthy questionnaire, and I had a long personal interview with each of the 200.

Ten Guides to Effective Listening

At the end of nine months of rather close and inductive study of these 200 freshmen, it seemed to us that ten factors emerged, clearly differentiating good and bad listeners. We reported in a number of articles what we called "the ten worst listening habits of the American people." In recent years the elimination of these bad habits, and the replacement of them with their counterpart skills, seems to have become the central concern of most listening training programs. Thus, we have ten significant guides to effective listening.

1. *Find areas of interest*

All studies point to the advantage in being interested in the topic under discussion. Bad listeners usually declare the subject dry after the first few sentences. Once this decision is made, it serves to rationalize any and all inattention.

Good listeners follow different tactics. True, their first thought may be that the subject sounds dry. But a second one immediately follows, based on the realization that to get up and leave might prove a bit awkward.

The final reflection is that, being trapped anyhow, perhaps it might be well to learn if anything is being said that can be put to use.

The key to the whole matter of interest in a topic is the word *use*. Whenever we wish to listen efficiently, we ought to say to ourselves: "What's he saying that I can use? What worthwhile ideas has he? Is he reporting any workable procedures? Anything that I can cash in, or with which I can make myself happier?" Such questions lead us to screen what we are hearing in a continual effort to sort out the elements of personal value. G.K. Chesterton spoke wisely indeed when he said, "There is no such thing as an uninteresting subject; there are only uninterested people."

2. *Judge content, not delivery*

Many listeners alibi inattention to a speaker by thinking to themselves: "Who could listen to such a character? What an awful voice! Will he ever stop reading from his notes?"

The good listener reacts differently. He may well look at the speaker and think, "This man is inept. Seems like almost anyone ought to be able to talk better than that." But from this initial similarity he moves on to a different conclusion, thinking "But wait a minute...I'm not interested in his personality or delivery. I want to find out what he knows. Does this man know some things that I need to know?

Essentially we "listen with our own experience." Is the conveyor to be held responsible because we are poorly equipped to decode his message? We cannot understand everything we hear, but one sure way to raise the level of our understanding is to assume the responsibility which is inherently ours.

3. *Hold your fire*

Overstimulation is almost as bad as understimulation, and the two together constitute the twin evils of inefficient listening. The overstimulated listener gets too excited, or excited too soon, by the speaker. Some of us are greatly addicted to this weakness. For us, a speaker can seldom talk for more than a few minutes without touching upon a pet bias or conviction. Occasionally we are roused in support of the speaker's point; usually it is the reverse. In either case overstimulation reflects the desire of the listener to enter, somehow, immediately into the argument.

The aroused person usually becomes preoccupied by trying to do three things simultaneously: calculate what hurt is being done to his own pet ideas; plot an embarrassing question to ask the speaker; enjoy mentally all the discomfiture visualized for the speaker once the devastating reply to him is launched. With these things going on, subsequent passages go unheard.

We must learn not to get too excited about a speaker's point until we are certain we thoroughly understand it. The secret is contained in the principle that we must always withhold evaluation until our comprehension is complete.

4. *Listen for ideas*

Good listeners focus on central ideas; they tend to recognize the characteristic language in which central ideas are usually stated, and they are able to discriminate between fact and principle, idea and example, evidence and argument. Poor listeners are inclined to listen for the facts in every presentation.

To understand the fault, let us assume that a man is giving us instructions made up of facts A to Z. The man begins to talk. We hear fact A and think: "We've got to remember it!" So we begin a memory exercise by repeating "Fact A, fact A, fact A...."

Meanwhile, the fellow is telling us fact B. Now we have two facts to memorize. We're so busy doing it that we miss fact C completely. And so it goes up to fact Z. We catch a few facts, garble several others and completely miss the rest.

It is a significant fact that only about 25 per cent of persons listening to a formal talk are able to grasp the speaker's central idea. To develop this skill requires an ability to recognize conventional organizational patterns, transitional language, and the speaker's use of recapitulation. Fortunately, all of these items can be readily mastered with a bit of effort.

5. *Be flexible*

Our research has shown that our 100 worst listeners thought that note-taking and outlining were synonyms. They believed there was but one way to take notes — by making an outline.

Actually, no damage would be done if all talks followed some definite plan of organization. Unfortunately, less than half of even formal speeches are carefully organized. There are few things more frustrating than to try to outline an unoutlinable speech.

Note-taking may help or may become a distraction. Some persons try to take down everything in shorthand; the vast majority of us are far too voluminous even in longhand. While studies are not too clear on the point, there is some evidence to indicate that the volume of notes taken and their value to the taker are inversely related. In any case, the real issue is one of interpretation. Few of us have memories good enough to remember even the salient points we hear. If we can obtain brief, meaningful records of them for later review, we definitely improve our ability to learn and to remember.

The 100 best listeners had apparently learned early in life that if they wanted to be efficient note-takers they had to have more than one system of taking notes. They equipped themselves with four or five systems, and learned to adjust their system to the organizational pattern, or the absence of one, in each talk they heard. If we want to be good listeners, we must be flexible and adaptable note-takers.

6. *Work at listening*

One of the most striking characteristics of poor listeners is their disinclination to spend any energy in a listening situation. College students, by their own testimony, frequently enter classes all worn out physically; assume postures which only seem to give attention to the speaker; and then proceed to catch up on needed rest or to reflect upon purely personal matters. This faking of attention is one of the worst habits afflicting us as a people.

Listening is hard work. It is characterized by faster heart action, quicker circulation of the blood, a small rise in bodily temperature. The overrelaxed listener is merely appearing to tune in, and then feeling conscience-free to pursue any of a thousand mental tangents.

For selfish reasons alone one of the best investments we can make is to give each speaker our conscious attention. We ought to establish eye contact and maintain it; to indicate by posture and facial expression that the occasion and the speaker's efforts are a matter of real concern to us. When we do these things we help the speaker to express himself more clearly, and we in turn profit by better understanding of the improved communication we have helped him to achieve. None of this necessarily implies acceptance of his point of view or favorable action upon his appeals. It is, rather, an expression of interest.

7. *Resist distractions*

The good listeners tend to adjust quickly to any kind of abnormal situation; poor listeners tend to tolerate bad conditions and, in some instances, even to create distractions themselves.

We live in a noisy age. We are distracted not only by what we hear, but by what we see. Poor listeners tend to be readily influenced by all manner of distractions, even in an intimate face-to-face situation.

A good listener instinctively fights distraction. Sometimes the fight is easily won — by closing a door, shutting off the radio, moving closer to the person talking, or asking him to speak louder. If the distractions cannot be met that easily, then it becomes a matter of concentration.

8. *Exercise your mind*

Poor listeners are inexperienced in hearing difficult, expository material. Good listeners apparently develop an appetite for hearing a variety of presentations difficult enough to challenge their mental capacities.

Perhaps the one word that best describes the bad listener is "inexperienced." Although he spends 45 per cent of his communication day listening to something, he is inexperienced in hearing anything tough, technical, or expository. He has for years painstakingly sought light, recreational material. The problem he creates is deeply significant, because such a person is a poor producer in factory, office, or classroom.

Inexperience is not easily or quickly overcome. However, knowledge of our own weakness may lead us to repair it. We need never become too old to meet new challenges.

9. *Keep your mind open*

Parallel to the blind spots which afflict human beings are certain psychological deaf spots which impair our ability to perceive and understand. These deaf spots are the dwelling place of our most cherished notions, convictions, and complexes. Often, when a speaker invades one of these areas with a word or phrase, we turn our mind to retraveling familiar mental pathways crisscrossing our invaded area of sensitivity.

It is hard to believe in moments of cold detachment that just a word or phrase can cause such emotional eruption. Yet with poor listeners it is frequently the case; and even with very good listeners it is occasionally the case. When such emotional deafness transpires, communicative efficiency drops rapidly to zero.

Among the words known thus to serve as red flags to some listeners are: mother-in-law, landlord, redneck, sharecropper, sissy, pervert, automation, clerk, income tax, hack, dumb farmer, pink, "Greetings," anti-vivisectionist, evolution, square, punk, welsher.

Effective listeners try to identify and to rationalize the words or phrases most upsetting emotionally. Often the emotional impact of such words can be decreased through a free and open discussion of them with friends or associates.

10. *Capitalize on thought speed*

Most persons talk at a speed of about 125 words a minute. There is good evidence that if thought were measured in words per minute, most of us could think easily at about four times that rate. It is difficult—almost painful—to try to slow down our thinking speed. Thus we normally have about 400 words of thinking time to spare during every minute a person talks to us.

What do we do with our excess thinking time while someone is speaking? If we are poor listeners, we soon become impatient with the slow progress the speaker seems to be making. So our thoughts turn to something else for a moment, then dart back to the speaker. These brief side excursions of thought continue until our mind tarries too long on some enticing but irrelevant subject. Then, when our thoughts return to the person talking, we find he's far ahead of us. Now it's harder to follow him and increasingly easy to take off on side excursions. Finally we give up; the person is still talking, but our mind is in another world.

The good listener uses his thought speed to advantage; he constantly applies his spare thinking time to what is being said. It is not difficult once one has a definite pattern of thought to follow. To develop such a pattern we should:

1. Try to anticipate what a person is going to talk about. On the basis of what he's already said, ask yourself: "What's he trying to get at? What point is he going to make?"
2. Mentally summarize what the person has been saying. What point has he made already, if any?
3. Weigh the speaker's evidence by mentally questioning it. As he presents facts, illustrative stories and statistics, continually ask yourself: "Are they accurate? Do they come from an unprejudiced source? Am I getting the full picture, or is he telling me only what will prove his point?"
4. Listen between the lines. The speaker doesn't always put everything that's important into words. The changing tones and volume of his voice may have a meaning. So may his facial expressions, the gestures he makes with his hands, the movement of his body.

Not capitalizing on thought speed is our greatest single handicap. The differential between thought speed and speech speed breeds false feelings of security and mental tangents. Yet, through listening training, this same differential can be readily converted into our greatest single asset.

Questions:

1. Nichols raises an important and pervasive problem when he notes that "Quantitatively speaking, America has built her school system upside down." The least used skills are given the most emphasis and the most used skills are given the least emphasis. Examine your own college catalog with particular reference to required courses. Is what Nichols says true of your college's required curriculum? What changes do you feel should be made?
2. Examine your own listening habits in relation to the ten guides to effective listening. Which of these do you follow regularly? Which do you fail to follow? Why?
3. Most textbooks devoted to effective speaking assert that it is the responsibility of the speaker to make the listeners listen. Nichols, however, argues that it is the listener's responsibility to listen attentively. Whom do you feel bears the primary responsibility, speaker or listener? Is there any advantage to both the speaker and the listener feeling that the major responsibility is their own?
4. Experiment with different systems of note-taking while listening to speeches or lectures (for example, outlining the entire talk, jotting

down key words and phrases, noting main ideas). Which system works best for you? In what ways does the effectiveness of the system of note-taking depend upon the type of speech given?

5. Nichols notes some words which he says serve as "red flags," words which arouse emotional reactions and prevent efficient listening. Of course, those words which are emotion-arousing to one person may not be to another person. And certainly the effects which certain words have change with time. Make a list of those words which are particularly emotion-arousing for you. Why do they have the effects they do? Compare your list with those of other students. What factors might account for the similarities and differences in these lists? Of what value is it for the listener to be aware of the possible causes and effects of these words? Of what value is such awareness to the speaker?

6. It appears that one of the greatest obstacles to improving our listening skills is that we feel that we are efficient listeners — when we want to be — and that listening ability really cannot be improved significantly anyway. Examine your own attitudes and beliefs concerning listening and listening training. What factors do you suppose contributed to the formation of these attitudes and beliefs? Are these attitudes and beliefs the products of rational decision-making or, at the other extreme, are they merely "conveniences" we use to avoid the hard work involved in listening and in its improvement?

Through its national advertisements, the Sperry Corporation has proved how strongly it feels about the importance of listening as a communication skill. Dr. Lyman Steil prepared Sperry's listening profile.

Your Personal Listening Profile

Lyman K. Steil

Toward Better Listening

Thank you for your interest in listening. If listening is ever to receive the attention it deserves...in schools, homes, businesses...it will come about because concerned people like you have made themselves heard in the silence that surrounds the subject.

At Sperry, we've emphasized good listening for many years. Research shows that it's been important to our success and is one of our greatest strengths in the marketplace. We're proud of that—but we aren't satisfied that we're listening, understanding and responding as well as we can.

That's why Sperry's corporate advertising theme, **we understand how important it is to listen,** is more than a slogan. It expresses a basic management philosophy and is fundamental to the way we do business. We're dedicated to listening effectively and responding in the right way to the people who have direct interest in the products and performance of the company.

Long before the advertising program was conceived, Sperry had stressed the importance of listening and responding in its personnel development courses, management conferences, small group meetings, roundtable discussions and other continuing programs.

But because the training covered other aspects of communications as well, it was felt that more concentrated attention should be devoted

From Sperry Corporation Listening Program materials by Dr. Lyman K. Steil, Department of Rhetoric, University of Minnesota and Communication Development, Inc. for Sperry Corporation, Copyright 1979. Reprinted by permission of Dr. Steil and Sperry Corporation.

specifically to the development of listening skills.

Additional training was prepared by Sperry's own senior management development specialists, and listening classes are being conducted for our personnel.

They are tailored to the special needs of our managers who supervise the work of others, our marketing executives and other employees as well.

The Sperry instructors who conduct the classes received orientation to make them more familiar with the subject matter and how to teach it effectively.

The training in listening has four objectives:

- To build an awareness of the importance to business of listening.
- To increase understanding of the nature of listening and its impact on the total communications process.
- To diagnose listening abilities and practices.
- To develop skills and techniques to improve listening effectiveness.

Group participation is emphasized, rather than lectures by the instructor. Also employed are film, videotape, audiotape, individual self-evaluation, testing of abilities, analysis of listening case situations and role playing in small groups.

Attendance at each session ranges from 16 to 24. That assures a good level of interchange during the group participation exercises without making the size of the class unwieldy.

The training covers understanding the listening concept and its various elements. It concentrates on specific on-the-job applications showing how Sperry employees in various real-life situations can do a better job of responding — the end product of the listening process.

Real listening occurs in four stages — sensing (hearing the message), understanding (interpreting it), evaluating (appraising it) and responding (doing something with it).

Intelligent, sincere response is central to the Sperry philosophy, and is, in fact, the ultimate point of the training.

We believe the training we are doing in this field is appropriate for Sperry and the employees who receive it. Other institutions have different environments, requiring different approaches. So we do not provide training aids or other materials used in our own internal programs to outside organizations or individuals.

However, many books, articles, films and other materials are available on various aspects of listening. Current books on the subject are listed elsewhere in this pamphlet. We at Sperry really believe **we understand how important it is to listen.** And we encourage those interested in developing their own programs on better listening to do so, using these and other sources.

Facts About Listening

1. First of all, you should know what we mean by "listening."

It's more than just hearing. That's only the first part of listening... the physical part when your ears *sense* sound waves. There are three other parts equally important. There's the *interpretation* of what was heard that leads to understanding, or misunderstanding. Then comes the *evaluation* stage when you weight the information and decide how you'll use it. Finally, based on what you heard and how you evaluated it, you *react*. That's listening.

2. Before we can become good listeners, it helps to know why people talk to each other.

There are four basic types of verbal communication. There's the "getting-to-know-you" or the "building of relationships" kind of talk which is called *phatic* communication. Next, there's *cathartic* communication which allows the release of pent-up emotion and often amounts to one person spilling his or her troubles on concerned, caring ears. Then there's *informative* communication in which ideas, data or information is shared. Last of all is *persuasive* communication where the purpose is to reinforce or change attitudes or to produce action.

3. Listening is our primary communication activity.

Studies show that we spend about 80% of our waking hours communicating. And, according to research, at least 45% of that time is spent listening. In schools, students spend 60% - 70% of their classroom time engaged in listening. And in business, listening has often been cited as being the most critical managerial skill.

4. Our listening habits are not the result of training but rather the result of the lack of it.

The following chart shows the order in which the four basic communication skills are learned, the degree to which they are used and the extent to which they are taught. Listening is the communication skill used most but taught least.

	Listening	Speaking	Reading	Writing
Learned	1st	2nd	3rd	4th
Used	Most (45%)	Next Most (30%)	Next Least (16%)	Least (9%)
Taught	Least	Next Least	Next Most	Most

5. Most individuals are inefficient listeners.

Tests have shown that immediately after listening to a 10-minute oral presentation, the average listener has heard, understood, properly evaluated and retained approximately half of what was said. And within 48 hours, that drops off another 50% to a final 25% level of effectiveness. In other words, we quite often comprehend and retain only one-quarter of what is said.

6. Inefficient and ineffective listening is extraordinarily costly.

With more than 100 million workers in America, a simple ten dollar listening mistake by each of them would cost a billion dollars. Letters have to be retyped; appointments rescheduled; shipments reshiped. And when people in large corporations fail to listen to one another, the results are even costlier. Ideas get distorted by as much as 80% as they travel through the chain of command. Employees feel more and more distant, and ultimately alienated, from top management.

7. Good listening can be taught.

In the few schools where listening programs have been adopted, listening comprehension among students has as much as doubled in just a few months.

How Well Do You Listen?
(A Personal Profile)

Here are three tests in which we'll ask you to rate yourself as a listener. There are no correct or incorrect answers. Your responses, however, will extend your understanding of yourself as a listener. And highlight areas in which improvement might be welcome...to you and to those around you. When you've completed the tests, please turn to page 106 to see how your scores compare with those of thousands of others who've taken the same tests before you.

Quiz 1

A. Circle the term that best describes you as a listener.

Superior Excellent Above Average Average Below Average Poor Terrible

B. On a scale of 0-100 (100 = highest), how would you rate yourself as a listener?

_____

(0-100)

Quiz 2

How do you think the following people would rate you as a listener? (0-100)

Your Best Friend   _____

Your Boss   _____

Business Colleague   _____

A Job Subordinate   _____

Your Spouse   _____

Quiz 3

As a listener, how often do you find yourself engaging in these 10 bad listening habits? First, check the appropriate columns. Then tabulate your score using the key below.

Listening Habit	Almost Always	Usually	Some-times	Seldom	Almost Never	Score
1. Calling the subject uninteresting						
2. Criticizing the speaker's delivery or mannerisms						
3. Getting over-stimulated by something the speaker says						
4. Listening primarily for facts						
5. Trying to outline every-thing						
6. Faking attention to the speaker						
7. Allowing interfering distractions						
8. Avoiding difficult material						
9. Letting emotion-laden words arouse personal antagonism						
10. Wasting the advantage of thought speed (daydreaming)						

The table header spans: **Frequency** (Almost Always, Usually, Some-times, Seldom, Almost Never) and **Score**.

Total
Score _____

Key
For every "Almost Always" checked, give yourself a score of **2**
For every "Usually" checked, give yourself a score of **4**
For every "Sometimes" checked, give yourself a score of **6**
For every "Seldom" checked, give yourself a score of **8**
For every "Almost Never" checked, give yourself a score of **10**

Profile Analysis

This is how other people have responded to the same questions that you've just answered.

Quiz 1

A. 85% of all listeners questioned rated themselves as *Average* or less. Fewer than 5% rate themselves as *Superior* or *Excellent*.

B. On the 0-100 scale, the extreme range is 10-90; the general range is 35-85; and the *average* rating is 55.

Quiz 2

When comparing the listening self-ratings and projected ratings of others, most respondents believe that their best friend would rate them highest as a listener. And that rating would be higher than the one they gave themselves in Quiz # 1...where the average was 55.

How come? We can only guess that best friend status is such an intimate, special kind of relationship that you can't imagine it ever happening unless you *were* a good listener. If you weren't, you and he or she wouldn't be best friends to begin with.

Going down the list, people who take this test usually think their bosses would rate them higher than they rated themselves. Now part of that is probably wishful thinking. And part of it is true. We *do* tend to listen to our bosses better...whether it's out of respect or fear or whatever doesn't matter.

The grades for colleague and job subordinate work out to be just about the same as the listener rated himself...that 55 figure again.

But when you get to spouse...husband or wife...something really dramatic happens. The score here is significantly lower than the 55 average that previous profile-takers gave themselves. And what's interesting is that the figure goes steadily downhill. While newlyweds tend to rate their spouse at the same high level as their best friend, as the marriage goes on...and on...the rating falls. So in a household where the couple has been married 50 years, there could be a lot of talk. But maybe nobody is *really* listening.

Quiz 3

The average score is a 62...7 points higher than the 55 that the average test-taker gave himself in Quiz #1. Which suggests that when listening is broken down into specific areas of competence, we rate ourselves better than we do when listening is considered only as a generality.

Of course, the best way to discover how well you listen is to ask the people to whom you listen most frequently. Your spouse, boss, best friend, etc. They'll give you an earful.

10 Keys to Effective Listening

These keys are a positive guideline to better listening. In fact, they're at the heart of developing better listening habits that could last a lifetime.

10 Keys to Effective Listening	The Bad Listener	The Good Listener
1. Find areas of interest	Tunes out dry subjects	Opportunitizes; asks ''what's in it for me?''
2. Judge content, not delivery	Tunes out if delivery is poor	Judges content, skips over delivery errors
3. Hold your fire	Tends to enter into argument	Doesn't judge until comprehension
4. Listen for ideas	Listens for facts	Listens for central themes
5. Be flexible	Taking intensive notes using only one system	Takes fewer notes. Uses 4-5 different systems, depending on speaker
6. Work at listening	Shows no energy output. Fakes attention.	Works hard, exhibits active body state
7. Resist distractions	Is easily distracted	Fights or avoids distractions, tolerates bad habits, knows how to concentrate
8. Exercise your mind	Resists difficult expository material; seeks light, recreational material	Uses heavier material as exercise for the mind
9. Keep your mind open	Reacts to emotional words	Interprets color words; does not get hung up on them
10. Capitalize on fact thought is faster than speech	Tends to daydream with slow speakers	Challenges, anticipates, mentally summarizes, weighs the evidence, listens between the lines to tone of voice

"Listening" Reading List

Banville, Thomas G. *How to Listen — How to Be Heard.* LC 77-17961. 1978. (ISBN 0-88229-332-X). Nelson-Hall.

Barbara, Dominick A. *Art of Listening.* (Illus.). 1974 (ISBN 0-398-00086-7). C.C. Thomas.

Note: All references are listed in this order: Author; Title; Library of Congress No. (LC); International Standard Book No. (ISBN); Publisher.

Carin. *Creative Questioning & Sensitivity: Listening Techniques.* 2nd ed. 1978 text ed. (ISBN 0-675-08421-0); media (ISBN 0-675-08485-7). Merrill.

Cassie, Dhyan. *Auditory Training Handbook for Good Listeners.* LC 75-26439. 1976 pap. text ed. (1762). Interstate.

Crum, J.K. *Art of Inner Listening.* 1975. pap. (ISBN 0-89129-092-3, PV092). Pillar Bks.

DeMare, George. *Communicating At The Top.* 1979. John Wiley & Sons. Price Waterhouse & So.

Duker, Sam. *Listening Bibliography.* 2nd ed. LC 68-12630. 1968. (ISBN 0-8108-0085-3). Scarecrow Press.

— *Listening: Readings.* 1966. LC 68-22752. Scarecrow Press.

— *Listening: Readings. Vol. 2.* 1971. (ISBN 0-8108-0364-X.) Scarecrow Press.

— *Teaching Listening in the Elementary School: Readings.* 1971 Scarecrow Press.

Ernst, Franklin H., Jr. *Outline of the Activity of Listening.* 3rd ed. 1973. softbound (ISBN 0-916944-09-3). Addresso'set.

— *Who's Listening — Handbook of the Listening Activity.* LC 73-84380. 1973. (ISBN 0-916944-15-8). Addresso'set.

Erway, Ella, A. *Listening: A Programmed Approach.* 2nd ed. 1979.

Faber, Carl A. *On Listening.* 1976. (ISBN 0-918026-02-4).

Friedman, Paul. *Listening Processes: Attention, Understanding, Evaluation.* 1978. National Education Association.

Geeting, Baxter & Corinne Geeting. *How to Listen Assertively.* (Illus.). 1978. (ISBN 0-671-18365-6), Monarch.

Girzaitis, Loretta. *Listening: A Response Ability.* LC 72-77722. (Illus.). 1972. pap. (ISBN 0-88489-047-3). St. Marys.

Goldstein, H. *Reading & Listening Comprehension at Various Controlled Rates.* Columbia University Teachers College. Contributions to Education: No. 821). Repr. of 1940 ed. (ISBN 0-404-55821-6). AMS PR.

Hirsch, Robert O. *Listening: A Way To Process Information Aurally.* Gorsuch Scarisbrick, Pub.

Johnson, Ida Mae. *Developing the Listening Skills.* 1974. (ISBN 0-914296-18-3). Activity Rec.

Keller, Paul W., Charles T. Brown. *Monologue to Dialogue.* 1973. Prentice-Hall.

Koile, Earl. *Listening As a Way of Becoming.* LC 76-48520. 1977. (ISBN 0-87680-510-1). Word Bks.

Kratoville, Betty L. *Listen, My Children, & You Shall Hear, Bk. 1.* LC 68-29770. 1968. pap. (1044); pkg. of 20 extra grading sheets (1045). Interstate.

Langs, Robert. *The Listening Process.* 1978. (ISBN 0-87668-341-3). Aronson.

Lorayne & Lucas. *The Memory Book.* Ballantine Books.

Lundsteen, Sara W. *Listening: Its Impact on Reading and The Other Language Arts.* 1971. NCTE-ERIC — Urbana, Ill.

Mills, Ernest P. *Listening: Key to Communication* (Vardamann Management & Communication Ser.). (Illus.). 1974. pap. (ISBN 0-442-80021-5). Van Nos Reinhold.

Moray, Neville. *Listening & Attention.* lib. bdg. (ISBN 0-88307-409-5). Gannon; pap. (ISBN 0-14-080066-2). Penguin.

Morley, Joan. *Improving Aural Comprehension.* Student's Workbook, Teacher's Book of Readings. LC 70-185904. 1972. tchr's bk. or readings. (ISBN 0-472-08666-9); student's wkbk (ISBN 0-472-08665-0). U. of Mich. Pr.

National Education Association & Stanford E. Taylor. *Listening (What Research Says to the Teacher Ser.)*. 1973. pap. (ISBN 0-8106-1012-4); filmstrip (ISBN 0-8106-1118-X). NEA.

Nichols, R. & L.A. Stevens. *Are You Listening?* 1957. (ISBN 0-07-046475-8). McGraw-Hill.

Plaister, T. *Developing Listening Comprehension for ESL Students: The Kingdom of Kochen.* 1976. (ISBN 0-13-204479-X); tapes (ISBN 0-13-204495-1). Prentice-Hall.

Russell, David H. & Elizabeth F. Russell. *Listening Aids Through the Grades.* LC 59-8373. 1959. pap. text ed. (ISBN 0-8077-2080-1). Tchrs. Coll.

Spearritt, Donald. *Listening Comprehension, a Factoral Analysis.* (Australian Council for Educational Research). 1962. Verry.

Steil, Lyman K., Larry Barker. *Effective Listening: Developing Your Ear-Q.* 1980. Gorsuch Scarisbrick, Pub.

Stocker, Claudell S. *Listening for the Visually Impaired: A Teaching Manual.* 1974. pap. (ISBN 0-398-02936-9). C.C. Thomas.

Templer, J.C. *Further Listening Comprehension Texts.* (gr. 9-12). 1972. pap. text ed. (ISBN 0-435-28728-1); tchr's ed. (ISBN 0-435-28729-X). Heinemann Ed.

—*Listening Comprehension Tests.* (gr. 9-12). 1974. pap. text ed. (ISBN 0-435-28736-2); tchr's ed. (ISBN 0-435-28737-0). Heinemann Ed.

Weaver, Carl H. *Human Listening: Process and Behavior.* 1972. Bobbs-Merrill.

Wolvin, Andrew D., Carolyn Gwynn Coakley. *Listening Instruction.* (No. 334). SCA/ERIC 1979.

Yates, Virginia. *Listening and Note-taking.* 2nded. 1970. McGraw-Hill.

And a Final Word About Listening

We at Sperry feel strongly that listening is an important...and often neglected...communication skill.

Listening is just as active as talking, although most people believe the primary responsibility for good communications rests with the speaker. But think how much better we could communicate if both the listener and the speaker took at least 51% of the responsibility for successful communications!

Questions:

1. Classify your listening skills in the following settings:
   a. at church.
   b. talking with your best friend.
   c. talking with a new acquaintance in a bar.
   d. having a conversation with one of your parents on the telephone.
   e. talking with an attractive member of the opposite sex.
   f. listening to a policeman who has stopped you for speeding.
2. Do you consider yourself a good listener? Why or why not?
3. In what situations are you most affected by bad listening habits?

Section II

Experiencing Speech Communication

Introduction

Speech, as indicated throughout the first section, is an exchange of symbols. The critical terminology in the preceding statement is "exchange." We can communicate endlessly about communication. We can discuss symbols and symbol systems, language acquisition, communication theory, complementary communication processes, etc.; yet the central aspect of communication is inherent in the experience itself. Therefore, the most poignant approach to a survey of speech communication resides in the examination of the various forms of human interaction, namely: intrapersonal communication, interpersonal communication, small group communication, and public speaking. Our concerns range from the individual in private counsel all the way to the individual communicating in the most public of settings. The readings selected are designed to give both an overview of the particular communication form as well as some directions for improving your own communication skills.

The first form, intrapersonal communication, was not a concern of speech communication scholars until the late sixties. Until that time such concerns were thought to rest primarily in the realm of psychology. In fact, as late as 1972 a colleague of ours wrote a dissertation proposal dealing with theories of the "self" and was informed by one of his committee members that "speech communication is not concerned with the 'self'." To most of us in the field, the statement is ludicrous. Since the time of the Hellenistic philosophers we have based our concern in the realm of "self." Quintilian's dictum that good oratory involves "a good man speaking well" implies that selfhood is an integral aspect in the act of speaking. While Quintilian's concern may have rested only in the realm of ethics, the principle nevertheless implies that good oratory is rooted in self knowledge. It follows, therefore, that any form of communication requires some degree of self understanding, and to that end speech communication experts must seek to discover as much as possible about the inner life of human beings.

Intrapersonal communication is concerned with the inner life of the individual as it relates to his/her communication processes. Self-talk is vital to an individual's well being as well as his/her ability to interact successfully in society. Therefore, the speech communication scholar wishes to know as much as possible about how we communicate with ourselves, the various forms of self-talk, the positive and negative effects of the process, and the means for improving intrapersonal communication. For these reasons a study of "self" is imperative to an understanding of intrapersonal communication since self-concept and self-talk are inseparable.

Interpersonal communication is also a recent area of study in speech communication. Prior to the 1970's, speech communication researchers were concerned primarily with the nature of rhetoric as it manifests itself in the public arena. In other words, most of the scholarly works in the field were devoted to analyses of speakers and their speeches. Other concerns centered in the area of skills improvement in public speaking, oral interpretation, group discussion, and debate.

In the early seventies a book entitled, *Reaching Out* by David W. Johnson alerted some speech communication experts to the need for concern in this area. From our predilection with the question, "What are the necessary ingredients to create understanding and attitude change?", we widened our parameter to include consideration of the question, "What does it mean and how does it feel to be understood?" We became aware that communication on the dyadic level is a crucial concern and merits the same amount of attention as the other forms of communication.

Like any new field of study, the discipline of interpersonal communication has floundered in its development. Growing "like Topsy," the subject matter in this area has ranged from the general area of interpersonal to highly specialized areas such as medical and family communication. Lacking a theoretical body of knowledge in speech communication, researchers borrowed concepts from clinical psychology, humanistic psychology, social psychology, anthropology, and sociology. At the same time several scholars were seeking to formulate a philosophy as a means of centralizing concerns in the field. This has led to the development of two major groups — the experimentalists and the humanists.

Regardless of the philosophy, interpersonal communication centers its concerns in one-to-one communication. The original approach (a moralist application of principles from humanistic psychology) has given way to concerns over the processes and skills involved in interpersonal communication. We are concerned with the interaction of "normal" persons engaged in daily communication in their various settings. We are concerned with assisting individuals in improving the quality of their lives through improving their ability to communicate in all situations.

Small group communication represents a traditional area of concentration. Originally termed group discussion, categories of investigation included: formulation of problems for discussion, the study of research techniques, the study of evidence, the study of reasoning, and the study and practice of rational problem solving. Closely aligned with debate, this area was a mainstay for departments of speech throughout the nation between the years 1920 and 1965. Speech majors were expected to become proficient in the processes mentioned above. This emphasis was so marked that discussion teams from university speech deparments competed in tournaments throughout the country.

The important aspect of the above discussion is the philosophy represented in the activity. During this period the guiding principle for all speech departments was the assumption that good communication involved the study and development of skills in rational decision making. Such emphasis it was felt was the only means of nurturing and preserving mankind's most precious commodity — freedom of speech. The goal was to create enlightened communicators capable of participating in rational group decision making in a democratic environment.

Since the sixties the concerns in group interaction have shifted toward group dynamics. We have become increasingly interested in the processes which occur at the group level. "How and why people act in groups," has become a key interest in the field of group communication. Many experimental studies have been conducted in an effort to discover the patterns in group interaction. In addition to these interests, psychology moved into the era of sensitivity groups, and speech communication followed suit with the inclusion of concerns over the individual's ability to interact in groups as a means of raising self esteem and improving basic communication skills.

Small group communication now claims all of the concerns discussed above. The more recent concerns have merit, but so do the interests of the past. In fact, concerns with rational decision making and group interaction processes are complementary since they afford the student the opportunity to study group activity as both observer and participant.

Public speaking is the most widely known area in the field of speech communication. In fact, if you asked anyone outside the field what speech teachers do, you would probably get an answer such as "They teach public speaking, of course." And, in fact, though our interests have become markedly diversified in the past twenty-five years, our concerns are still rooted in the oral tradition exemplified by public address. The Aristotelian postulate remains the axiom on which our interests rotate. The rhetor, Aristotle postulated, is engaged in "the art of discovering all the available means of persuasion."[1] We are as

[1]Lane Cooper, The Rhetoric of Aristotle. New York: D. Appleton-Century Company, 1932.

teachers of public address engaged in the study and practice of the oral tradition of suasion. We are concerned with all the elements which are involved in that process.

Until the late fifties the study of public address was centered in the five canons of classical rhetoric — "inventio," "dispositio," "elocutio," "memoria," "pronuntiatio." *Inventio* was considered the chief canon for it contained most of the necessary ingredients in researching and developing the speech. Aristotle designated these elements under the category of "proofs," a term referring to the suasive devices available to the speaker. Artistic proofs were those created by the speaker called "ethos," "pathos," and "logos."

"Ethos" is the Greek term Aristotle used to designate the element we now refer to as speaker credibility. As Aristotle indicated, this is the most significant of proofs, for unless the audience views the speaker as knowledgeable and trustworthy, all other proof is nullified. "Pathos" refers to motivational appeals — those appeals designed to involve the audience at the emotional level. "Logos" refers to logical appeal — the attempt by the speaker to create the perception that his/her arguments are logically valid.

"Proofs" not controlled by the speaker are termed "inartistic." They constitute the materials called evidence which the speaker uses to prove his/her points. The other canons refer to components familiar to anyone who has had a course in public speaking. "Dispositio" refers to organization, "elocutio" represents concerns of style or language usage, "pronuntiatio" means delivery components, and "memoria" (the canon rarely included) is concerned with the process of memory.

These axioms formed the basis for almost all the principles discussed in public speaking texts and classes until the fifties. In the next few years, Carl Hovland and his associates at Yale University changed the pattern of thinking about public address components for years to come. In a series of experimental studies beginning in 1953, Hovland sought to discover the factors which affected persuasion. This group of social psychologists studied speaker credibility and motivational appeals to discover the efficacy of traditional concepts.[2]

The study of public speaking was revolutionized. Suddenly, after years of operating on principles which had become sacrosanct, scholars in other fields began testing those very principles. Hence, scholars in speech communication began conducting experimental studies of their own in a renewed effort (using modern techniques) to discover "all the available means of persuasion."

Though these efforts have shifted dramatically since the late fifties, there is still an emphasis on experimental study in the area of public speaking. Furthermore, though some traditionalists in our discipline

[2]Carl Hovland, Irving Janis, and Harold Kelley, *Communication and Persuasion.* New Haven: Yale University Press, 1953.

have resisted the encroachment of scientism into the humanities arena, we have all gained knowledge from both the traditional as well as the behavioral studies. Yet, no matter how we approach the subject, our basic concern in public speaking still resides in the dictum of Quintilian's—a good person skilled in speaking.

As stated previously, it is through speech communication that we discover, test, express and stimulate meaning. We are surrounded by the process on all levels and the study of speech communication is the study of that total involvement. As Kenneth Burke so aptly observed in *Permanence and Change:*

> Our speculations may run the whole gamut, from play, through reverence, even to an occasional shiver of collective metaphysical dread— for always the eternal enigma is there, right on the edges of our metropolitan bickerings, stretching outwards to interstellar and inwards to the depths of the mind. And in this staggering disproportion between man and no-man, there is no place for forgetting that men build their cultures by huddling together, nervously loquacious, at the edge of an abyss.[3]

---

[3]Kenneth Burke, *Permanence and Change.* Los Altos, California: Hermes Publications, 1954, p. 351.

How She Resolved to Act

"I shall be careful to say nothing at all
About myself or what I know of him
Or the vaguest thought I have—no matter how dim,
Tonight if it so happen that he call."

And not ten minutes later the doorbell rang
And into the hall he stepped as he always did
With a face and a bearing that quite poorly hid
His brain that burned and his heart that fairly sang
And his tongue that wanted to be rid of the truth.

As well as she could, for she was very loath
To signify how she felt, she kept very still,
But soon her heart cracked loud as a coffee mill
And her brain swung like a comet in the dark
And her tongue raced like a squirrel in the park.

Merrill Moore

Reprinted by permission of Ann Leslie Moore.

In this article, the author delineates theories of the self to explain the development of a pragmatic model of intrapersonal communication. Termed a rhetorical model, this construct was created in the belief that it provides a means for examining the individual's self talk.

Intrapersonal Communication

The Development of a Rhetorical Model

Marcus L. Ambrester

Have you ever watched someone walking along a busy sidewalk in a conversation with him or herself? You assumed that this person was engaged in some form of self-talk because you observed his/her lips moving. What was your reaction? Weren't you shocked to see someone so boldly talking to himself in public? You may have concluded that the person was eccentric or drunk or even psychotic.

Nevertheless, even though this behavior is considered strange in our culture, we all engage in self-talk continuously. We are very careful to avoid moving our lips because that is the social taboo; yet we are constantly making plans, solving problems, daydreaming, reasoning etc. through the self-talk process called intrapersonal communication.

We are engaged in what many writers refer to as the internal rhetorical wrangle. We are, as George H. Mead and Kenneth Burke both contend self-persuading creatures who constantly address ourselves as orators address an audience. Mead characterizes the process as "an I addressing its Me." This intralogue is so automatic with us that we take it for granted. For instance, suppose your best friend asks you how well you like her new dress and you really think it looks unbecoming. Your wrangle would begin. A part of you might say, "Tell her she looks like a circus clown." Another part would counsel, "Don't say that, stupid, you'll lose her friendship." The wrangle could (and often does) go on and on thusly: "Remember you have to be honest," "I can't afford to be honest"; "Tell her it looks okay"; "No, she'll see through that." By the time you answer you will have per-

suaded yourself that what you say to her is the most appropriate
response in this situation. Nevertheless, you will have undergone a
very rapid, well practiced internal rhetorical wrangle. By rhetorical
wrangle we mean a highly complex system of self persuasion. We will
discuss this process in more detail later in the article.

Though most of us are somewhat aware of our own self-talk, until
recent years very little effort was expended by academicians to study
this process. In observing the problem, Frederick Perls, a renowned
gestalt psychologist queried:

> Do we have a built-in dictator who is making decisions, a council of
> concensus, a government with executive power? Is there an uncon-
> scious, or emotions, or a computing brain, which does the job? Is there
> a God, a soul permeating the body and taking charge of all its require-
> ments and goals with infinite wisdom?
>
> We don't know! We can only make up fantasies, maps, models, work-
> ing hypotheses, and check out every second as to their correctness
> and reliability. And if we know, what good will it do?
>
> . . . .
>
> Out of the fog of ignorance, are there emerging any building stones for
> a reliable, complete, applicable, and unified theory of man and his
> functions?
>
> Some, not too many yet. But enough to give us reliable guidance for our
> specific purpose. (1972, pp. 68-69)

After a rather thorough search for a workable model demonstrating
the functions of self-talk, we sought with the help of a colleague Glynis
Strause to develop a model of our own. That quest began with an
attempt to analyse the emergence of the "self."

The Development of the Self

It would be presumptuous to attempt to offer a complete explanation
of personality development. Instead, our interest centers in the
development of internal rhetorical selves which affect our decision
making process and control the roles we create to satisfy social norms.
This brief explanation represents the results of years of testing various
aspects of personality theories to arrive at a rhetorical perspective on
personality development.

The most basic perspective for the development of the "self" rests in
Freud's theory of identification. Freud theorized that the child
developed through his/her direct association with parents or
guardians. This development is based on the process of identification.
Freud argued that the child, in an effort to either maintain succor
and/or avoid punishment, identifies with the parent figure. This identification process which is all pervasive, results in modeling behavior. In
other words, Freud postulated that the child recognizes early in life

that his/her needs are met by the parent. Consequently, in order to insure continuance of need gratification, the child begins a rhetorical process of parental ingratiation. S/he "reasons" in his early stages that gratification may best be obtained and maintained by "acting like" the parent figure. Thus identification leads to imitation and then to acting the parental role at all levels.

As the child identifies with and imitates the parent figure his/her self-concept begins to form. The early form of the self-concept is that of one who is attached to the love objects — mother and father. Hence, the whole emergence of the self is dependent upon the degree to which the child can assimilate and act out the actions and values of the parent. For Freud, this whole process was centered in his theory of the oedipal and electra complexes. Neo-Freudians have attempted to demystify the theory by demonstrating that the identification process is simply a natural link between parent and child in which the child emulates the parent to gain and maintain acceptance and love.

One of the inherent features of this rhetorical theory of personality development resides in the concept of value formation. As the child is rehearsing his/her role based on mother and father s/he is introjecting the values of the parents. In other words, if dad sits in front of the television set and proclaims each time a person from a minority race appears that "the #%#*#% are taking over the country," his child sitting by him will soon be proclaiming the same thing. The child will be taking on his/her father's value system as a part of his/her identification process. Consequently the child's value system is linked directly to the self-concept. This appears to be a principle reason that we cling tenaciously to many of our early values. To deny them would strike a blow at our self-concept.

As we develop our sense of self through the process of identification, we are creating inherent conflicts. There is the self that wants to have his/her needs gratified, there is the self that seeks to maintain the parental tie and there is the self that attempts to maintain equilibrium among these warring factions. These warring factions form the basis for our internal rhetorical wrangle which we will discuss in detail shortly.

Of course Freud pioneered the work in the inner world of the self with his development of the theory of the "id," "ego" and "superego." As you may recall from your study of psychology, the watershed theory on which most of the other theories rest is the comprehensive philosophy of Sigmund Freud. In the Freudian construct the "id" represents that part of the individual which, as Kenneth Burke puts it "knows no, 'no'". The "id" seeks need gratification at any cost. The "suprego" on the other hand is composed of the "shoulds" and "should nots" superimposed upon the individual by parental figures. The "ego" maintains contact with the external environment and attempts to stabilize the "this is who I am" concept in face of the debilitating information from the "superego" and the socially unacceptable information from the "id."

Freud set the stage for the examination of our internal rhetorical wrangle with his books *The Interpretation of Dreams* and *Jokes and Their Relation to the Unconscious.* In both works (in different ways) he attempted to illuminate the process of the "id" engaged in circumventing the repressive pressure of the "superego." Yet Freud's ultimate purpose was to investigate and understand the workings of the individual's inner world as a gateway to unlock the secrets of neurosis and psychosis. His discussions of the internal rhetorical wrangle are therefore concentrated in the direction of his study. However one of the keys he left us to the hidden world of intrapersonal communication is found in his study of jokes. Throughout his book Freud discusses the means (through joke creating, telling, and responding) the individual uses to allow the "id" to circumvent the repressions of the "superego." In other words, Freud contends that the things you consider funny represent a window to your repressions.

This fascinating theory points to a rhetorical process operating within the individual. The "id" is constantly engaged in the art of discovering the means to circumvent the "superego" and convince the "ego" that everything is "okay." Beyond this basic process, Freud's theory offers little further insights into the internal rhetorical wrangle.

Taking their cue from Freud, and for that matter Jung, many psychologists interested in the inner world of the individual have attempted to shed more light on the inner workings of the self. However, since much of their work has centered in the study of psychosis, the acquired information is of little interest or value to the average person engaged in a search for more understanding of intrapersonal communication.

However, the school of psychology led by Carl Jung took a different perspective. Jung, basing his philosophy in existentialism and phenomenology, fathered a school of psychology called "humanistic" which centered in the study of the whole individual and his/her environment and sought to discover the keys to healthy personality rather than psychosis.

Espousing this philosophy are psychologists such as Erick Fromm, Milton Rokeach, Gordon Allport, Frederick Perls, as well as modern "pop" psychologists including Eric Berne, Thomas Harris, Manuel Smith, and Wayne Dyer. These persons and others of the humanist school of psychology have developed models and theories of the inner life of the "normal" individual.

The most popular model from this school in the past twenty years is the model developed by Berne and further popularized by Harris in his book *I'm Okay, You're Okay.* This model called the transactional model is characterized by three inner selves—the "parent," the "adult," and the "child." Based on the Freudian model, the authors seek to portray the inner life of "normal" persons. This transactional model has been extremely popular in working with individuals who manifest normal anxieties about their abilities to function in society. While the model is extremely workable in this area, the creation of the "parent," "adult," and "child" was based on interpersonal rather than intrapersonal concerns. Hence a need for a workable intrapersonal model still exists.

The Model of Intrapersonal Communication

In 1980 Marcus Ambrester and Glynis Holm Strause developed a model of intrapersonal communication processes based in both the Freudian and Jungian schools of psychology. The Ambrester/Strause model of intrapersonal communication evolved from the gradual enlightened perspective that, while most of the psychoanalytic models give credence to the idea that we are involved in constant self-talk, the examination of the phenomenon is truncated at best. Furthermore, our own field of interpersonal communication has centered in perception rather than the process of self persuasion. The model attempts to represent intrapersonal communication particularly during times of personal conflict. Such a model is always subject to alteration; yet the important fact remains that this attempt represents one of the first forays into the inner communicative life of the individual. We are attempting to depict the ways in which we actually communicate with ourselves — the ways we find to persuade ourselves and then portray the roles we wish to portray to others.

The Ambrester/Strause Rhetorical Model of Intrapersonal Communication

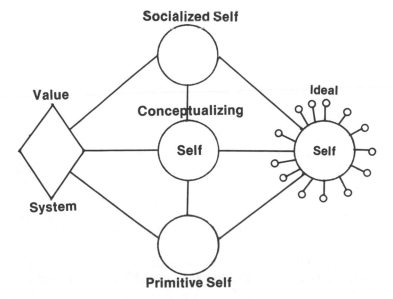

The rhetorical model of intrapersonal communication should be considered a complete interdependent system. All the components function autonomously while simultaneously relying upon interaction for their existence. The selves are therefore characterized by their indentification with each other as well as their alienation. Before we examine the process of intrapersonal communication depicted by the model, we must first explain the nature of each of the components. Remember that these descriptions are highly speculative. Yet they are, nevertheless, based on compilations of many psychoanalytic theories.

The principal entities in the rhetorical model constantly engage in the act of discovering all the available means of persuasion as follows:

1. Socialized self discovers and employs all the necessary means to persuade the person to act in socially acceptable manners and "repent" for social "failures";

2. Primative self discovers and employs all the necessary means to persuade the person to act in any manner required to meet his/her most basic needs and deny responsibility for such action;

3. Conceptualizing self discovers and employs all the necessary means to persuade the person to act in ethically valid manners (congruent with the value system) and project an "ideal self" consistent with his/her self-concept (allowing for consciously purposeful manipulative roles).

This brief explanation of the selves demonstrates their most basic functions. The following discussion presents a more detailed explanation of their nature and symbolic action.

The Socialized Self

The socialized self (SS) is a highly articulate being. Growing from your identification processes with parents and others, the SS becomes your internal guardian. SS is a put-down artist. S/he likes to find every means possible to debilitate your conceptualizing self (CS). S/he majors in utilizing devices which make you feel less than satisfied with yourself. SS is past and future oriented. S/he says, "You remember how you hurt your poor mother's feelings that time. You really are a slob when you do things like that." S/he also says, "You know you have to be prepared for that interview coming up. Of course, you'll blow it as usual; but, you've at least got to try, dummy." SS is never satisfied no matter how hard you try to please him/her. There's always more you should do, more you should have done, and all those things you should not have done. SS talks most when you are making decisions. S/he tells you the "Right" course of action to follow.

S/he represents the ethical dimension of sociability. S/he lets you know what other people will think, or are thinking of you. S/he tries to keep you "in line." When you don't stay in line, s/he is waiting with a barrage of rhetorical devices to make CS feel guilty.

SS seeks at all times to fulfill the rhetorical identificatory motives. "If you want to be loved," s/he says, "you must be pretty or handsome or witty or charming." Other rhetorical methods might include these scenarios: "Look in that mirror. Just look! Is that not a mess? How do you expect anyone to care about you if you don't take more pride in your appearance? In another instance s/he might assert, "Boy! You really blew it that time, dummy. Nobody laughed at that dirty joke. I'm sure they were offended. They don't appreciate dirty jokes, stupid. No wonder those people kinda drifted away and left you alone. You really turned them off. I'm sure you won't be invited back to one of their parties. They don't like you, since you really don't know how to act. You'll never have any friends with your penchant for saying the wrong thing at the wrong time.

SS seems to use suasive sorieties. Beginning with the incident itself, SS employs debilitating devices and follows them all the way to our worst fears, finally pronouncing the ultimate failure. The success or failure of SS largely depends on the strength of CS to analyze the situation and tell SS. to "cool it."

SS has so many devices for keeping us sociable, it would be impossible to touch on even a fraction of them. The repertoire is as diversified as needed to protect the introjected values. SS seems to be with us always, and even though we may seem to blunt his/her impact on certain matters by denying attempted guilt induction, we continue to experience some of the effect of SS's rhetorical bombardment throughout our lives.

The Primitive Self

Like the socialized self, the primitive self is highly articulate and given to suasive devices. Evolving from your drive for personal need gratification, PS is concerned with persuading you that your needs must be served. Countering the oppressive bombardment of SS, PS develops devices which are centered in the moment. The only ethic to which PS ascribes is the ethic of "my needs." "If I want it," PS argues "it is good." Therefore, PS uses rhetorical strategies to fulfill this ethic. In fact, you may be familiar with phrases like: "I really deserve this break, since I've worked so hard."; "Go ahead, steal the candy. No one is looking."; "Whatever the cost to your associates, you need the promotion, so if you have to spread a few rumors about your rival, that's okay." Obviously, we may not give in to the urgings of PS all the time but s/he is forever present designing rhetorical strategies for need gratification. If you see a person to whom you are attracted PS will probably say, "Go to this person, tell him/her how attractive they are. Try to get them to see how desirable you are. Use all your charms to win him/her." PS's rhetoric is endless. S/he seeks every possible device to meet his/her needs.

PS seeks to satisfy some basic rhetorical motives. One of the basic rhetorical needs is to rescue the self concept from the debilitating effects of SS's strategies. One of the chief means of meeting this need is through the process of projection. "In all honesty," PS proclaims, I didn't have anything to do with wrecking that person. I've been programmed by my parents since birth to get ahead at any cost. It is simply a condition of my upbringing. I didn't have anything to do with it." The objective of this procedure is to take all blame away from the individual by casting it onto a real or imagined scapegoat.

Another function of PS is to meet the rhetorical self-discovery needs. The self-discovery needs serves to preserve our "role." If your self-concept is jeopardized, PS will begin a series of suasive devices aimed at restoration. "If people understood me better they would not treat me this way," "The only reason I let them humiliate me was to get them to show their true colors." "He may think I am incompetent, but the truth is he's the really stupid one." PS will employ any rhetorical devices necessary to rebuild the sense of self esteem.

PS likes to play. PS would play all the time if allowed total freedom. However, SS prevents such freedom and PS has to find justification for the need to play. "I owe it to myself to break. I've worked hard all week and all work and no play makes Jack a dull boy." "I'm not joining this intramural soccer team because I like it; I'm joining for the good of the team. if they don't have me, they would definitely finish last in the division."

One final strategy used by PS is controvertability of terms. "Controvertability of terms" is a Burkeian concept which refers to the ability to transliterate a fairly noxious activity into something noble. On the social level, we can change the negative connotation of war by controverting it to a "means of keeping the peace" or more familiarly "freeing the world for democracy." In both cases, the process points away from the actual activity to some entelechial motive which "raises" the activity to a higher status. This process, in psychological terminology, is a specialized form of projection.

At the intrapersonal level, PS applies the strategy to take off any guilt-inducing pressure from SS. PS, when confronted with the following situation might rhetorically handle it in the following manner:

> You have told a friend that you will go with her boyfriend to a party since she is to be out of town and doesn't want the boyfriend "on the prowl" in her absence. As it happens, you not only go to the party with the boy, you wind up going to his apartment after the party and "make out" with him for some time. While SS is working diligently to make you feel like the lowest form of humanity, PS is applying the aforementioned strategy, as follows. "My gosh, you did this for your friend's own good. What better way for her to find out that her friend is a louse. In fact, you know that you can't even like this guy. You knew from the beginning that he was worthless, and you had to find a way to demon-

strate this fact to your friend. S/he may not understand now, but she'll thank you for this one of these days." As you can see, this rather clever device allows PS to rescue us from the dregs of guilt induction. The realism of the reasoning power of CS can sometimes nullify the potential effectiveness of such rhetorical self-deception. PS has an equal quantity of rhetorical strategies to match those of SS. However, it seems that in many instances when we allow PS to "win," we become victims of the oppression of the SS. This assertion implies another aspect of the two warring entities—their relative strengths ebb and flow with changing situations and beliefs.

The Conceptualizing Self

This entity is perhaps the most articulate of the selves. The conceptualizing self (CS) is a very complex personage. At one level, it acts in the form of the Freudian ego, in that it represents the self conceptualizing self. CS contains the self-concept. CS says, "This is who I am." This self concept is frequently in jeopardy and CS uses all necessary means of persuasion to maintain high self esteem. Hence CS functions to control self-esteem through its "reasoning processes," which is another capacity of CS. Through its most basic function, contact with the external environment, CS interprets events through the capacities for categorization, analysis, logic, imagination, and decision-making. CS says, "I am viewing this event and interpreting the event in relation to me."

CS also functions to sort through all the incoming and introjected data to make judgments about self. The process is dynamic in that it goes on at all times. Some of the functions at this level can be represented in the following statements which CS makes: "This is how I see myself in this situation at this moment."; "This seems to be the role which I must (or choose) to play in this situation at this time."; "This is how I perceive others perceiving my role in this situation at this particular time." ad infinitum.

CS contains the analytical part of our intrapersonal communication. Suppose you went to high school in a place you despised. You were called endearing names such as "Bucktooth," "Skinny," or "Slouch," and you hated these labels because they represented rejection to you. Suppose your senior year your parents moved and you experienced the new birth of being in a new school, finding yourself accepted and liked. Then one evening the phone rings, you answer, and the voice at the other end says, "Hi, Bucktooth, guess who just moved to town?" At this, your SS would start, "I told you that your happiness wouldn't last, stupid." Your PS would cop out saying, "Poor me, I never get a break. Everything sad happens to me because my parents did a poor job in rearing me." The wrangle ensues to the point that CS must say, "Wait a minute. What has really happened? Is this the end of the world, or can I survive as I have in the past?" CS immediately begins searching analytically to restore self-concept from the automatic reaction to a stressful stimulus by SS and PS.

Another function of CS is its capacity for verbalization. Thought is a form of self-talk and CS engages in the process freely. If you are going to do a simple task like pick up a rake and take it outside to rake the yard, you probably say, "now I am picking up the rake. I am beginning to rake the yard." Planning is another function. CS prepares for things which are ahead by talking through them or creating mental images. Thanks to this function of CS we can plan the route we are going to take on a trip while we are getting ready to leave. We can also build a bridge, write a sonata, plan a tournament, prepare a lesson, etc. In some cases, we learn to do this so effortlessly that we are hardly aware of the process we go through to achieve our objectives. Memory also falls into this function of the CS. CS calls to mind events for purposes of simple nostalgia; but, most of the time the memory function serves to revive knowledge which we have stored. This is a valuable function since it allows humans to become time-binders, as Alfred Korzybski suggests. He alleges that by virtue of our linguistic capacity, humankind can remember the past and plan for the future. This function is one of the most important attributes of the conceptualizing self.

One more principal function of CS must be mentioned — the capacity to identify to the point that we can create roles which are quite similar to the model itself. This is the principal function in personality development and serves to assist us in meeting the most basic needs. This capacity of the CS allows us to create and perform any roles necessary to meet our needs and serves as the genesis for the development of the ability to create, maintain, and repair our self-concept. This is the heart of the identity system which forms the foundation of self-esteem.

The Ideal Self

Unlike the three selves previously discussed, the ideal self is not an entity in its own right. In one sense, the ideal self is an extention of the conceptualizing self. Since CS has direct contact with the external environment, it is in the best position to formulate an ideal self which serves two major functions. The IS is an identificatory measurement for the CS. The IS represents the perfected version of the "you" toward which you strive. This aspect of the IS is attached to the SS in the sense that SS both helps set up and maintain that image and simultaneously lets CS know at all times how far short you fall in your efforts to reach this ideal. PS is attached to IS by virture of its basic disdain for the entity. PS would rather not have an ideal by which to measure itself. PS goes about the business of trying to demonstrate to CS how IS is, in fact, being reached at the present.

The IS's other function rests in the projection of public selves to others in an effort to convince them that we are the person we appear to be. To better understand this process, compare your most private self with the self which you display to others. You will note that there are essential differences. This is not to imply that there is something wrong with the act of creating and maintaining an IS. The IS is the means we have of securing and maintaining social acceptance. This process is a highly sophisticated rhetorical procedure through which we assess the situation and then carefully select an IS to complement the demands placed on us by the situation. It is this related function of the IS, in conjunction with CS, which forms a second projection of IS. We do not simply play a role. We are far more complex beings than that. We select, prepare, sustain, and repair many different roles. For this reason, the IS forms satellite-like clusters which function as varying role functions displayed by the person. We are not the same person in every situation. We have to adapt roles to "fit" the situation. In essence, through the CS's interpretation of situations, we create these roles. Furthermore, as we experience the actual performance of the role, CS makes determinations concerning the effectiveness of the specific role and adjusts accordingly. This function of CS includes interpreting the situation and saying, "I'll be damned if I'll play that game!" or "I chose to accept this role in this situation."

The Value System

As we stated earlier in our discussion of identity formation, self-concept is linked directly to the value system according to proponents of identification theory. As the child identifies with the parent, s/he acts roles portrayed by the parent. This role taking process appears to be all pervasive in that the child not only acts like the parent, s/he also imitates the parents' verbalizations. The child proclaims the same beliefs that the parent proclaims. These values are called "introjected values" because they result from relationship rather than rationality or experience.

These introjected values are a part of the development of self-concept since they evolve from an identification with the parent. Therefore, those initial values are so closely linked to the child's need for love and fears of rejection that they become a part of the psyche. Hence, an attack on someone's basic values represents an attack upon his/her sense of worth. It is probably for these reasons and others that the individual's most basic values are so difficult to change. In an effort to protect those values, we form arguments to support them and therefore protect our self-esteem. The arguments do not have to stand any test of logic, they simply must satisfy the person that s/he has adequately defended his/her beliefs.

Obviously, as we develop and find other persons with whom we iden-tify, we alter our values based on the normative factors operating in the groups we value. Nevertheless, when we persuade our selves that an introjected value is no longer valid to meet our needs, we do so only after a severe rhetorical wrangle.

Perhaps the most accepted theory of values is that of Milton Rokeach who developed a three-layered system. Rokeach designated three levels of personal ethics — beliefs, attitudes, and values. Explaining his model, Rokeach states, "A belief is a simple proposition...inferred from what a person says or does, capable of being preceded by the phrase, 'I believe that'". (1968, p. 111). Attitudes, Rokeach alleges, are more complex in that they represent an organization of beliefs supporting a common subject. Values are the most introjected of all since they are central and enduring. Values have the capacity, according to Rokeach, to influence actions as well as decisions.

Looking at the Rokeach system, we would allege that attitudes develop as argumentative constructs designed to protect the value system and consequently the sense of self-worth. Beliefs are simply another extention of that same process.

Regardless of how we interpret the value system several postulates are important to the process of intrapersonal communication: (1) The value system is the chief resource for SS in his/her fight to force the individual to act in socially acceptable manners; (2) The value system is a chief resource for PS in his/her fight to justify socially unacceptable thoughts and actions; (3) The value system is the chief concern in CS's constant struggle to render actions and attitudes congruent through rhetorical strategies.

The Intrapersonal Rhetorical Wrangle

We have offered a rhetorical model, but the question of the viability of such a model is still unanswered. Facing this problem for some years, we eventually determined that the best test rested in the ability to apply the model on the part of the students who were asked to internalize the concept. Consequently, this portion of our discussion has been produced by students who found situations in their own lives that were quite applicable. This intralogue represents a typical example of the workings of intrapersonal communication.

Intralogue: "To Study or Not to Study, That Is the Question."

Situation: You have an examination scheduled tomorrow in a subject area which you have to endure rather than enjoy. You have reacted accordingly by not exactly devouring the books — so, realistically, in order to pass this course, you need a good grade on this exam.

Scene: "It's eight o'clock in the evening and you are seated at your desk, book open.

PS: "I'm so hungry!

SS: You're not hungry, idiot, you're just trying to find an excuse for not studying.

PS: No, really. I'm hungry. If I had a pizza, I could come back here and really hit the books.

SS: You always say that dummy. You know that doesn't work. You'll just find another excuse.

PS: No, I won't. I'm more true to my word than some I could name. Come on, let's go get a pizza and a beer and then get back to work.

CS: (intervening at this point) That really sounds like a reasonable request. After all, I really haven't had much to eat today.

SS: I won't say I told you so till I get a chance and then, of course, I'll say I told you so.

Scene: You go to the pizza parlor, "accidentally" meet a friend, have a pizza and several beers (PS tried to keep count but just forgot), and return to your room an hour later than part of you had planned. You return to your desk.

PS: I'm so tired and sleepy.

SS: I told you so!

PS: Now wait a minute. I work hard. I go to school, hold a job, keep this place clean, and try to keep my friends happy. I have every right to be tired.

SS: Sure, babe, rave on. What did I tell you before you left for that pizza? Did I not say that you would not do your work when you returned? Huh, smarty, tell me! I want to hear you eat crow, fat mouth!

PS: Get off my back. I'm tired and don't deserve this kind of treatment. You're just trying to make me feel guilty for something over which I really have no control. Look, just let me rest. It'll all come out in the wash. If not, who gives a damn anyway.

SS: You'd better give a damn, lazy. Your poor parents have complete trust in you.

PS: Hey! Don't try to lay that trip on me. Mom always says that I need more rest.

CS: (intervening once again) I suppose I could sleep now and get up early in the morning and study. Then the material will be fresh on my mind when I get to the exam.

SS: You know what will happen. How many times have you tried this before? Did it work? Of course not! Why? Because you're an inevitable loser. You'll just never make it. Wait and see!

Scene: Your alarm goes off as set at 4:00 a.m.

PS: I'm so sleepy. Turn off that awful noise!

SS: Get up! Get up! Get up!

CS: Was this really a reasonable solution?

PS: Let's sleep on it.

Scene: You wake up at 8:55 a.m. Your test begins in five minutes. You dress on the run. All the way to class SS has his/her say.

SS: I told you so, dummy. I knew you'd oversleep. Now you're going to pay. You'll see. You're really going to blow this test.

Scene: You finish the test in the full knowledge that you did indeed fail. As you are walking back to your room, SS really has a "field day."

SS: I told you so. You really flunked didn't you? You blew it again. You're really a first class loser!

PS: I couldn't help it. It really wasn't my fault. For one thing, the test was totally unfair. I thought it would be short answer, not multiple choice!

SS: The truth is you didn't think. In fact, you never think. You really don't have the capacity for rational thought processes. Remember what mother said? She told you that you would never make it with your attitude. See how right she was. You failed again. You'll just never make it. You're definitely not college material. Why don't you give up and start packing your bags!

PS: Leave me alone. It wasn't my fault. I could have cheated if the teacher hadn't stared at me. He hates me! I want my mommy! Everybody always picks on me and I'm really very fragile. Leave me to myself!

CS: How do I sort through this chaos? Am I really a loser? Can I not find a way to overcome this failure? Right now, I certainly don't like myself very much.

This example is only one of hundreds like it. We find ourselves engaging in this process frequently. The problem that we encounter in many cases is that we end our wrangle in a manner similar to the one above. We use our own self-persuasion process to ego-debilitate ourselves. For this reason, we wish to offer a few suggestions which may help you to alter your rhetorical wrangle.

Altering the Rhetorical Wrangle

Although there are no easy answers to reducing the negative effects of the internal rhetorical wrangle, some suggestions are in order. Many of us, by virtue of our lack of knowledge of the process, fall prey to this quite human phenomenon. One student approached me at the end of a class in which we had discussed this process and declared, "I have been aware for years of my intralogue. I even conducted an extensive search through the literature of psychology to try to find out what was going on. This is the first time that I have realized that everyone is engaged in self-persuasion. I was really convinced that I was severely neurotic." Although the example may be extreme, the point remains that many of us experience the negative effects of our own wrangle. The following suggestions may offer some new insights or at least present some alternatives.

1. Recognize the functioning of SS, PS, and CS. The simple recognition of this complex process can be helpful. Like the student in my class, once you acknowledge your wrangle as natural for loquacious creatures, you reduce your apprehension.

2. Recognize the inevitability of the process. While recognition of the process is important, it will not cause the wrangle to abate. You will most likely never rid yourself of the turmoil. Once you acknowledge this fact, however, you will rid yourself of any compulsive need to rid yourself of this "curse."

3. Record your rhetorical wrangles. Make a written record of your self-talk during and after decision making situations. In so doing you will begin to recognize patterns that develop in certain types of situations. You can begin to examine the degree to which you are allowing your "socialized self" to make unrealistic demands or create guilt. You may also recognize the ultimate rhetorical effect on your self-esteem in those instances when you are persuaded by "primative self."

4. Subject your wrangle to your own rational scrutiny. Ask yourself several questions which may create a different perspective.

A. *What is the worst thing that could happen?*
Answering this question by the more rational "conceptualizing self" can often demonstrate that the "doom and gloom" pronouncements of the "socialized self" are unrealistic.

B. *If the worst happens, can I handle it?*
The answer is generally yes. Whereas, you may have allowed your "socialized self" to convince you that all is lost, your answer to this question will usually diminish SS's suasive effect.

C. *What is the true nature of the problem?*
Rather than allowing yourself to be victimized by PS who will attempt to cast blame on everyone else and therefore blur the problem, attempt to assess the reality of the situation. Simply attempt to determine what has actually transpired rather than drawing inferences from the events.

D. *What are my alternatives in this situation?*
Make a list of alternatives to the apparent solution afforded by the situation. In all probability you will discover many options available to you that have been obscured by your internal wrangle.

5. Learn to accept personal responsibility for your actions. Do not confuse this suggestion with the usual social admonition to "face responsibility." Actually that which society deems as responsible is often the anathema of personal responsibility. For example, if a person alleges that he/she has assumed so much responsibility that they are overburdened, he/she is not accepting responsibility. He has created a self-persuasion which allows PS to argue, "It really wasn't my fault that I failed. People place so much responsibility on me that I can't get it all done. I'm always being victimized by others."

Accepting personal responsibility is quite simple in theory. It implies accepting the consequences of your actions prior to taking those actions. Thus if you decide to engage in an extended conversation with your friend and make it to work late, you would say, "I chose to do this and will therefore accept the consequences of my actions." Such a position requires the rational activity of CS. It is most difficult to accept such responsibility in many situations, yet this concept is the most valid in quelling the negative effects of the self-persuasion process.

6. Do not expect magical solutions. The suggestions offered above are just that, they are not panaceas. In fact, some of the suggestions may not work for you at all. Yet, even if they should offer some answers for you regarding the rhetorical wrangle, the self-persuasion process in which you engage has evolved throughout your development and will take time to alter. If you want to change, begin as soon as you like; but don't expect overnight success. Be patient with yourself and count on many set-backs. You can change your self-persuasion over time with concentration and self-acceptance.

Our attempt in this article has been to acquaint you with a rhetorical perspective regarding self-talk. As we have emphasized throughout, the model we have developed is a speculative construct based in other theories. Nevertheless, we have found the model to be quite instrumental as a vehicle for demonstrating the various rhetorical strategies we employ in the act of self-persuasion.

References

1. George H. Mead, *Mind, Self and Society.* Chicago: University of Chicago Press, 1934.
2. Kenneth Burke, *A Rhetoric of Motives.* Berkeley: University of California Press, 1950.
3. Frederick Perls. *Gestalt Therapy Verbatim.* New York: Bantam, 1976.
4. Sigmund Freud, *Interpretation of Dreams.* trans. by A.A. Brill. New York: Modern Library, 1950.
5. Sigmund Freud, *Wit and Its Relation to the Unconscious.* trans. by A.A. Brill. New York: Modern Library, 1938.
6. Sigmund Freud, *New Introductory Lectures in Psychoanalysis.* trans. and ed. by J. Strachey. New York: Norton, 1966.
7. Thomas A. Harris, *I'm OK — You're OK.* New York: Harper and Row, 1969.
8. Eric Berne, *Games People Play.* New York: Ballantine Books, 1964.
9. Milton Rokeach, *Beliefs, Attitudes, and Values.* San Francisco: Jossey Bass, 1968.
10. R.D. Laing, *The Politics of Experience.* New York: Ballantine, 1968.
11. Frederick Perls, *In and Out of the Garbage Pail.* New York: Bantam Books, 1972.

Questions:

1. To what extent does the intralogue in the article coincide with your own self talk?

2. Can you write an intralogue based on a recent experience to depict the rhetorical wrangle in which you engaged? Which "self" "won"? How did the other selves act? Did the wrangle continue? How did the wrangle change after the initial resolution? Did you ever discover a satisfactory means for quelling the turmoil? What was the nature of that process?

3. Can you think of other ways of altering your internal rhetorical wrangle other than those mentioned in the article?

4. What other forms of self-talk do you use? Which of these processes are helpful and which harmful to your self concept?

Gail Sheehy's bestseller, Passages, *deals with the predictable crises of adult life. In this intriguing chapter, which treats one stage of human growth to the next, the author examines the early struggles involved in the development of the "self."*

"Breast to Breakaway"

Gail Sheehy

Drinking, sex playing, competitive sports, hot rodding, street-ganging, joining the army, joining the Peace Corps, joining sororities and fraternities, smoking dope, popping pills, backpacking through Rajasthan, religious quests, rioting, streaking, seeking bliss consciousness — each of these experiments satisfied something of young people's need to test their capacities and seek their own truth. The context offered by history varies when each of us is ready to take the step away from home, but the inner shift demanded by this passage remains the same.

In gradually detaching ourselves from the family, we initiate the search for a personal identity. This is usually thought of as a crisis of adolescence. Yet the full achievement of identity is not merely a matter of deciding who we are and what we are going to do in the world; those decisions are subject to change over the course of a lifetime. There is a more highly refined dimension of growth that is only possible and appropriate after we have had time to profit by years of life experience. It is called by Jung *individuation,*[1] by Maslow *self-actuali-*

---

[1] The individuation process, a major contribution to psychological theory by Carl Jung, is explained concisely by Jolande Jacobi in *The Psychology of C.G. Jung* (1973 edition), p. 107. "Taken as a whole, individuation is a spontaneous, natural process within the psyche; it is potentially present in every man, although most men are unaware of it. Unless it is inhibited, obstructed, or distorted by some specific disturbance, it is a process of maturation or unfolding, the psychic parallel to the physical process of growth and aging."

zation, by others *integration* or *autonomy*. I speak of it in this book as *gaining our authenticity*. By that I mean the arrival at that felicitous state of inner expansion in which we know of all our potentialities and possess the ego strength to direct their full reach.

From the broad perspective of the life cycle, how long does this take?

We are children until we reach puberty. We are adolescents until we reach that point in our twenties when we take hold of a provisional identity. And somewhere between the late thirties and early forties when we enter midlife, we also have the opportunity for true adulthood, whereupon we proceed either to wither inside our husks or to regather and re-pot ourselves for the full flowering into our full authenticity.

If you have already left home, you will probably be muttering to yourself, "What is this nonsense? I *am* an adult!" "Don't I earn a paycheck?" "Aren't I taking care of a child of my own?" "Don't I live my life as I please, no matter what my parents think?" These and other external demonstrations of becoming an adult are easy to point out. The complicated steps of internal growth are another matter.

Each child arrives in the world an outlaw. He strives to center the universe about himself and to make it what he wants it to be: his own inner circle. For the first few months of life, this is easy. The infant is the world, and there is no awareness of "self" as distinct from "other."

Gradually, though dimly, this first circle comes to include primitive images of the caregiver—the first other—usually the mother. The baby cries out to its caregiver, who responds by feeding, soothing, and removing discomforts. Naturally, the need and response will not always dovetail. This allows the child to make his first rough reckoning of the balance he must expect in life between satisfaction and discontent. With the discovery that most of his needs will in time be met, the child gains the fundamental resource from which his development will proceed: a sense of basic trust.[2]

This trust becomes the cushion enabling a new kind of exchange, in which both the self and the other are acknowledged; psychologists call it *mutuality*. An early example of mutuality can be seen when a baby smiles. The mother returns the smile, whereupon the child rewards her with an even more enthusiastic response. The essence of mutuality is that each needs the recognition of the other to complete the transaction. The child has now written the first page in a long story of intimate exchanges.

---

[2]It was Erikson who stated, "For the first component of a healthy personality, I nominate a sense of basic trust." *Psychological Issues* (1959), pp. 55-56. In a later essay, "The Golden Rule and the Cycle of Life" (1964), he wrote about mutuality, not as a separate phase, but as an on-going process governed by the sense of basic trust established in early infancy. "The fact is that the mutuality of adult and baby is the original source of the basic ingredient of all effective as well as ethical human action: hope."

Our Merger and Seeker Selves

With the debut of the first separate sense of self about the age of two, we are endowed with an extraordinary gift: the makings of our own individuality. The price of cultivating this seed is separation, the gradual and painstaking process of separating the inner reality of *me* from the glorified images of *them*. Therein lies the rub. Glorification of our parents is encouraged by the very fact of our dependence on them, and our consequent need to cast them as the omnipotent Strong Ones.

Something in us yearns to remain an infant fused with mother, yearns to drive off anything strange and indulge only our own cravings for pleasure or power. The urge is so strong that now and then the young child is willing to forego his own inner imperatives and dissolve his budding distinctiveness. Why not? So long as we bathe in our own egocentric circle, we know nothing of problems. We can only know problems when forces in our inner life come into opposition. And that happens when the self begins to divide.[3]

It helps to think of these forces as under the management of two different sides of the self, as different as two floor managers on opposing sides of a bill in Congress. The impulse on one side of us is to merge. Its manager might be called our *Merger Self*. The opposing impulse is to seek our individuality; that side is our *Seeker Self*. These impulses are driven by contradictory wishes that set up the push-pull underlying all steps of development.

One is the universal wish to be attached to another, to restore somehow the beatific closeness with mother, for in that fusion would lie perfect harmony, absolute safety, and endless time. The Merger Self is born of the frustration with our early discovery that we are indeed separate and distinct from our caregiver. It triggers a desire to totally incorporate the other, any "other" who becomes the source of love and pleasure. And this desire, writes psychoanalyst Edith Jacobson, "probably never ceases to play a part in our emotional life."[4]

---

[3]Mahler has proposed that for the first three months of life the infant has no awareness of self and other. As the infant becomes aware that its needs are met from without, the next phase — symbiosis — is entered, although the mother is still assumed to be part of the self. Somewhere around the age of 2 the child moves into the phase Mahler has termed separation-individuation, which allows the gradual building of an individual identity. See Mahler (1953 and 1963) and the discussion by Blanck and Blanck of Mahler's developmental scheme in *Marriage and Personal Development* (1968), p. 49.

Peter Blos proposes that the first stage of individuation is completed toward the end of the third year of life with the attainment of object constancy. He sees adolescence as the second stage of individuation: "Not until the termination of adolescence do self and object representations acquire stability and firm boundaries." *The Second Individuation Process of Adolescence* (1967), pp. 162-187.

[4]Quote from Jacobson in *The Self and the Object World* (1964), p. 39.

John Bowlby, the distinguished British psychoanalyst whose lifework has been to examine effects on children of separation from parents, has now carried his thesis from

Identification is a form of imitating the other. Grandly we totter in mother's high heels. Faithfully we reproduce father's shaving ritual with an invisible razor. Behind thousands of such imitations of our parents that we perform in the first few years of life lies the desire to preserve maximum closeness with our original love sources.

How touchingly and transparently we display this longing to be attached to another throughout life! In the ecstasy of sexual union we come closest to recapturing the feeling of fusion. Not only does love-making appease the potential rages gathered from daily evidence of our differentness, we can also luxuriate, however briefly, in a state of timeless harmony reminiscent of that original state when self and other seemed as one. The capacity to reach out and empathize with others, to feel as they might feel without letting our own reality intrude, also depends upon allowing temporary fusions. The Merger Self then, in its constant effort to restore closeness, desires always a safe, tight fit.

The Seeker Self is driven by the opposite wish: to be separate, independent, to explore our capacities and become master of our own destiny.* This impulse is fueled in early childhood by our delight in awakening capabilities. Once we can walk, we want to walk without holding anyone's hand, to crawl up the stairs, to crawl *down* the stairs despite baby gates and solemn warnings concerning our imminent self-destruction. The renegade in us is opposed not only by the "don'ts" handed down by our parents, but also by their implicit instructions on what it means to be good and bad. And so, we also use identifications as the shortcut to learning how to behave as if we were grown-ups. Along the way we internalize countless images of ourselves as the "Strong Ones" we want to be like.

Most contemporary theorists agree that the intake of these earliest identifications is at the center of our psychological development.[5] No matter how old we are, our self-image is never entirely independent of these early images of our parents.

If the Merger Self is indulged too early, it can lead us into a no-risk, no-growth position. But once we are beyond the suspicion, or the fear,

---

infancy into adulthood. He argues in *Separation* (1973) that the child's emotional life is dominated by one theme — his need for closeness to the mother — and that all anxiety is basically a "realistic" fear of separation from the mother. In his third volume of the "Attachment and Loss" series, he hopes to demonstrate that the individual's ongoing need to defend against the threat of loss can explain most ramifications of personality.

*In this book, I have stayed away from the difficult and loaded terms *id, superego,* and *ego.* I have used a different formulation (the Seeker Self and the Merger Self) to describe two sets of forces always at loggerheads inside us over the questions of how far and how fast we shall grow. They are in no way meant to be interchangeable with Freudian concepts.

[5]Jacobson, Blos, and Roy Schafer (*Aspects of Internalization,* 1968) all posit that some mechanism of internalization or identification is at the center of psychological development.

of letting our distinctiveness be lost in attachments to others, it is our merger side that enables us to love intimately, share unselfishly, express tenderness, and experience empathy.

If the Seeker Self is left unbridled, it will lead us to a self-centered existence in which genuine commitments can have no place, and in which efforts to achieve individual distinction are so strenuous that they leave us emotionally impoverished.

It is only by getting the two sides to work in concert that eventually one becomes capable of both individuality and mutuality. But this is not merely an intramural competition.

The Inner Custodian

As soon as it becomes clear that a second circle — the magic circle of family — surrounds and restricts us, we run into another force that attempts to direct our development. All of us must learn as children, for instance, how to get across the street without being hit by a car. The process goes something like this:

"Stop! Don't run into the street!" shouts the mother the first time the curious child runs ahead of her toward the traffic at the end of the block. Startled by her tone of alarm, the child stops short. After one or more excursions to the same corner, the child halts before the curb and parrots exactly the mother's words: "Me 'top, wait for Mommy." The child does not cross the street. But now, instead of the control coming from outside, there is a controlling presence inside: a phantom parent. The command of the other has been partially incorporated into the self.

By taking in the "Don't cross the street" prohibition and thousands of other forms of behavior through identification, we all end up with a constant companion we might call our *inner custodian.* It curtails our freedom and in that respect is a dictator. But in exchange, it can foretell the future ("You'll be hit by a car if you cross on the red") and so also protects us from danger; therefore, it is a guardian as well.

The inner custodian has other powers beyond the familiar cautionary ones. Our parents also tell us throughout childhood: "Watch me; be like me," or in some cases, "Don't be like me." Directly or indirectly, a father may communicate the message: "If you don't go to medical school and become a doctor, you won't be respected." By the same token, a mother whose lot is to be a domestic may drum into her child the directive: "Study your English, Maria. Read. Learn. Do you want to grow up and be a maid like me?"

From then on throughout much of life, even when things are running smoothly outside, our internal world may be in a state of agitation over the competing urges of the Seeker and Merger Selves, as well as the face-off with the inner custodian.*

---

*In psychoanalytic terms, we are talking now about the concepts of self and object that originated with Freud. On first exposure, such concepts are infuriatingly abstract. Beyond the abstract words, though, their profundity eventually makes it possible to stretch

Eventually, of course, we all violate the "Don't cross the street" taboo. Violating it is the only way to end up with a judgment based on our own experience. Dangerous or not, we must find out if it's possible both to cross the street *and* to avoid being hit by cars.

The first time we make it safely to the other side of the street on our own, the authority on that particular subject begins to shift from the inner custodian to the self. Imagine our self compartment overtaking an inch or so from the compartment controlled by our phantom parent. By experimenting, we find out how to watch for speeding cars and what to do if we get caught in the middle when the light changes. Now we are on the way to trusting our own dictates and relying on our own guardianship, so that eventually we can play in the big traffic of the world. We no longer hear Mother's voice telling us to stop. It is what psychiatrists call an *integrated identification*. Each time we confront that archaic directive with the truth of our own experience, we become freer to enjoy riding a bike, taking the bus to school alone, and some of us eventually to attempt skiing, skin diving, or piloting a plane.

Learning to cross the street is comparatively easy. Coming to trust our own judgment in volatile matters such as sex, intimacy, competition, the choice of friends, loves, career, ideology, and the right values to pursue is a much longer and more demanding process.

Breaking Away from the Inner Custodian

By the time we are ready to leave home, we have learned to administer the protections of the inner custodian and to choose directives for ourselves — or so we think. It is this internalized protection that gives us a sense of insulation from being burned by life, from being bullied by others (and even into midlife, from coming face to face with our own absolute separateness). The illusion can serve us well while we are young, but it is also very tricky.

This inner custodian is a two-faced image. Like the self, it has two sides. The benevolent side of our internalized parent is felt to be the *guardian* of our safety. The *dictator* side of our internalized parent has the menacing face of an administrator of shoulds and should-nots. Its influence is prohibitive.

Think of Janus, the ancient god of entrances and exits. His two bearded profiles, back to back and looking in opposite directions, represent two sides of the same gate. But is inside the gate safety or entrapment? Is outside the gate freedom or danger? This is a riddle

---

a person's biography over a theoretical framework and to see the underdesign of a person's development along with some of the original sources of snags and knots. I have tried to put the theory in less abstract terms, substituting "inner custodian" for "object," and to apply it to the stages of adult life to add a deeper dimension to the tasks we face in each passage.

with which we struggle throughout life, for the answer is yes, no, both, and not entirely either.

Particularly in the Pulling Up Roots passage, in which we are shedding an old familiar life system for the first time and feeling exposed and uncertain, we are tempted to take on the form of our phantom parent along with all its weaknesses. We fool ourselves by insisting that it is our choice alone or that we are really quite different. This can be a step backward on the way to a progressive solution, as we shall see. However, many who allow themselves to lapse into this form and accept passively the identity proffered (directly or indirectly) by the family, wind up locked in.

None of us wants to go too far, too fast beyond the value system of our inner custodian, to become too much an individual. Because then we cannot crawl back into the sanctuary when the growing gets rough. This is the conundrum of Pulling Up Roots, indeed, of all the decades well into the middle of the fifth.

The passage in which we are earnestly in transit between the intimate circle of family and the adult world extends roughly from the ages of 18 to 22. The tasks during this time are to locate ourselves in a peer group role, a sex role, an anticipated occupation, an ideology or world view. We generally begin at this stage by claiming control over at least one aspect of our lives that our parents can't touch. Parents can offer lessons and clubs and family trips to Yosemite or the Caribbean, but in the giving somewhat contaminate almost anything they give because it is an extension of their rules and values.

Each time we master an undertaking that replaces the parental view of the world with our own evolving perspective, we overtake another inch or so from our inner custodian. But it is not so simple as a one-to-one transfer. Underlying each of these tasks, there is also the fundamental conflict *within us*: while our Seeker Self urges us to confront the unknown and take chances—pushing the young person to all manner of extremes—our Merger Self beckons us back toward the comforts of safety and the known—and the possibility of locking in prematurely.[6]

---

[6]After noting, in one life story after another, the dynamic interplay of forces I came to describe as the Seeker and Merger selves, I discovered that Abraham H. Maslow had also written about two competing forces in explaining his theory of growth. The reader should be aware that Maslow has talked about it, but in my opinion his formulation is too black and white. "Every human being has both sets of forces within him. One set clings to safety and defensiveness out of fear, tending to regress backward, hanging on to the past, *afraid* to grow away from the primitive communication with the mother's uterus and breast, *afraid* to take chances, *afraid* to jeopardize what he already has, *afraid* of independence, freedom and separateness. The other set of forces impels him forward toward wholeness of Self and uniqueness of Self, toward full functioning of all his capacities, toward confidence in the face of the external world at the same time that he can accept his deepest, real unconscious Self." Quote is from Maslow's *Toward a Psychology of Being* (1968), p. 45.

A First Solo Flight

On the brink of the Pulling Up Roots passage, the familiar universe seems stale. The conviction is that *real* life is somewhere out there, away from family and school, "waiting to happen to me." Young people who can't wait to put a continent between themselves and their parents and childhood friends are impelled by the desire to defeat the power the family still has to reclaim them. In extreme cases, they choose authoritarian spiritual groups that demand total allegiance and a complete break with past associations. The attractions are the promise of absolute truth, repudiation of parents, and a substitute for the safety of home.

Donald Babcock, the young man we met in Chapter Two who was about to repeat his father's pattern, provides an example of how the Merger Self can overwhelm before the Seeker Self has a chance to kick up its heels.

Donald was graduated from the Hotchkiss prep school and then entered Yale because that was the *family destiny*. If the father is Joseph P. Kennedy, the family destiny is that the eldest son become president. If the mother is Judy Garland, that the daughter be a star. In many instances, the family destiny will define, not a particular occupation, but rather a certain value to strive for: intellectual achievement, creative independence, contribution to one's race, or sheer self-reliance. At the gateway to the twenties, the young person will have to figure out some way to incorporate this parental mandate with his own inner imperatives (or reject it for the time being) if he is to cultivate his own budding distinctiveness.

After finishing his first year at Yale, Donald's motto was loud and clear: "I have to get away from my parents." The getaway vehicle was his parents' car. He wasn't looking for an authoritarian family or for spiritual levitation; he was simply seeking the *real* experience of driving across the country to take a summer job in California. Like most Americans of an age to leave home, Donald set out swaddled in the magical protection we all carry along from childhood. Most of us at that age believe we should have all the powers we presume our parents to possess. We, too, should be able to forecast the future and know where absolute safety lies.

"Be sure to rotate drivers," were his father's final instructions. "That way, nobody will fall asleep at the wheel."

They were going ninety when they left the road. They had just rotated drivers: *I don't know what happened I was asleep at the time I woke up hanging from a seat belt staring at my friend's bloody face I tried to move but nothing would, not my back, my neck, my wrist, oh Jesus, we just laid out there in the desert for two hours.* He could hear others crying from somewhere else in the metal squash. He didn't know it then, but his neck was broken. And also his back.

With all the illusory protection the 19-year-old carries on his first solo excursion, not even this temporary paralysis can be believed. After all, the hero always walks out of the debris, blood-crusted but grinning, and oh what a story to tell some beautiful girl.

"The accident was a setback for me in a lot of ways. I couldn't take the job I had waiting in California. In fact, I couldn't do much of anything. That accident ended my athletic career. I lost fifty pounds. And I was back in a dependent state, living at home again, needing a lot of care. My father would come back after he checked into the office and shave me. My mother would come home during the day from her job; my grandmother was always looking in. It was kinda nice, it brought the whole family closer together. But after a few weeks, it began to drag on. I was immobilized in traction."

Donald's assumption that he could stand on his own two feet had been knocked out from beneath him, although as he saw it from this stage, it was only temporary. It meant that he would have to be propped up a little bit longer by his parents. When fall semester began, he wasn't strong enough to go back to school.

"My father came through with a job for me as a security guard on a museum estate. As a Republican committeeman, he has a lot of jobs to give out. I was against the idea, but here I was in a back brace. My job was to keep people out. Nobody ever came in except horseback riders. Looking back at it, it's weird, but the accident was probably a good thing. In that I got a chance to meet Bonnie."

Bonnie loves to tell the tale of their meeting in an enchanted forest.

"My place to ride on the estate was the Wonderland. I called it that because all the shurbs were shaped like animals. I would get off my horse and let her graze while I wandered under the giant pine trees and around the perfect little pond. It was a place for fantasies. For me, it was love at first sight. I saw somebody there, a boy, sitting against a tree and playing his harmonica. He looked so *passive*. When I rode away, I just couldn't forget his face. I had to go back every day."

What better fairy tale than to bring life to a slightly wasted swain?

For Donald, banished to seclusion in a forest inhabited only by scuttling creatures and small, nervous birds, Bonnie's appearance was a vision of strength. She was the certainty of youth that he had misplaced. How recklessly she galloped toward him bareback; yet dismounting from her horse, she was so ineffably feminine, blonde, soothing as butter on burned fingers.

"She was beautiful. We met in the woods every day for three weeks. Then I had an operation. I was trying to take care of myself. I knew I had to wear a back brace for two more months. I was still literally a cripple. I felt—powerless."

Bonnie didn't know about the back brace until their first public date. She led him to an amusement park. "He was trying so hard to impress me by going on all these crazy rides that I love. Suddenly I realized that this man was in agony. I knew he didn't want mothering... but even now I tell him that he shouldn't be sleeping on a waterbed.''

How strange it all was for Donald. What a startling contradiction to the syllogism he had worked out for his life before the accident. About not getting married for seven years after graduation, he had been absolutely definite. He was a modern man. But then, abruptly, he had again become a boy, one who needed taking care of. His own parents would not do. To allow such a lapse would be to risk falling back into the old childhood dependency. By transferring the need to a girl his age, Donald could replace the soothing functions of his family. We are all particularly susceptible to "take care of me" contracts at such times. Donald, being now the very picture of 22, settles for a far simpler explanation: "Love is a strange thing."

It seems that his need to recover a sense of safety led Donald to give up his own vision of how to make his way in the world. Almost to the wire before graduation from Yale, he was engrossed in oceanographic research and determined to make an original contribution to the energy problem. But instead of carrying out his plan to go to graduate school, he decided to marry Bonnie a week after finishing college and go into business—just like his father. Although his father welcomed this repetition of the family pattern, Donald's mother was disturbed by it. She tried to search her son's mind for the kind of marriage he envisioned.

Donald told her, "This may surprise you, but I really would like a marriage pretty much like yours."

"That's flattering to hear," his mother admits, "but Donald hasn't a clue about what a marriage like ours is. He's seen what he wanted to see. How can my son know what it's like to live with a lack of communication?" Although Donald tells her he hasn't altogether abandoned the idea of graduate work but wants first to "take a shot at the big time" and build financial security, his mother foresees for him a duplication of the narrow, risk-fearing path taken by the man she married.

Ken Babcock didn't dare wrestle with identity questions when he was a young man either. Today, his is the slugged face of a man who has led with his chin for a quarter century in the big ring of American business. Always a contender but never quite champion, never imagining what it would be like to say what he really felt. It is only in middle age that Ken Babcock has broken out of the I-must-become-president mold mandated by *his* father. Only at 48, for the first time, is he beginning to feel comfortable living within his own contours while asking, uncertainly, for confirmation that what he has become is enough.

And so while his son Donald has also avoided any early turbulence by passively accepting the family destiny *in toto*, it is but a temporary comfort. Heading off an identity crisis at this passage only inhibits one's development. Other young people who can accept the experience of a crisis at this turning point generally emerge stronger and more in control of their destinies.

Author's Note

The basic source on concepts of self and object representations, from which my description of the "inner custodian" is derived, is Freud, particularly his paper, *On Narcissism: An Introduction* (1914), and *The Ego and the Id* (1923). Most helpful in understanding these concepts is Edith Jacobson's monograph, *The Self and the Object World* (1973), which was officially sponsored by the Journal of the American Psychoanalytic Association. Discussions with Roger Gould were provocative in applying the concepts to individual biographies.

The clearest explanation of the process of identification appears in Robert White's *The Enterprise of Living* (1972).

Questions:

1. How are the "seeker/merger selves" in Sheehy's theory related to the "socialized/primitive selves" in the previous article?

2. In what situations do you find your "merger self" most prominent? In what situations does your "seeker self" emerge?

3. To what extent have you experienced the process of "breaking away from your inner custodian"? How has this process affected your intrapersonal and interpersonal communication?

4. If you have not already experienced a "Pulling Up Roots" passage, does the idea appear exciting or frightening? If you have experienced such a passage, what surprised you about your reactions to it?

If you have ever alleged that someone "hurt your feelings," you may be making a very inaccurate judgment. In this article, Narcisco and Burkett argue that most of our concepts about feelings are derived from a misuse of the abstracting process.

Myths of Feeling

John Narcisco and David Burkett

When I'm driving down the street and I notice another car in my lane coming toward me, I may experience many things happening in my body. My heart may beat faster, my pulse quicken, my hands perspire, and my stomach lurch. These are physiological responses to a situation typically described *not* in these physical terms but as the experience of feeling scared or frightened.

Operationally, I would be clearer and more accurate if I described what is really happening: "I am perspiring, my heart is beating faster, my pulse is racing, and my stomach is lurching."

I've learned to think "scared" or "frightened" with the presence of these correlated physical occurrences. Each of us experiences visceral reactions which occur in response to the stimulus of a particular situation, like the car on a path toward me. We have also learned to tie these occurrences to an abstract symbol. The problem is that we tend to make the abstract symbol the reality, and we call that a feeling. In actuality, we don't *feel* scared or frightened, we *think* and physically react scared or frightened.

In addition to making the abstract symbol the reality, we often behave in certain ways *because* of that so-called reality. For example, the common assumption is that when a person is angry he does something *because* of the anger. He might slam the door, and he might claim that "anger" made him do it.

From the book *Declare Yourself* by John Narcisco and David Burkett. © 1975 by John Narcisco and David Burkett. Published by Prentice-Hall, Inc., Englewood Cliffs, New Jersey 07632.

To me, slamming the door is the anger.

This is not a new view. Many readers may be familiar with the James-Lange theory of the emotions and the often quoted line that demonstrates that theory: "We are not running because we are afraid; we are afraid because we are running."

An essay by William James written in 1884 ("What Is Emotion?") further describes this theory of emotions. "Common sense," James writes, "says we lose our fortune, are sorry and weep; we meet a bear, are frightened and run; we are insulted by a rival, are angry and strike." The James-Lange hypothesis states that this sequence is not correct. James writes that "the one mental state is not immediately induced by the other, the bodily manifestations must first be interposed between, and the more rational statement is that we feel sorry, because we cry, angry because we strike...." He also writes: "Our natural way of thinking about these standard emotions is that the mental perception of some fact excites the mental affection called the emotion, and that this latter state of mind gives rise to the bodily expression.

There are actual physiological feelings, of course.

When I was a youngster, I explored my world through physiological events called feelings, namely pressure, pain, cold, and warm. These are areas of scientific study in physiology and psychology. As I grew older, I continued to use the word "feelings," but I carried it over to what probably could better be described intellectually, in terms of thinking. Most people fall into this same trap.

I'm sure you have heard people say things such as "What do you *feel* the Astro's chances are to win the pennant?" or "Do you *feel* this product will sell?" or "Do you *feel* you know what's going to be on the examination?" In each case, the more appropriate word is not "feel" but "think." The process is intellectual.

This misuse of the abstract symbol often makes interpersonal relationships more difficult, and I believe I can demonstrate this in discussing what I call the four myths of feelings. Most people practice these myths; perhaps you do too.

The first myth is that feelings are involuntary, that they happen to us without forewarning, no matter what we do.

I'm sure you've heard someone say "I'm angry, and I just can't help it." The person really is saying that he has a right to be angry under these particular circumstances, and that anyone in the same situation also would be angry.

I don't think of feelings as being involuntary.

Suppose a couple is arguing. The argument becomes more heated. Both the husband and wife are shouting when suddenly the telephone rings. The wife walks to the phone, picks up the receiver, and says, in a very pleasant voice, "Hello. Yes, this is Helen; so nice of you to call. Oh, he's just fine. We'd be delighted to come, and thank you for the invitation. Good-bye."

She replaces the receiver, then returns to resume the argument in its original intensity.

If the situation calls for it, we can turn off anger and turn on pleasantness. We can decide how to behave.

I think we learn that feelings are involuntary when we are children. What does a mother say to her child when the child is not getting what he wants for some reason? She might say something such as "I'm sure you must be very angry, and I don't blame you. I'd be angry too." The child learns that anger is natural under the circumstances. It is logical and to be expected.

Robert McKinley, the psychiatrist, tells a poignant story of a youngster, two or three years of age, who is experiencing a severe thunderstorm for the first time. The child is playing in his room when he hears a large clap of thunder. Mother, in the next room, calls to him: "Are you okay?"

The child, quite naturally, thinks to himself that for some reason, probably because of the thunder, he's not supposed to be okay.

"Why?" he calls back from his room.

"Didn't you hear that thunder? Aren't you afraid?"

And, he thinks, I guess I am afraid. I'm *supposed* to be afraid of the thunder.

In the future when a storm produces more severe thunder and lightning, the child—now afraid—rushes to his mother and is comforted. The mother has taught her child to be afraid of thunder. Fear is part of the thunder, and he soon learns that fear and perhaps other feelings are involuntary.

Parents often assume that children should have the same feelings that they have been taught to have, and rather than teach the child to handle the situation, they teach him to feel as they did or do.

A youngster may be taught to fear snakes through his father's fear of snakes. If he is thus taught, he is likely to have certain reactions when he sees a snake. He will "think" snake, and there will be a correlated, physiological printout that may include a quickening of his heartbeat, increased flow of perspiration, perhaps even nausea. He will say he "feels" frightened. He may think he has no other choice.

However, if he learns more about snakes, which ones are dangerous and which ones are harmless, his physiological responses may be modified by these new experiences. A diamondback rattler might call up the old printout of nausea, sweating, and increased pulse rate, but he may respond to the situation differently rather than "feel" fear. He may experience the same physiological printout—the "fear," as he calls it—but he can respond more effectively to the situation because of his additional learning. Eventually the feeling of fear (actually the behavior of fear) will be extinguished by the repetition of the stimulus without some associated negative happening which he now understands better.

And upon recognizing a garter snake, he probably won't experience much physiological change at all because he has learned that garter snakes are not dangerous.

The change is in the "feeling" reaction occasioned by new learning, that is, in the way the youngster thinks.

So, although most of us are taught that feelings are involuntary, I think it can easily be shown that they are not. I *decide* how to behave in any situation as I have learned to do. If I am to change how I behave, therefore, I have to learn some new options.

The second myth is that feelings are caused by something outside ourselves.

I talked with a student not long ago. He told me that he was having trouble getting to his 8 a.m. class.

"I just can't get up for my eight o'clock," he said.

"Does some actual force keep you in bed?" I asked him.

"Well, no."

"Then I'd like you to change one word in your original sentence. Try saying 'I *don't* get up for my eight o'clock class.'"

The word "can't," I explained, implies an outside force, a kind of demon or spirit or monster of some type that has the student in his grip.

It reminds me of the comic line "The devil made me do it."

"What might happen," I said to the student, "if you did go to your eight o'clock class?"

"Well, I might get called on for my Spanish assignment, and I wouldn't like that," he said.

No outside force prevented the student from getting to his eight o'clock class, but I believe he was using a get-my-way behavior. The payoff was not having to face the professor or the class. The strategy was to blame the problem on an outside force that made the student helpless.

Perhaps you've heard someone say "*You* have made me angry."

In other words, an outside force—another person—has visited anger upon this individual.

This is another example of using feelings as a get-my-way behavior. The person really is saying "I am angry, and it's your fault. Change what you are doing so I won't have to be angry anymore."

Few interpersonal forces render us actually helpless. And, because we can choose how we behave from among the learned options, the more accurate response might be that "I am responding in the only way I have learned to react to what you have done" or "I have decided to behave to what you have done by this option from among those I possess."

Notice the pronoun "I," the first person singular. Using "I" stresses that the speaker is responsible for his own selection of choices from among those he has learned. This is a crucial point that I will discuss later in more detail.

I recall a father telling me of an incident in his home.

After a difficult day, he settled in his den to read the evening newspaper. Just as he was getting comfortable, his children, six and eight years of age, came into the room doing what youngters their age do — teasing one another, playing a game with shouts.

The father told me later how he jumped to his feet and yelled at the youngsters. "You make me furious," he cried.

In attempting to get his children to be quiet so he could read his newspaper, he probably expressed "anger" which had descended upon him. He was claiming that the cause of that anger was something outside himself, his children's behavior.

The more accurate response might have sounded this way: "I have decided to shout and complain in response to what you kids are doing in hopes that you will stop it."

There were other alternatives to what the father actually did. The father could have accepted the fact that the children were doing predictable, and therefore understandable, behavior to which he needn't have responded with anger. He could have had the children play in another room. He could have gone to another room to read. He could have decided to postpone his reading and play with the children instead.

Other alternatives to his shouting were possible, but the father — believing, as most people do, that feelings are involuntary and are caused by something outside himself — crossed out additional alternatives or refused to look for them.

And his shouting may have been successful. The option he selected undoubtedly was one that had worked for him before, or he would not have used it in this instance. Get-my-way techniques often work, and we continue using them because they do. The problem is that they may make our relationships with other people ineffective, awkward, and unclear as they require us to be helpless, to suffer, or to become angry. The fewer alternatives a person sees to a situation, the more limited he is in his response.

This matter of options or alternatives is a crucial one. In our culture, we often say a person is "sick" or "mentally ill" when he simply doesn't act the way we act. Some would claim he needs therapy. Could it not be that the person doesn't see the options we do or that we don't see the options he does? We may not be aware of the other's alternatives, and one of us may need to learn them. Perhaps we should call this education rather than therapy, with all its additional implications.

Last December, a woman told me that she "couldn't help but be hurt when her daughter told her she wasn't coming home for Christmas."

The hurt, she claimed, was caused by something outside herself.

"You hurt me when you say that" indicates that the mother had *decided* to be hurt in response to the daughter's decision. The "hurt" was the mother's attempt to get *her* way, inviting the daughter to change what she was doing, in other words — to come home for the holiday not because the daughter wanted to, but because she had been taught to be responsible for her mother's feelings.

Had the daughter changed her mind and come home, which she did not do, she would have been practicing what undoubtedly had been her early training. She would have complied with her mother's desires in order to prevent hurt to her mother and avoid guilt feelings in herself.

It's my belief that no one can hurt another person psychologically. One can provide a behavioral stimulus, but the other person must elect to be hurt by that stimulus. It is *his decision.*

If his training is such that he has only the option to be hurt in the particular situation, then he will behave that way. The point is that there are options other than to be hurt. Those options must be learned.

I asked the mother to consider what might have happened if she hadn't been hurt.

"Well, I suppose the world wouldn't have come to an end," she said. "I probably would have had a more enjoyable Christmas, and so would my daughter. And I would have accepted my daughter's invitation to visit her for New Year's, instead of brooding and feeling rejected and let down." The mother was aware of other options, but she hadn't stopped to consider them.

Our feelings are not caused or controlled by things or persons outside ourselves without our permission.

Our training in terms of feelings is that we must have them and we must express them, which leads us to the third myth.

The third myth is that feelings can be shared.

Again, the crucial issue is what we think feelings are. Feelings, in my opinion, are thoughts and associated physical reactions manifested in covert and overt behavior, such as a faster heart beat, a quickened pulse, blotched skin, or other reactions, including verbal ones.

I *can* share words that I use to describe the physical reactions that I experience. When I do that, I am sharing my unique perception of those physical reactions I have. I'm talking now about my subjective reality.

My subjective reality cannot be shared directly with someone else's subjective reality. I can provide stimuli for the other person in the form of words, grimaces, and other overt physical reactions, but the other person must experience these in his own unique way and make meaning of them in his own subjectivity.

Philosophers and psychologists call this realm of subjectivity the "phenomenological field" of the individual, and phenomenological fields cannot directly interact.

I am not denying that feelings as experiences are realities. Without question, these experiences occur. But because they do not exist in objective reality, they can't be shared.

Most of us attempt to share them with hypothetical constructs, those abstract symbols like "anger," "fear," "love," "hate." These we call feelings.

We also often associate the words "like" and dislike" with feelings. I propose a different view of these words to disconnect them from feelings and to recognize them as a means of evaluation. To say "I *like* something," then, means that I have a response somewhere on the positive side of my evaluation continuum.

The popularity of sensitivity training in the mid-1960s came about because many people believed feelings could be shared and indeed needed to be shared. They practiced a kind of "abscess theory." The approach was that the abscess of "anger" or "alienation" or whatever had to be "lanced"—expressed—in order for healing to occur.

Many sensitivity sessions actually were instructional period which frequently taught participants more skillful get-my-way techniques!

In a particular sensitivity group, a young man sobs. A typical approach would be to allow him to continue sobbing. Finally the group leader might say, "John, it seems as though you have some very deep feelings." And John continues crying, the sobbing becoming louder and louder, reinforced by the attention being given it.

Compare that approach with one in which someone says simply, "John, something must not be happening in your life that you want to happen. What is it?"

Now John isn't under the control of outside forces; he can decide how to behave. While he can share his sobbing (an operational event) and also his thoughts in words in response to the question and to the situation (another operational event), he cannot share feelings.

The Fourth myth is that we can be responsible for one another's feelings.

The subjective life of the individual is that and no more. What he experiences within himself in any situation is his alone. How he labels that experience is the result of what he has learned. It is uniquely his.

If he thinks that feelings are not involuntary and are not caused by something outside himself, then it follows that his behavior is a matter of choice among his learned options.

P.W. Bridgman suggested in *The Way Things Are* (Cambridge, Harvard University Press, 1959) that in writing scientific papers, authors should use first person singular. Bridgman reasoned that because the scientist was the observer, he would write "I have observed such and such" rather than "It was observed that such and such happened."

Bridgman's idea is deceptively simple and enormously significant. No two people observe an event in quite the same way, and only by using the pronoun "I" can responsibility be assigned to the responsible person.

Philosophers for centuries have argued that each of us lives in a world of his own. And, as Bridgman wrote: "Not only do I see that I cannot get away from myself, but I see that you cannot get away from yourself. The problem of how to deal with the insight that we never get away from ourselves is perhaps the most important problem before us."

In interpersonal relationships, I believe first person singular is most appropriate because it places responsibility clearly.

If I say to another person, "I do not like what you did," then no contradiction is possible. No one can correct me because my perception and what I have decided to think about it is mine alone. The other person may, however, suggest that I received only a portion of the information, or that I received it unclearly for one reason or another. In such a case, the meaning of the message may be tentative until it can be negotiated. It also is legitimate for me to perceive the message quite differently from the way the other person perceives it.

On the other hand, if I say "You have made me angry," then "you" may very well contradict me by responding with something such as "No, I didn't." In fact, I am eliciting a defensiveness and also inviting "you" to attempt a control of me by your helplessness, suffering, or anger.

Only I am responsible for my behavior. Only I can change what I do. However, when I change my behavior, I may give the other person in the relationship the opportunity to evaluate his behavior and perhaps modify it.

In the example of the schoolteacher and his "defiant" student, Tim, in Chapter 2, when the schoolteacher concentrated on his behavior and not on Tim's, he sought to change himself. That destroyed the payoff (his anger behavior) which he had previously furnished Tim. Tim, within a few days, re-evaluated his own behavior and changed it.

Unfortunately, most of us have learned to place the emphasis on the other person, to work on the behavior of other people rather than to concentrate on our own.

Get-my-way behavior is based on feelings, such as helplessness, suffering, and anger. Such behavior is designed to convince the other person in the relationship that he is responsible and that he must change the situation, what he is doing, so that I don't have to feel this way anymore.

Parents and teachers could contribute toward solving the problem of self-responsibility by encouraging youngsters to make more use of first person singular. This would help young people to experience their own unique and individual worlds and begin accepting responsibility for their own distinctive here-and-now experiences.

In consulting with businessmen and educators, I have noted how few of them write letters to clients and associates in the first person singular. Every time "I" is avoided, there is the distinct possibility that we are avoiding experiencing ourselves and refusing to take responsibility for what we do.

(Incidentally, the reader may now understand this book's being written in the first person singular, even though there are two authors.)

When seen in the light of the discussion on these pages, the four myths of feelings in example form might sound like this:

    a. feelings are involuntary:

       "I feel angry
          and I can't help it."

    b. feelings are caused by something outside myself:

       "You caused it,
          and it's all your fault."

    c. feelings can be shared:

       "I've told you about it."

    d. we can be responsible for one another's feelings:

       "Now it's your responsibility
          to make me feel okay again."

Let me pose a question to you.

What is your definition of a close relationship?

Is it possible that your definition requires that you must practice the four myths of feelings?

If so, you may want to take another look at your definition. You may want to learn some new options.

Questions:

1. What is meant by "phenomenological field of the individual"?
2. Why do the authors refer to feelings as physiological events?
3. Do you believe you can decide how to behave in all situations?
4. To what extent are you capable of accepting responsibility for your own feelings?
5. Is it difficult to accept the concepts in this article? Why or why not?

In one of the most understandable treatises in the discipline, John Powell categorizes and explicates the levels of interpersonal communication. Not only does he designate some of the problems in dyadic encounter, the author also offers some interesting solutions.

Interpersonal Encounter and the Five Levels of Communication

John Powell, S.J.

Someone has aptly distinguished five levels of communication on which persons can relate to one another. Perhaps it will help our understanding of these levels to visualize a person locked inside of a prison. It is the human being, urged by an inner insistence to go out to others and yet afraid to do so. The five levels of communication, which will be described a little later, represent five degrees of willingness to go outside of himself, to communicate himself to others.

The man in the prison—and he is Everyman—has been there for years, although ironically the grated iron doors are not locked. He can go out of his prison, but in his long detention he has learned to fear the possible dangers that he might encounter. He has come to feel some sort of safety and protection behind the walls of his prison, where he is a voluntary captive. The darkness of his prison even shields him from a clear view of himself, and he is not sure what he would like in broad daylight. Above all, he is not sure how the world, which he sees from behind his bars, and the people whom he sees moving about in that world, would receive him. He is fragmented by an almost desperate need for that world and for those people, and, at the same time, by an almost desperate fear of the risks of rejection he would be taking if he ended his isolation.

The prisoner is reminiscent of what Viktor Frankl writes in his book,

Man's Search for Meaning, about his fellow prisoners in the Nazi concentration camp at Dachau. Some of these prisoners, who yearned so desperately for their freedom, had been held captive so long that, when they were eventually released, they walked out into the sunlight, blinked nervously and then silently walked back into the familiar darkness of the prisons, to which they had been accustomed for such a long time.

This is the visualized, if somewhat dramatic, dilemma that all of us experience at some time in our lives and in the process of becoming persons. Most of us make only a weak response to the invitation of encounter with others and our world because we feel uncomfortable in exposing our nakedness as persons. Some of us are willing only to pretend this exodus, while others somehow find the courage to go all the way out to freedom. There are various stages in between. These stages are described below, under the headings of the five levels of communication. The fifth level, to be considered first, represents the least willingness to communicate ourselves to others. The successive, descending levels indicate greater and greater success in the adventure.

Level Five: Cliché Conversation

This level represents the weakest response to the human dilemma and the lowest level of self-communication. In fact, there is no communication here at all, unless by accident. On this level, we talk in cliches, such as: "How are you?...How is your family?...Where have you been?" We say things like: "I like your dress very much." "I hope we can get together again real soon." "It's really good to see you." In fact, we really mean almost nothing of what we are asking or saying. If the other party were to begin answering our question, "How are you?" in detail, we would be astounded. Usually and fortunately the other party senses the superficiality and conventionality of our concern and question, and obliges by simply giving the standard answer, "Just fine, thank you."

This is the conversation, the noncommunication, of the cocktail party, the club meeting, the neighborhood laundromat, etc. There is no sharing of persons at all. Everyone remains safely in the isolation of his pretense, sham, sophistication. The whole group seems to gather to be lonely together. It is well summarized in the lyrics of Paul Simon in *Sounds of Silence* used so effectively in the movie, *The Graduate*:

> "And in the naked night I saw
> Ten thousand people, maybe more,
> People talking without speaking,
> People hearing without listening,
> People writing songs that voices never shared.
> No one dared
> Disturb the sounds of silence."

Level Four: Reporting the Facts about Others

On this fourth level, we do not step very far outside the prison of our loneliness into real communication because we expose almost nothing of ourselves. We remain contented to tell others what so-and-so has said or done. We offer no personal, self-revelatory commentary on these facts, but simply report them. Just as most of us, at times, hide behind cliches, so we also seek shelter in gossip items, conversation pieces, and little narrations about others. We give nothing of ourselves and invite nothing from others in return.

Level Three: My Ideas and Judgments

On this level, there is some communication of my person. I am willing to take this step out of my solitary confinement. I will take the risk of telling you some of my ideas and reveal some of my judgments and decisions. My communication usually remains under a strict censorship, however. As I communicate my ideas, etc., I will be watching you carefully. I want to test the temperature of the water before I leap in. I want to be sure that you will accept me with my ideas, judgments, and decisions. If you raise your eyebrow or narrow your eyes, if you yawn or look at your watch, I will probably retreat to safer ground. I will run for the cover of silence, or change the subject of conversation, or worse, I will start to say things I suspect that you want me to say. I will try to be what pleases you.

Someday, perhaps, when I develop the courage and the intensity of desire to grow as a person, I will spill all of the contents of my mind and heart before you. It will be my moment of truth. It may even be that I have already done so, but still you can know only a little about my person, unless I am willing to advance to the next depth-level of self-communication.

Level Two: My Feelings (Emotions). "Gut Level"

It might not occur to many of us that, once we have revealed our ideas, judgments, and decisions, there is really much more of our persons to share. Actually, the things that most clearly differentiate and individuate me from others, that make the communication of my person a unique knowledge, are my *feelings* or *emotions.*

If I really want you to know who I am, I must tell you about my stomach (gut-level) as well as my head. My ideas, judgments, and decisions are quite conventional. If I am a Republican or Democrat by persuasion, I have a lot of company. If I am for or against space exploration, there will be others who will support me in my conviction. But the *feelings* that lie under my ideas, judgments, and convictions are uniquely mine. No one supports a political party, or has a religious conviction, or is committed to a cause with my exact feelings of fervor or apathy. No one experiences my precise sense of frustration, labors

under my fears, feels my passions. Nobody opposes war with my particular indignation or supports patriotism with my unique sense of
loyalty.

It is these feelings, on this level of communication, which I must
share with you, if I am to tell you who I really am. To illustrate this, I
would like to put in the left-hand column a judgment, and in the right-
hand column some of the possible emotional reactions to this judgment.
If I tell you only the contents of my mind, I will be withholding a great
deal about myself, especially in those areas where I am uniquely
personal, most individual, most deeply myself.

Judgment	Some Possible Emotional Reactions
I think that you are intelligent.	...and I am jealous.
	...and I feel frustrated.
	...and I feel proud to be your friend.
	...and it makes me ill at ease with you.
	...and I feel suspicious of you.
	...and I feel inferior to you.
	...and I feel impelled to imitate you.
	...and I feel like running away from you.
	...and I feel the desire to humiliate you.

Most of us feel that others will not tolerate such emotional honesty in
communication. We would rather defend our dishonesty on the
grounds that it might hurt others, and, having rationalized our phoni-
ness into nobility, we settle for superficial relationships. This occurs
not only in the case of casual acquaintances, but even with members of
our own families; it destroys authentic communion within marriages.
Consequently, we ourselves do not grow, nor do we help anyone else to
grow. Meanwhile we have to live with repressed emotions — a dangerous and self-destructive path to follow. Any relationship, which is to
have the nature of true personal encounter, must be based on this
honest, open, gut-level communication. The alternative is to remain in
my prison, to endure inch-by-inch death as a person.

We will say more of this level of communication, after describing the
first and deepest level of communication between persons.

Level One: Peak Communication

All deep and authentic friendships, and especially the union of those
who are married, must be based on absolute openness and honesty. At
times, gut-level communication will be most difficult, but it is at these
precise times that it is most necessary. Among close friends or between
partners in marriage there will come from time to time a complete emotional and personal communion.

In our human condition this can never be a permanent experience.

There should and will be, however, moments when encounter attains perfect communication. At these times the two persons will feel an almost perfect and mutual empathy. I know that my own reactions are shared completely by my friend; my happiness or my grief is perfectly reduplicated in him. We are like two musical instruments playing exactly the same note, filled with and giving forth precisely the same sound. This is what is meant by level one, peak communication.

"Rules" for Gut-Level Communication

If friendship and human love are to mature between any two persons, there must be absolute and honest mutual revelation; this kind of self-revelation can be achieved only through what we have called "gut-level" communication. There is no other way, and all the reasons which we adduce to rationalize our cover-ups and dishonesty must be seen as delusions. It would be much better for me to tell you how I really feel about you than to enter into the stickiness and discomfort of a phony relationship.

Dishonesty always has a way of coming back to haunt and trouble us. Even if I should have to tell you that I do not admire or love you emotionally, it would be much better than trying to deceive you and having to pay the ultimate price of all such deception, your greater hurt and mine. And you will have to tell me things, at times, that will be difficult for you to share. But really you have no choice, and, if I want your friendship, I must be ready to accept you as you are. If either of us comes to the relationship without this determination of mutual honesty and openness, there can be no friendship, no growth; rather there can be only a subject-object kind of thing that is typified by adolescent bickering, pouting, jealousy, anger and accusations.

The classic temptation in this matter, and it would seem to be the most destructive of all delusions in this area of human relations, is this: we are tempted to think that communication of an unfavorable emotional reaction will tend to be divisive. If I tell you that it bothers me when you do something you are accustomed to do, I may be tempted to believe that it would be better not to mention it. Our relationship will be more peaceful. You wouldn't understand, anyway.

So I keep it inside myself, and each time you do your thing my stomach keeps score 2...3...4...5...6...7...8...until one day you do the same thing that you have always done and all hell breaks loose. All the while you were annoying me, I was keeping it inside and somewhere, secretly, learning to hate you. My good thoughts were turning to gall.

When it finally erupted in one great emotional avalanche, you didn't understand. You thought that this kind of reaction was totally uncalled for. The bonds of our love seemed fragile and about to break. And it all started when I said: "I don't like what she's doing, but it would be better not to say anything. The relationship will be more peaceful."

That was all a delusion, and I should have told you in the beginning. Now there has been an emotional divorce, all because I wanted to keep the peace between us.

Rule one: Gut-level communication (emotional openness and honesty) must never imply a judgment of the other. I am simply not mature enough to enter into true friendship unless I realize that I cannot judge the intention or motivation of another. I must be humble and sane enough to bow before the complexity and mystery of a human being. If I judge you, I have only revealed my own immaturity and ineptness for friendship.

Emotional candor does not ever imply a judgment of you. In fact, it even abstains from any judgment of myself. For example, if I were to say to you, "I am ill at ease with you," I have been emotionally honest and at the same time have not implied in the least that it is your fault that I am ill at ease with you. Perhaps it is my own inferiority complex or my exaggerated concept of your intelligence. I am not saying it is anyone's fault, but simply giving a report of my emotional reaction to you at this time.

If I were to say to you that I feel angry or hurt by something you have done or said, it remains the same. I have not judged you. Perhaps it is my own self-love that has made me so sensitive, or my inclination to paranoia (a persecution complex). I am not sure, and, in most cases, I can never be sure. To be sure would imply a judgment. I can only say for sure that this has been and is my emotional reaction.

If I were to tell you that something you do annoys me, again I would not be so arrogant as to think that your action would annoy anyone. I do not even mean that your action is in any way wrong or offensive. I simply mean that here and now I experience annoyance. Perhaps it is my headache or my digestion or the fact that I did not get much sleep last night. I really do not know. All that I know is this, that I am trying to tell you that I am experiencing annoyance at this moment.

It would probably be most helpful in most cases to preface our gut-level communication with some kind of a disclaimer to assure the other that there is no judgment implied. I might begin by saying, "I don't know why this bothers me, but it does...I guess that I am just hyper-sensitive, and I really don't mean to imply that it is your fault, but I do feel hurt by what you are saying."

Of course, the main thing is that there is *in fact* no judgment. If I am in the habit of judging the intentions or motivation of another, I should try very hard to outgrow this adolescent habit. I simply will not be able to disguise my judgments, no matter how many disclaimers I make.

On the other hand, if I am really mature enough to refrain from such judgments, this too will eventually be apparent. If I really want to know the intention or motivation or reaction of another, there is only one way to find out: *I must ask him.* (Don't pass this by lightly. You don't have x-ray eyes either!)

Rule two: Emotions are not moral (good or bad). Theoretically, most of us would accept the fact that emotions are neither meritorious nor sinful. Feeling frustrated, or being annoyed, or experiencing fears and anger do not make one a good or a bad person. Practically, however, most of us do not accept in our day-to-day living what we would accept in theory. We exercise a rather strict censorship of our emotions. If our censoring consciences do not approve certain emotions, we repress these emotions into our subconscious mind. Experts in psychosomatic medicine say that the most common cause of fatigue and actual sickness is the repression of emotions. The fact is that there are emotions to which we do not want to admit. We are ashamed of our fears, or we feel guilty because of our anger or emotional-physical desires.

Before anyone can be liberated enough to practice "gut-level communication," in which he will be emotionally open and honest, he must feel convinced that emotions are *not moral* but simply *factual.* My jealousies, my anger, my sexual desires, my fears, etc., do not make me a good or bad person. Of course, these emotional reactions must be integrated by my mind and will, but before they can be integrated, before I can decide whether I want to act on them or not, I must allow them to arise and I must clearly hear what they are saying to me. I must be able to say, without any sense of moral reprehension, that I am afraid or angry or sexually aroused.

Before I will be free enough to do this, however, I must be convinced that emotions are not moral, neither good nor bad in themselves. I must be convinced, too, that the experience of the whole gamut of emotions is a part of the human condition, the inheritance of every man.

Rule three: Feelings (emotions) must be integrated with the intellect and will. It is extremely important to understand this next point. The non-repression of our emotions means that we must experience, recognize, and accept our emotions fully. It does not in any way imply that we will always *act on* those emotions. This would be tragic and the worst form of immaturity, if a person were to allow his feelings or emotions to control his life. It is one thing to feel and to admit to myself and to others that I am afraid, but it is another thing to allow this fear to overwhelm me. It is one thing for me to feel and to admit that I am angry and another to punch you in the nose.

...For example, I may feel a strong fear of telling you the truth in some given matter. The fact is, and it is neither good nor bad in itself, that I am experiencing fear. I allow myself to feel this fear, to recognize it. My mind makes the judgment that I should not act on this fear, but in spite of it, and to tell you the truth. The will consequently carries out the judgment of the mind. I tell you the truth.

However, if I am seeking a real and authentic relationship with you, and wish to practice "gut-level" communication, I must tell you something like this: "I really don't know why...maybe it's my streak of cowardice...but I feel afraid to tell you something, and yet I know that

I must be honest with you...This is the truth as I see it...."

...It should be obvious that, in the integrated person, emotions are neither repressed nor do they assume control of the whole person. They are recognized (What is it that I am feeling?) and integrated (Do I want to act on this feeling or not?).

Rule four: In "gut-level" communication, emotions must be "reported." If I am to tell you who I really am, I must tell you about my feelings, whether I will act upon them or not. I may tell you that I am angry, explaining the fact of my anger without inferring any judgment of you, and not intending to act upon this anger. I may tell you that I am afraid, explaining the fact of my fear without accusing you of being its cause, and at the same time not succumbing to the fear. But I must, if I am to open myself to you, allow you to experience (encounter) my person and tell you about my anger and my fear.

It has been truly said that we either *speak out* (report) our feelings or we will *act them out.* Feelings are like steam that is gathering inside of a kettle. Kept inside and gathering strength, they can blow the human lid off, just as the steam inside the kettle will blow off the lid of the kettle.

We have already referred to the verdict of psychosomatic medicine that repressed emotions are the most common cause of fatigue and actual sickness. This is part of the "acting out" process. Repressed emotions may find their outlet in the "acting out" of headaches, skin-rashes, allergies, asthma, common colds, aching backs or limbs, but they can also be acted out in the tension of tightened muscles, the slamming of doors, the clenching of fists, the rise of blood pressure, the grinding of teeth, tears, temper tantrums, acts of violence. We do not bury our emotions *dead*; they remain *alive* in our subconscious minds and intestines, to hurt and trouble us. It is not only much more conducive to an authentic relationship to report our true feelings, but it is equally essential to our integrity and health.

The most common reason for not reporting our emotions is that we do not want to admit to them for one reason or another. We fear that others might not think well of us, or actually reject us, or punish us in some way for our emotional candor. We have been somehow "programmed" not to accept certain emotions as part of us. We are ashamed of them. Now we can rationalize and say that we cannot report these emotions because they would not be understood, or that reporting them would disturb a peaceful relationship, or evoke an emotionally stormy reaction from the other; but all of our reasons are essentially fraudulent, and our silence can produce only fraudulent relationships. Anyone who builds a relationship on less than openness and honesty is building on sand. Such a relationship will never stand the test of time, and neither party to the relationship will draw from it any noticeable benefits.

Rule five: With rare exceptions, emotions must be reported at the time that they are being experienced. It is much easier for most of us to report an emotion that is a matter of history. It is almost like talking about another person when I can talk about myself a year or two years ago, and admit that I was very fearful or very angry at that time. Because they were transient emotions and are now gone, it is easy to dissociate these feelings from my person here and now. It is difficult, however, to recapture a feeling once it has passed into my personal history. We are very often puzzled by such previous emotions. "I don't know why I ever got so excited." The time to report emotions is the time when they are being experienced. Even temporary deferral of this report of emotions is unwise and unhealthy.

All communication must obviously respect not only the transmitter of the communication but also the receiver who is to accept the communication. Consequently, it could occur that, in the integration of my emotions, my judgment may dictate that this is not the opportune moment to report my emotional reaction. If the receiver is so emotionally disturbed himself that he could hardly be in a receptive mood, and my report would only be distorted somehow by his turbulent emotional state, it may be that I will have to defer this report.

But, if the matter is serious enough and the emotions strong enough, this period of deferment cannot be too long nor can I be frightened or bullied into complete repression of emotions. Note that this period of deferment should never be a long one, and it would seem that in most cases it would be a rare thing.

Also, it would seem to be a valid exception to this rule to defer or eliminate this report in the case of a passing incident with a chance acquaintance. The gruff manner of a bus driver may irk me, without this being the occasion for me to stand nose to nose with him and tell him about my emotional reactions to him. In the case of two people, however, who must work or live together or who want to relate deeply, this emotional reporting at the time of the emotions is vitally important.

The Benefits of "Gut-Level" Communication

The obvious and primary benefit of "gut-level" communication will be a real and authentic relationship and what we have called a true "encounter" of persons. Not only will there be mutual communication of persons and the consequent sharing and experiencing of personhood, but it will result in a more and more clearly defined sense of self-identity for each of the parties in the relationship.

Today, many of us are asking: "Who am I?" It has come to be a socially fashionable question. The implication is that I do not really know my own self as a person. We have said that my person is what I think, judge, feel, etc. If I have communicated these things freely and openly, as clearly as I can and as honestly as I can, I will find a noticeable growth in my own sense of identity as well as a deeper and more authentic knowledge of the other. It has come to be a psychological truism that I will understand only as much of myself as I have been willing to communicate to another.

The second and very important result of such communication is that, having understood myself because I have communicated myself, I will find the patterns of immaturity changing into patterns of maturity. I will change! Anyone who sees the *patterns* of his reactions, and is willing to examine them, may come to the realization that these are patterns of hypersensitivity or paranoia. At the moment the realization penetrates him, he will find the pattern changing. Notwithstanding all that we have said about emotions, we must not believe that emotional patterns are purely biological or inevitable. *I can and will change my emotional patterns,* that is, I will move from one emotion to another, if I have honestly let my emotions arise for recognition and, having honestly reported them, judge them to be immature and undesirable.

For example, if I consistently and honestly report the emotion of "feeling hurt" by many small and inconsequential things, it will become apparent to me in time that I am hypersensitive and that I have been indulging myself in self-pity. The moment that this becomes clear to me, really hits me, I will change.

In summary the dynamic is this: We allow our emotions to arise so that they can be identified; we observe the patterns in our emotional reactions, report and judge them. Having done these things, we instinctively and immediately make the necessary adjustments in the light of our own ideals and hopes for growth. We change. Try this and see for yourself.

If all this is true, and you have only to experience it to know its truth, it is obvious that the little phrase we have used so conveniently, "I'm sorry, but that's the way I am," is nothing more than a refuge and delusion. It is handy if you don't want to grow up; but if you do want to grow up, you try to rise above this fallacy.

The third benefit of "gut-level" communication is that it will evoke from others a responsive honesty and openness, which is necessary if the relationship is to be interpersonal, mutual. Goldbrunner, a psychiatrist, somewhat boastfully claims that he can gain instant access to the deepest parts of anyone within a matter of minutes. His technique is not to begin by probing with questions for this only makes the insecure person more defensive. The theory of this psychiatrist is that if we want another to be open with us, we must begin by opening up ourselves to him, by telling the other honestly and openly of our feelings.

Person is resonant to person, Goldbrunner insists. If I am willing to step out of the darkness of my prison, to expose the deepest part of me to another person, the result is almost always automatic and immediate: The other person feels empowered to reveal himself to me. Having heard of my secret and deep feelings, he is given the courage to communicate his own. This, in the last analysis, is what we meant by "encounter."

> *I have seen "being real" act sometimes like a new kind of religion, a new form of self-justification, a new perfectionism, or even a perverse new snobbery. I experienced this recently when I found myself arguing against someone else's truth on the grounds that his truth professed to be universal whereas I knew all·truth to be personal. I was in effect shouting down his throat: "You shouldn't be telling me what I shouldn't be."— or — "I won't accept your not believing in acceptance." I also sense that I am misusing the idea of being real whenever I discover myself anxiously weighing my words and actions, that is, whenever I am being careful to be "real." When I do this I am only playing a new role—the role of the "real person." Calculation does not enter into being real. Concern with appearance does not enter into it. Being real is more a process of letting go than it is the effort of becoming. I don't really have to become me, although at times it feels this way—I am already me. And that is both the easiest and the hardest thing for me to realize.*
>
> Hugh Prather

Questions:

1. Is "noncommunication" the same as a "duologue"?
2. How can one seek shelter in gossip?
3. Can you identify the "level" at which you spend most of your time while conversing? Identify the conversational "levels" of your closest friends and/or associates.
4. Can you remember the last time you experienced "peak" communication?
5. How many "cliche" conversations have you heard today? Where do you most often experience this level in your own conversations? With whom?

Small group communication has been a major area of communication study for the past 20 years. Realization of the importance of social interaction in family and problem-solving groups, training sessions, committees, and various small group units has led theorists to close analyses of small group communication.

Methods of Group Interactions

Donald Klopf

Because we are likely to engage frequently in learning and problem-solving discussions, we devote a major portion of the chapter to both of those formats and processes. There are, however, other forms of small group interaction in which we participate and we will describe those also, considering them as special forms of public and private discussion.

With respect to the formats, they should not be thought of as line-by-line recipes to be followed in all of their details. Rather, they should be recognized as conceptual models against which practice can be compared with the expectation that better group interaction will result.

Some people are annoyed by the idea of a plan or format which has to be walked through because they like to emphasize spontaneity, individuality, creativity, permissiveness, and so on. Yet others are enthused about programs which give the sort of direction and guidance characteristic of the ones in this chapter. These people stress efficiency, predictability, security, and order. Neither attitude holds here. The need for formats comes from the nature of groups themselves. When a number of people work together to achieve a common purpose, there has to be enough definition of what needs to be done so that the members know how to participate, can guide their own behavior, and can learn from the responses of others.

From *Interacting in Groups* by Donald W. Klopf, 1981. Reprinted by permission of Morton Publishing Company.

For the beginners, the steps suggested in the formats which follow should be slavishly followed and, in the process, hopefully the beginners will internalize the procedures. Then, after gaining familiarity with the steps, variations can be made while following the main track. Ultimately they might want to develop a different sequence and try it out, keeping in mind that one of the principal qualities of poor group discussion is lack of direction with the topics discussed arising fortuitously or at the insistence of a dominating member.[1]

The formats which follow are meant to be procedural tools which relate to the goal of learning. In each case they provide an outline of a logical sequence that a group can follow in order to reach its goal. For each format to be effective in group discussion, a mandate must be derived from the group so that each can be put into operation with the consent and support of the members.[2]

Learning Through Discussion

Earlier we offered a general description of learning groups which encompassed all types and sorts. Now we need to be more specific since we will concentrate on one type in this section—the classroom learning group. First, we review the three principal types and show how they differ from each other.

Types of Learning Groups

One type is a form of the experiential group—experiential groups being groups formed for the explicit purpose of helping group members through participation.[3] Learning groups of this type include sensitivity training groups, T-groups ("T" stands for "training"), and human relations groups, groups which function for one or several of these purposes: to gain understanding of group influences on the members' responses, to obtain feedback about the effects of members' behavior, and to facilitate group communication.[4]

Another type of learning group is called the enlightenment group, a group which meets to exchange ideas, learn new methods, and expand knowledge. Business and professional people, teachers, and scientists are among groups of people who find it useful to meet regularly at conventions, workshops and seminars to share knowledge and to become informed about new discoveries, insights and facts concerning their sphere of work. Hobby groups and most educational groups are counted also among enlightenment learning groups.[5]

---

[1]Herbert A. Thelen, "Introduction," *Learning Thru Discussion*, Wm. Fawcett Hill (Beverly Hills: Sage Publications, 1969), 10-12.

[2]Wm. Fawcett Hill, 22.

[3]Marvin E. Shaw, *Group Dynamics: The Psychology of Small Group Behavior*, 2nd ed. (New York: McGraw-Hill Co., 1976), 446.

[4]Shaw, 338.

[5]Dean C. Barnlund and Franklyn S. Haiman, *The Dynamics of Discussion* (Boston: Houghton Mifflin Co., 1960), 24-26, provide a fuller analysis of this type.

The third type, the classroom learning group is the one we will attend to here because of its pervasiveness in school systems and because of its value in helping students learn more and faster. It is the group organized by the instructor to maximize learning. As such, it focuses on the subject matter of the course for purposes of attitude formation, opinion-sharing, and mastering difficult topic material.

In a sense, the classroom learning group can be viewed as a form of the enlightenment group since it too is related to expanding knowledge and to informing others. But the classroom group is confined to the school setting whereas the enlightenment group can be found in a variety of settings.

On the other hand, the similarity between the classroom group and the experiential group is not as strong. The classroom group differs from the experiential group as it deals only with the subject matter of a course while the experiential group centers on the behavior of group members, offering a means for learning new behavioral skills and changing ineffective ones.

The Learning Group Discussion Format

In order to participate in classroom learning group discussions, the group members must do their homework, in this case reading the material assigned for discussion, otherwise the talk will be worthless. Admittedly some materials will be more readily understood than others. Then, the group should devote its time to those not completely understood rather than beating to death the materials everyone understands. Occasionally, the assignment will be so difficult, no one comprehends it. In such instances the text should be consulted once again, or, if that does not help, the instructor should be questioned.

When engaging in class discussion this five-step format can be followed:

1. *Define the terms and concepts.* Before discussing the subject matter in detail, each member should understand the meaning of the terms and concepts used most by the author. Many subjects rely on a jargon or vocabulary peculiar to those authors writing in the area, and mastering this specialized language may be half of the course. Hence considerable time could be legitimately spent on this step as long as the group does not extend the definitions into a resume of the whole assignment. Stick to defining only the vital terms and concepts by observing this procedure: (1) list the terms and concepts needing definition; (2) define each using examples whenever possible; and (3) check each person to see that a common understanding of the meaning is held by all.

2. *Determine the overall meaning of the reading.* The goal in this step is to agree on what is the writer's aim, purpose or objective for the

reading material being discussed and what are the major topic areas. Since most writers usually state the purpose somewhere in the material, identifying it should not consume much time. It is important, however, for all of the group to agree on what the author intended. Also, determining the topic areas may not require a great deal of time since most textbook authors divide a chapter's subject matter in clearly discernable topic areas. When this is not the case, a close analysis is necessary to isolate the topic areas. The vital point here is to decide which topics are difficult to comprehend and which ones deal with subject matter easily understood by the group. The topics least understood should form the basis for the discussion in the next step.

3. *Discuss the major topics.* In this step the group talks about what the author wrote by covering in detail the topics identified in the previous step. For each topic, the group can discuss the main ideas; the statements that explain, prove, illustrate, or exemplify the main ideas; questions raised by the main ideas; and the sub-ideas and questions they raise. As they discuss, the members must restrict their talk to what was written; their opinions about the materials are not to be stated yet. Since this is the most crucial step in learning, about half or three quarters of the discussion should be devoted to it.

4. *Apply the new knowledge.* Knowledge should not only be accumulated, it should be integrated into what the members already know and its personal value to the students should be recognized. Some subjects, speech communication for instance, have very direct personal application and students can easily figure out their relevance to everyday life experiences. Other subjects may have less personal application but may supply intellectual stimulation useful to the students. The group should take the time to decide how to use what is learned and this step provides that opportunity. To do so, the group could try these techniques: speculate about how the material could be used; give examples of how it might be applied; and compare the members' reasons for thinking it useful with those of an expert, the instructor, for example, or the author, if the author states them in his or her writing.

5. *Evaluate the subject matter.* Much of the time group members have feelings about what they are assigned to read and these feelings should be expressed. However, the expression should wait until the discussion's end when everyone has understood the content. The reason for waiting until this step is that few groups learn much about a reading if they begin their discussion by expressing their personal feelings. When they start by expressing their feelings, the discussion centers on their gripes about the materials and not on the content. The opinions are important but the content of the materials should have first priority. When they are ready for this step, the members can

express their feelings about the main ideas, the validity of the supporting materials, the usefulness of the reading, and the author's writing
style.[6]

Steps in Group Learning

   I. Define the Terms and Concepts
   II. Determine the Overall Meaning
   III. Discuss the Major Topics
   IV. Apply the New Knowledge
   V. Evaluate the Subject Matter

Discussing a classroom reading assignment takes time and groups
using the format just explained are apt to waste valuable minutes
getting started and then have to rush through the final steps. A wiser
course of action would be to allocate a certain number of minutes to
each step, moving on when the allotted time has expired. In our estimation, the first step, defining terms and concepts, should be given about
10 percent of the available time, depending upon the complexity of the
subject matter. The second step determining the meaning, deserves no
more than 10 percent while the bulk of the time, approximately 60
percent, should go to the third step, that of discussing the major topics.
The fourth and fifth steps, applying and evaluating the subject
material, should each be given no more than 10 percent of the time. Of
course, this time scheme should be adapted to the subject matter. With
complex materials, more time may have to be devoted to the first and
third steps as understanding the material is the principal goal in
learning. The other steps are consequently shortened.

Problem Solving in Groups

Problem solving is as system of arranging and organizing the thinking of the group's members so that it will have the greatest usefulness
or value to the group. The format described later in this section provides a method of reaching that goal. Before describing it, we should
understand the problem-solving process and to do so we can begin by
noting the nature of problems.[7]

Problems

Practically all human problems have three elements—a goal, obstacles to achieving that goal, and a point when we become aware of

---

[6]Wm. Fawcett Hill, 22-31, is the source from which the five steps are extracted. Much
of the explanation comes from Donald W. Klopf and Ronald E. Cambra, *Personal and
Public Speaking* (Denver: Morton Publishing Co., 1980), 122-124.

[7]John W. Keltner, *Interpersonal Speech Communication: Elements and Structures*
(Belmont, Calif.: Wadsworth Publishing Co., 1970), 154-159, serves as the source of this
explanation.

the obstacles. For example, the sorority sisters want to change an out-dated initiation procedure (goal). As they meet to discuss the change (point of encounter), several members vehemently oppose the change (obstacles). In dealing with the problem, the girls must cope with all three elements of the problem. The goal may be strong or weak; they may want the change right now or they may be willing to wait for a more favorable time. If they are willing to wait, then the point of en-counter, the meeting, can be postponed to another, perhaps more for-tuitous time. If not, the problem has to be faced immediately. The problem stems from the obstacles to the achievement of the goal, the obstacles being the girls who oppose the change and their reasons for doing so. In order to reach the goal, the obstacles have to be overcome.

For a problem to exist, therefore, there first must be a goal the group considers worthy of achieving. The goal may be simple, for instance, wanting to limit group meetings to one hour, or complex, such as raising enough money to build a new clubhouse. But whatever the goal is, in order for a problem to exist, the goal must be blocked, hindered, opposed, resisted or restrained in some way by some person, regula-tion, thing, or combination. Without these obstacles, there is no prob-lem. In other words, problems are created by obstacles which hinder the achievement of goals.

Important also is the third characteristic of a problem, the point of encounter, when the group becomes aware of the obstacles between the members and the goal. The circumstances surrounding the point of encounter help determine its seriousness. Time may be a factor. In the sorority example, the girls who oppose a change in the initiation procedure may not be as steadfast if they have other, more important things to do. Their opposition may be token, merely voicing their objec-tions, as they want to get on with whatever else interests them more. With a lot of time at their disposal, they may engage in an extensive debate on the subject, forcing the others to deal with a much larger problem.

Understanding the three characteristics of a real problem is easier said than done. Usually what we perceive is the symptoms of a problem and we try to treat these without examining the goals and the obstacles preventing the achievement of the goals. We can illustrate this point with the common headache. When we get one, most of us swallow a few aspirin to ease the pain. When we do so, we probably are treating the symptoms of what could be more complex obstacles to our goal of maintaining good health. Headaches are symptoms of many prob-lems — eye strain, fatigue, a cold, brain tumors, and so on. The aspirin may temporarily ease the pain but the obstacles, in this case, the causes of the headache may still be present. We will not achieve good health until we treat the causes of the headache. Once the causes have been identified, the obstacles stand a better chance of being overcome and the problem solved.

In the investigation of the causes, we may come across certain conditions that must be met if we are to attain our goal. These conditions become the criteria by which we judge possible solutions to the problem and, once the criteria are established, we can suggest possible solutions to the problem. The more solutions we come up with, the better chance we have for finding the best solution to the problem. The best solution is the one which meets the criteria most satisfactorily.[8]

This process of problem solving, therefore, proceeds from the point of encounter, which is to say the point when the problem first becomes known, to an understanding of the goals and obstacles. Next, the process involves establishing criteria, finding solutions, selecting the best solution, and carrying it out.

Types of Problems

Problems can be classified into three types—fact, value and policy —and it is helpful to describe each because some cannot be solved through discussion so groups will waste time talking about them. Others may involve heavy feelings and require special training to solve. Still others are appropriate for discussion.

Problems of Fact. A problem of fact concerns something that is, was, or will be so, and refers to events, happenings, or objects. There are two types of facts—*accepted* facts and *verifiable* facts. *Accepted facts* are those purported to have happened and are perceived to be true but the probability makes them discussable. For example, a group could discuss these problems: Are labor unions a cause of inflation in the United States? Can lower income famililies afford the cost of education? Were the American Indians' ancestors from the continent of Asia? Our discussion would center around the probable truth of each purported fact and such discussion would be useful for the purpose of sharing information, to reinforce important points in the minds of the group's members, or to learn different people's perceptions of the problem. When the purpose of the discussion, however, is purely informative, the facts discussed do not in themselves constitute a problem and the discussion is not problem-solving but enlightenment.

Verifiable facts, on the other hand, are ones that can be objectively verified. They can be checked out and the certainty of their truth or falsity can be readily established. As a consequence, there is no basis for discussion.

Problems of Value. Problems of value concern the desirability or worth of an idea, a person, or an action, and are subjectively determined. For example, the problem, "Is the military draft harmful to society?" involves attitudes and values and is not easily solved by finding the facts. The ultimate concern is the group's perception of what is harmful, a question of value which will be difficult to answer

[8]Keltner, 154-159.

unless all of the members can agree as to what harmful means. There is benefit from discussing problems of value since the members can share their feelings and attitudes. However, a value problem ordinarily has no real solution and the group may be wasting its time discussing one.

Problems of Policy. Problems of policy require that an action of some sort be taken. To determine what kind of action, facts can be brought to bear, reasoning may come into play and consensus can be readily obtained. For this reason, this type of problem is best suited for small groups to solve. Here are examples of policy problems: What should be done about inflation? What should the sorority's initiation policy be? Should athletic scholarships be abolished? How often should the group meet? Each requires objective analysis to uncover the goals and obstacles and each can call forth possible solutions.

The Standard Agenda

Whenever a group encounters a situation in which the attainment of a goal or goals is hindered in some fashion by one or more obstacles, the problem-solving process comes into play. The group can approach its problems in an orderly manner and enhance its chances of arriving at an effective solution, or, it can blunder through and with luck perhaps arrive at a proper solution.[9]

The following format was designed to help groups obtain effective solutions in an efficient and orderly fashion. We call it the standard agenda, although others refer to it by names such as the problem-solving sequence, the reflective pattern, and so on.[9]

An agenda is made up of the items of business which a group must act upon. A chairperson uses an agenda as a guide to the order in which specific items of business are to be taken up at a meeting and most chair persons find an agenda to be an indispensable reminder of what items are to be discussed in the course of the meeting.

The *standard agenda* has a similar purpose. It consists of the items essential to problem solving ordered in a systematic way. The standard agenda contains the steps we seem to more or less unconsciously follow when we think about a problem on our own. When we are thinking together in a group, we are apt to roam all around a problem and muddle through to a solution unless we organize our thinking. The steps of the standard agenda help a group to review a problem in an orderly fashion. The five steps are explained next.[11]

[9]Keltner, 302-303.

[10]Gerald M. Phillips, Doublas J. Pedersen, and Julia T. Wood, *Group Discussion: A Practical Guide to Discussion and Leadership* (Boston: Houghton Mifflin Co., 1979), present a detailed description of the standard agenda in Part II along with suggestions on how to execute each step.

[11]See Donald W. Klopf and Ronald E. Cambra, *Personal and Public Speaking* (Denver: Morton Publishing Co., 1980), 124-127, for a similar explanation.

1. *What is the problem?* In this step the group identifies the goal or goals which are not being met, examines the point of encounter or the situation in which the problem is occurring, and determines other aspects of the problem's nature. Answers to questions like the following should help the group obtain a better understanding of the problem.

1. *What is the situation in which the problem is occurring?*
2. *What in general is the difficulty?*
3. *How did the difficulty arise?*
4. *What is its importance?*
5. *What is the meaning of any terms that need clarifying?*

In speech communication classes, teachers often assign problems for the students to discuss. Typically, these are worded as questions and are problems of policy: Should the United States reform the electoral college system? Should the United States significantly increase its foreign military commitments? What changes, if any, should be made in the United States policy toward accepting political refugees? Should censorship be instituted to overcome the evils of pornography? The first aspect of dealing with problems of this type is defining terms. The members should arrive at a common understanding of what the key terms in the question mean. In the question, "Should/the United States/reform/the electroal college system?", the terms between the slash marks probably need to be defined. Take the term "United States" for example. Does this mean the federal government or the fifty states should take action? Or, does it mean the executive or legislative branches should initiate the action? Without a common understanding of the terms, the group could get bogged down in all sorts of semantic misconceptions of what the question actually means.

2. *What caused the problem?* In this step the group identifies the causes of obstacles to reaching the goals and examines the effects of the problem. For most problems, completing this step quite likely means analyzing the problem and gathering the facts about it. Research may be necessary—reading on the problem area or talking with those persons knowledgeable about it. In a previous chapter we described how to gather information and what types are useful so we should not need to repeat that process here. We should point out that a major factor in solving problems satisfactorily is finding the facts. All other factors being equal, securing the facts is the key to success.

Steps in Problem Solving

1. What is the problem?
2. What caused the problem?
3. What are possible solutions?
4. What is the best solution?
5. How can the best solution be carried out?

Answers to these questions are helpful in locating the facts:
1. *What effects show that a problem exists?*
2. *How serious are the effects?*
3. *What is causing the problem?*
4. *Are the causes inherent in the problem situation?*
5. *Have previous attempts been made to solve the problem?*

3. *What are possible solutions to the problem?* Knowing what caused the obstacles which prevent goals from being reached, the groups are about ready to propose ways of overcoming or eliminating these barriers, in other words, to suggest solutions to the problem. Before doing so, to insure that a group's solution does not cause more serious problems that already exist, the proper procedure is to develop a set of criteria or conditions that an acceptable solution must meet. One criterion obviously is that the solution corrects the causes of the problems. Other general criteria worth considering are: (1) Is the proposed solution workable? (2) Is it economical? (3) Is it the best possible way to solve the problem? (4) Will it produce more benefits than disadvantages? (5) Are the benefits significant ones? (6) Is the proposed solution just? (7) Is it moral? (8) Will it get the job done effectively? (9) Is it clear? (10) Will it be harmful in any way?

With the criteria established, the group seeks out and describes as many solutions as appear to have usefulness in the situation. It is often desirable to "brainstorm" at this stage in order to develop a large quantity of potential solutions. (Brainstorming is a discussion method we will explain in the next section.) Quantity is important; the quality of the solutions can be analyzed later when all possible solutions have been brought to light.

4. *What is the best solution to the problem?* In this step, each solution is evaluated in terms of the criteria established and the one best fulfilling the criteria should be chosen. These questions serve as guidelines in accomplishing this task:

1. *What is the exact nature of each solution?*
2. *How would it correct the problem?*
3. *How well would it remedy the problem?*
4. *How well would it satisfy the criteria?*
5. *Would a combination of solutions be best?*

5. *How can the selected solution be implemented?* The final step requires that the group decide how to carry out the solution chosen by the group as its best. There are several advantages in doing so. First, in deciding how to implement the solution, the group may uncover possible weaknesses. What often sounds like a good decision might prove inoperable and the members could find this out when they try to work

out a plan of action. Should the solution be unworkable, it can be abandoned in favor of one more likely to work. Second, the group forces itself to go beyond just talking about a solution. It has to do something about carrying it out. The adage, "action speaks louder than words," applies here. Talk is not enough in solving problems.

The responsibility for implementing the plan of action frequently is assigned to an individual, a sub-committee, or an action committee. When this is the case, the problem-solving group outlines the general features of the action plan which the action group then puts into operation. The standard agenda-performance system, explained in the next section, offers a way to implement solutions.

In the classroom where students are merely learning how to use the problem-solving method, this step might result in no more than setting up a plan of action. A group to carry out the plan will not be necessary, although this need not be the case. One instructor encouraged the students to implement their solutions. One group, for example, wanted to help children in underdeveloped countries and decided to send C.A.R.E. packages. They raised $1,000 for the packages. Another class group, also proposing to help children, adopted a Korean war orphan and paid the child's expenses for ten years, stopping when the child was old enough to earn her own living. Another raised a year's tuition expenses for a university debater. Others undertook similar ventures and saw them to fruition.

A group does not necessarily go through each of the five steps in the standard agenda automatically. Only the ones pertinent to the problem should be considered. Occasionally the members know what the problem is so that the group begins with the second step instead of describing the problem's nature. Once in a while, the solution is obvious and the group then concentrates on how to put it into operation. Usually the wisest course is to begin with the first step and this is especially true when the group is meeting for the first time to discuss a problem.

The standard agenda is not without weaknesses. It restricts creativity and it stops short of actual implementation of a solution. When rigidly followed, the standard agenda confines proposed solutions to ones which eliminate the causes of a problem. Other possible solutions are not considered, although using a method like brainstorming will help overcome this weakness. Likewise, the standard agenda serves to establish solutions but offers no provisions for implementing them. It works well, therefore, for policy-making groups but not for groups that have to take action on what they propose.

Other Methods of Interaction

In this section we describe some of the selected special forms of group discussion. Special forms of private discussion are explained first. These include the standard agenda — performance system, brainstorming, the problem census and role playing. Then special forms of public discussion are examined, including the buzz group, panel discussion, symposium, dialogue and interview.

Standard Agenda-Performance System

Groups are often charged with the dual responsibility of both solving a problem and carrying out the solution. The standard agenda-performance system (SAPS, for short) provides a method of handling that dual responsibility.[12] It weds the standard agenda, useful for solving problems, with a performance system, a procedure for implementing whatever solution a group settles upon.

SAPS involves ten steps, the first five of which are identical to those in the standard agenda. The remaining five set forth the procedure for executing the solution arrived at in the discussion using the standard agenda. The steps are:

1. *The nature of the problem.*
2. *The causes of the problem.*
3. *The proposed solutions to eliminate the problem.*
4. *The selection of the best solution to the problem.*
5. *The implementation of the best solution. (In this step the group decides to use the performance system procedure called for in the next five steps.)*
6. *The determination of the final objective and its tentative completion date.*
7. *The listing of the events in a time and task sequence that must occur before the final objective is reached.*
8. *The preparation of a diagram showing the events in a time and task sequence.*
9. *The completion of each event.*
10. *An evaluation of each event as it is completed.*

An illustration of how SAPS is used should give a better idea of what each step entails. Let us imagine that Alpha Beta Sigma fraternity needs to raise money to support its service projects. What should the members do to raise funds?

To help them solve this problem in a more logical fashion, the members use the standard agenda. They discuss the nature of their problem and its causes. They propose solutions, and pick the best solution. They decide to manufacture coconut shell buttons, widely used on

---

[12]This method combines the standard agenda with features of PERT)Program Evaluation and Review Technique), a mathematical decision-making method used by the United States Department of Defense in building the Polaris missile. A more elaborate dovetailing of the two methods is in Gerald M. Phillips and Eugene C. Erickson, *Interpersonal Dynamics in the Small Group* (New York: Random House, 1970), 21-24.

sports shirts and resort attire. A ready market exists in the United States and tropical regions throughout the world for all the buttons they can produce at a low price. Coconut shells are in abundance and, in many cases, are free for the asking.

Having decided on the solution through the standard agenda, they next face the matter of putting the solution in operation. Their goal now is to manufacture the buttons in the best way possible. The performance system phase of SAPS begins at this point.

First, they determine their final objective: to have 15,000 coconut shell buttons ready for delivery by June 30. With this objective in mind, they put together a list of all the events that must occur before the objective is reached. They name the events and organize them into a time and job sequence, as shown in the partial schedule in Figure 7-1. The dates represent the expected time of completion for each event.

Most groups using SAPS want to visualize what is supposed to happen at what time and in what sequence. From the list of events, the fraternity can diagram the sequence of events as suggested in Figure

Event Number	Event with Tentative Date	Preceding Events
1	Group discussion meeting adjourns, March 1	0
2	Sale of stock to raise funds Completed, April 1	1
3	Equipment purchased, April 15	2
4	Coconut shells obtained, April 15	2
15	Buttons polished, June 20	14
16	Orders for 15,000 buttons secured, June 25	9
17	Buttons ready for delivery, June 30	15, 16

Figure 7-1. Events in Manufacturing Coconut Buttons

7-2. Note that the numbers in the diagram correspond to the "event number" in the Figure 7-1 Schedule, and that the events are ordered in a time and task sequence. Thus, Event 1 comes first and Event 17 last. Events 3, 4, and 5 can be completed on the same date. Event 6 cannot be started until those three events are complete. Event 7 can begin anytime after Event 2 is completed but Event 7 has to be finished before Event 8 can begin, and so on.

By using SAPS the fraternity members are forced to think through the entire button producing operation before it starts. Once the operation is laid out in a step-by-step fashion, the members know what they have to do to meet their objective. They know they have the equipment, materials, space, and personnel they need. They also have a list of dates by which they must complete each step. They know the steps necessary to manufacture and sell the buttons. In other words, they have a plan ready to be put into operation.

Through SAPS the fraternity may evaluate and review its planning at three critical points: when the events are listed, and when they are placed in a time and task sequence, and when the diagram is prepared. As the group carries out each event, review and evaluation may also be necessary. The time schedule may be upset because one task took longer than anticipated or an event may not be completed because of inadequate machinery, poor training, and insufficient materials. In those cases, adjustments can be made. For example, suppose the fraternity discovers on June 1 that the salesmen have procured orders for 5,000 buttons and the prospects of reaching the 15,000 objective are dim. Production plans can be altered very easily. The buttons have not all been punched out yet and a cut-back can be made. The hole drilling and polishing steps can also be revised at this point. So SAPS has decided advantages of careful planning plus frequent review.

SAPS has several disadvantages. Used to carry out solutions to simple problems, it may bog down the whole operation. SAPS requires several hours of thought from the group planning to use it. With a simple solution that could be carried out in a couple of hours, its use seems burdensome and unnecessary. Occasionally the solution may be complex, but the group may be impatient or enthusiastic and want to jump right into action. SAPS may kill the group's desire. For human relations problems it has little value. But it is effective for complex problems technical in nature consisting of many steps needing to be coordinated.

Figure 7-2. Manufacturing Coconut Buttons: Diagram of Events Showing Time and Task Sequence

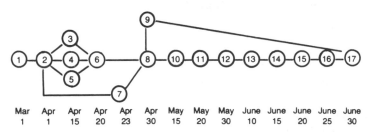

Brainstorming

The effectiveness of both the standard agenda and SAPS can be enhanced by using brainstorming, a method of small group interaction designed to generate a wealth of solutions with no restrictions or limitations on the kinds of solutions offered. Group members can express any ideas that pop into their heads without fear of having them immediately evaluated.

Informally, everyone practices brainstorming, as the following example suggests:

Mother:	Father won't be home for dinner tonight. He said we should eat out. Where should we go?
Coreen:	Any place?
Mother:	What do you suggest?
Dorothy:	The Belle Vue!
Mike:	The Rose Room!
Peter:	The Sky Lounge! A great view of the city!
Beth:	Chinese food! The Taikan-En!
Coreen:	The Azalea Coffee Shop! They've got hamburgers!
Mother:	Whoa! What ideas! Let's see. The Belle Vue is kind of expensive and we'd have to dress up. The Rose Room is on the other side of town—too far. The Sky Lounge only serves steaks. I want something else.
Coreen:	The Azalea!
Beth:	Taikan-En!
Mother:	What should it be? Chinese food or the Azalea's wide range of dishes?
Dorothy:	Azalea!
Mike:	Azalea.
Peter:	I guess I can get a steak at the Azalea.
Mother:	Beth, the Azalea has Chinese food also.
Beth:	O.K. Let's go there.

While the problem illustrated by this example is a simple one, it does demonstrate the brainstorming technique, that is having many ideas freely expressed. With a more complex and serious problem, of course, a more formal procedure would be appropriate, such as in these five steps:

1. *The statement of the problem.* The chairman or moderator announces the problem, gives the necessary background information, and answers questions about the problem if any are asked. In our illustration, the following dialogue represents this first step.

Mother:	Father won't be home for dinner tonight. He said we should eat out. Where should we go?
Coreen:	Any place?
Mother:	What do you suggest?

2. *The appointment of a recorder.* A group member is selected to write down on a chalkboard, or on some kind of a display board visible to all members, any and all ideas suggested by the group.

3. *The brainstorming period.* The members are free to state any ideas that come to mind whether or not they seem impractical, implausible or wild. No criticism is permitted during this period. Evaluation of any idea is suspended. Quantity of ideas is desired; the objective is to

get as many ideas as possible. Ideas already expressed can be built upon or elaborated but they cannot be evaluated. Note in the illustration above that each of the children had a solution: Belle Vue, Rose Room, Sky Lounge, Taikan-En, Azalea Coffee Shop. None were evaluated until all were voiced.

4. *The evaluation period.* At this step, each of the solutions is evaluated in terms of criteria now decided upon. The criteria tend to relate to the advantages and disadvantages of each solution. The advantages center on how well the solution solves the problem. Is the solution inexpensive yet of high quality? Can it be easily carried out? Do a majority of people favor it? The disadvantages stem from high cost, poor quality, impossibility to implement, lack of support, and so on. These evaluative remarks of the mother in the above illustration deal with advantages and disadvantages: *"The Belle Vue is kind of expensive and we'd have to dress up. The Rose Room is on the other side of town — too far. The Sky Lounge only serves steaks. I want something else."*

5. *The selection of the best solution.* The solution which seems to best fit the criteria is agreed upon. The Azalea Coffee Shop apparently found favor because it was near, had a wide range of foods, was informal, and was cheap.

Brainstorming makes it possible for a group to consider a great many solutions to problems without being hampered by restrictions or limitations of any sort. All ideas are accepted without challenge in an atmosphere of informality, permissiveness, and freedom from criticism. The solution eventually agreed upon results from the creative talents of all the members.

Brainstorming has its limitations. While it is a fruitful method of bringing out a great variety of ideas and of encouraging creativity, many of the suggestions produced can be frivolous and even downright ridiculous. Suggestions of this kind can slow down and disrupt the brainstorming session. With groups larger than fifteen members, brainstorming sessions can become unmanageable. Everyone speaks at once in their haste to get their ideas out. Brainstorming also tends to be of limited benefit to newly-formed groups. Since the members do not know each other well enough to express themselves freely, they tend to hold back their ideas. Brainstorming is more productive in small groups whose members have been together for some time.

As was the case with the standard agenda method, brainstorming is primarily suited to policy making groups. Brainstorming can produce some novel and imaginative solutions which, with some further refinement, can serve to eliminate problems. But brainstorming is not a very appropriate method when it comes to implementing a solution. Brainstorming can produce creative solutions, but it is not an effective method for translating those solutions into an organized plan of action.

The Problem Census

The problem census offers a group method of finding out the problems or aspects of a single problem that a group wishes to discuss. Used at the opening of a meeting, it serves to bring out the main issues and is worthwhile when discussion time is limited.

Examine this sample discussion taken from the opening discussion of a Ranier College Club meeting:

President: The business meeting of the Ranier College Club will now come to order. In the past few days, three or four members have mentioned problems to me that they consider to be important to all of us. Each of these problems, as I see them, would take a half hour or more to discuss. We don't have that much time. Also, you might not feel the problems are important. I think you should decide. Therefore, those of you who have problems worth our time, please state them briefly. The secretary will write them on the blackboard. Then we can vote for the one or two we'd like to consider today. Remember, the meeting adjourns in an hour and a half. Does anyone have a problem?

Treasurer: Yes. We have $5.28 in our treasury. Several bills are due. We need to raise some money.

President: OK! A money-raising project! The secretary has written that down. Anything else?

Secretary: I have one. Several members are delinquent in their attendance. The Constitution says they should be expelled. What should I do? There! It's on the board!

Sam Bird: All we have are dry business meetings. We need some good programs — social activities.

Doug Suhm: One of our purposes is to serve others. We haven't had a service project this year. Let's do some service.

President: OK. Four problems. Any more? No? You see them on the board. Which one, or ones, should we take up today and in what order?

Next, the President calls for a show of hands to establish the priority of the problems. The results are: 1. Sam Bird's problem; 2. Doug Suhm's; 3. the Secretary's; and 4. the Treasurer's. The President then begins the discussion with the first ranked problem. Bird's request for programs. Time permitting, the other three will be considered in turn.

The problem census usually take only a few minutes to conduct. It follows these five steps:

1. At the beginning of the meeting or discussion, the chairman presents the idea of the problem census and calls for member responses.

2. The members state the issues, topics, or aspects of a problem they feel are worth discussing.

3. Each problem, issue, or topic is recorded on a chalkboard.

4. By a vote, the members decide which problem they would like to discuss first, second, third, and so forth, until a priority is established.

5. The members discuss each problem in order until the meeting time is exhausted. Those not covered may be carried over to the next meeting.

Some problems are controversial and the members do not want to be identified as the persons responsible for bringing them up. In this case a written statement of the problem can be prepared and turned over to the chairman who reads it to the group without revealing the writer's name. For example, the Ranier's latest project failed and there are several reasons for the failure, all of which relate to an unkept promise to do an important task. To prevent embarrassment or possible retaliation to those who identify the culprits, the President calls for a secret poll and in this way the reasons for the failure, and the people involved, are brought out for discussion without identifying the informers.

Role Playing

A method of group involvement in which several members of a group act out imaginary human relations problems, *role playing* helps the members understand by dramatizing the problems. The dramatization tends to bring out aspects of the problem situations the members might not think about or be reluctant to talk about in an ordinary discussion.

To role play, some members of the group are called upon to act in a brief skit revolving around a problem involving human relationships. The actors are given a description of the problem situation and then they act out the situation, making up their lines as they proceed.

Little structure is given either to the plot or the characters played by the actors, although the problem is clearly defined and the actors have clues about the characters. To illustrate, the following problem was used by an instructor concerned about borrowing and lending class research notes:

> An honest student who does not want to do anything irregular has loaned his research notes for a class assignment to a friend. After the assignment is turned in, the teacher calls him in and accuses him of copying from his friend. Apparently his friend has used the notes in order to do his own assignment and both the lender's and borrower's assignments proved to be similar. What can the honest student do to clear up the accusation without implicating his friend?

To role play this situation, the instructor asked three students to play the roles, one as the lender, one the borrower, and one the teacher.

Two scenes were staged. The first showed the borrower requesting the notes and the other involved the lender being accused by the teacher of copying the paper. Through the dramatization of the incident, the class visualized the human trauma resulting from note-copying. Then, after a few minutes of role playing, the group discussed what occurred during the role playing.

Role playing, when used judiciously, usually creates interest and provides insights into people's behaviors that may otherwise be overlooked. Used frequently, it becomes boring, and it has hazardous elements as well. Caution must be used in choosing the actors. Some people are shy about performing before others and these persons should not be picked for fear of hurting their feelings. Some people enjoy acting before others so much that their performances call attention to the actors themselves and not to the roles they are supposed to be playing. They also should be avoided for fear of making a farce of the dramatization.

The Buzz Group

The previous types of discussion we said are most useful in *private* groups, those meeting without outsiders present as an audience. The next types are most useful in the meetings of *public* groups, ones open to the public in which an audience can participate. The *buzz* group method of discussion is a type which bridges the gap. It can be used in private group meetings and it can be used in meetings involving an audience as we shall see in the explanation which follows.

Several different labels have been attached to this method used by groups, especially larger ones, to facilitate discussion. Besides the buzz group, it is called the discussion cluster, the huddle, and *Phillips 66.* The last name comes from a practice followed by J. Donald Phillips, an authority in adult education at Michigan State University. Professor Phillips divided large groups into smaller groups of six people. Each group had six minutes in which to discuss some phase of the problem facing the larger group. (The Phillips' practice basically describes all types of buzz groups.)

The buzz group, the huddle, and the discussion cluster refer to the method of dividing a group into similar units to discuss a problem or some aspect of it. Thus, for example, a group of fifty could divide into ten sub-groups of five each, a group of fifteen into five sub-groups of three each, a group of six into sub-groups of two each, and numerous other variations are possible.

The method follows this procedure. After the sub-groups are established, the chairman gives each a single question to discuss or problem to solve. The sub-groups discuss their assignment in the time allowed. The results from each sub-group are reported to the large group and acted upon.

For illustration purposes, let us return to an earlier example, let us assume that the President of the Ranier College Club feels the time has come for the membership to talk over ways of raising funds to get the club out of debt. He wants the members to become personally involved and to actively participate in the discussion. But he foresees chaos if he throws the meeting open for general discussion. He decides to use the buzz group method.

After announcing the problem, the President splits the thirty-five members into seven groups of five each. He could ask each group to discuss the same problem or he could have each group discuss some phase of the problem. He elects to have the group discuss the same problem: "How can the Ranier College Club raise funds to pay its bills?"

He gives the seven groups twenty minutes to arrive at plans to raise funds. Each plan should be described in as much detail as possible. At the end of the stated time, a reporter from each group describes the group's plans to the entire membership. After the plans are stated, the President calls for an open discussion of ten minutes or so. The discussion is followed by a vote to decide what plan the members will support.

The buzz group method encourages participation from everyone in any size of audience. While a person may hesitate to actively take part when a group is large, he or she is less reluctant to do so if the group is composed of a few members. If the thirty-five Ranier College Club members discussed the fund-raising problem together, only the more forceful ones may get to speak. In the buzz groups, each member can voice his opinions if he wishes.

The buzz group method is useful when the chairman desires to focus attention on a number of specific, limited aspects of a problem. Each buzz group can deal with a single aspect and report its findings to the larger group for action. The Ranier College President did not choose to do so, but he could have broken the fund-raising question into smaller parts. After announcing the major problem, the need to raise funds, he might have assigned two buzz groups the topic "How to raise funds by selling things." Two other groups could deal with how to raise funds through conducting dances, shows, or movie programs. The remaining groups could work on how to raise funds by offering club member's services to cut grass, do odd jobs, and so forth.

The Panel Discussion

The panel discussion is a small group discussion conducted before an audience for a predetermined amount of time. It is normally followed by audience participation in the form of questions or comments. The function of the discussion is to provide the audience with expert analyses of a problem in order to increase their understanding of the problem's significant issues. The audience participation period permits the audience's members to express their views, to call for expert answers to their questions, to present additional information, and to vent their feelings.

To understand how a panel discussion proceeds, assume that a school conducts a weekly discussion program one afternoon a week. Topics of student interest are discussed, such as the value of grades, the need for a dress code, student-teacher relations, and a variety of other school concerns. The discussion follows the panel method and proceeds as follows:

1. After the topic is agreed upon and the panel members selected, they investigate the topic as much as possible in the time available. They become familiar with the topic's nature, analyzing and evaluating it to discover its principal features and its strong and weak points.

2. When the discussion is held, they arrange themselves before the audience. The chairman, who introduces the participants, announces the topic, and conducts the audience participation part of the discussion, sits on the side.

The Panel Discussion is Conducted Before an Audience

3. Before the audience, the panel carries on its discussion. There are no speeches as such. The panel members speak informally together about the topic with each one talking for no more than a minute or two at a time.

4. After thirty-five minutes or so of talk by the panel, the audience is invited to participate. They ask questions, supply additional information, and make other comments for approximately fifteen minutes. Adjournment follows.

The Symposium

Another method staged for an audience is the symposium, a series of short speeches on various aspects of the same topic delivered by several speakers. It, too, is followed by audience participation. Each speaker without interruption presents a different aspect of, or proposes a different solution to the problem introduced by the chairman of the symposium. The speeches serve to stimulate audience reaction which may come in the form of questions or comments. Like the members of a discussion panel, the symposium speakers should be experts in the problem area.

The procedure followed in organizing and conducting a symposium is quite simple. Each participant prepares a speech on one aspect of the chosen or assigned topic. For example, a group of students could conduct a spring symposium on summer jobs for students. One speaker could be appointed to research the ways of looking for and applying for summer employment. In her talk, she could discuss where to look for employment and how to get in touch with and interest prospective employers. Another speaker could talk about local opportunities, discussing specific businesses which usually employ students. Another speaker could talk about how to set up a private summer business, one which offers services like odd jobs, painting, lawn cutting, and the like. After each speaker has had his or her say, a chairman could summarize the three speeches. After the summary, the audience could participate by asking questions and offering comments or additional information.

The Symposium

In a symposium, the various speakers do not debate by arguing against each other's point of view. The entire purpose of a symposium is to enlighten the audience by splitting up a topic into manageable portions and then having knowledgeable people provide information on the portion assigned to them.

The Dialogue

Two persons are featured in this form of discussion, with both sharing the responsibility for the content material. The discussion usually is held in front of an audience. Speeches are avoided. Instead, the two converse together about some vital problem, a controversial issue, or a proposed plan of action. After a designated period, the audience may participate by questioning the performers or commenting on the subject matter.

One school club, the Bay View CO-ED Club, used the dialogue as a means of gaining information on subjects of vital concern to the members. The club membership consisted of young women and men who met for social purposes. While some of their meetings were fun-filled, others featured programs on more serious topics — contemporary events, social etiquette, interpersonal relations, for instance. The dialogue proved to be an effective way of examining the club's more serious concerns. It created interest and was easy to carry out. For presenting facts, opinions, and points of view, it allows for direct and informal communication; and, when experts are used, it heightens understanding of the subject matter. For example, the Bay View CO—ED Club planned a program on interpersonal relations and invited two experts to take part in a dialogue on the subject.

The dialogue, which was recorded, included this exchange between the two, Ms. Adler and Mr. Hawkins:

Ms. Adler: *Young men I talk to often mention the costs of a date. I know they spend a lot of money sometimes.*

Mr. Hawkins: *Young men may get a little unhappy about the money they spend on a date. A prom can run them a hundred dollars. They think they have to buy flowers, rent a tuxedo, get a car and pay for the gas, go someplace after. That plus a haircut, prom tickets, tips, runs into some money. And they frequently don't want to go. If they don't their girl will be mad, go with someone else, or they'll feel left out. They work hard to earn the money, and worse, if it's the first time out with the girl, they may never see her again.*

Ms. Adler: *Some events are costly — and occasionally a young man goes over his head. Many girls are content with inexpensive evenings and are eager to share costs. The splashy affairs are wonderful once in a while to get ready for and look back on. But the girl has expenses — and usually no way of earning money. For most girls, it's a once in a lifetime event and they enjoy the bustle of getting ready. A dutch-treat coke, movie, or television at home with friends is just as welcome. Attention is important, not always money.*

Mr. Hawkins: *Money does constantly come up so maybe we should check it out more deeply. I have some results of polls I have taken among the guys in our clubs. By presenting their ideas, you and I will have some issues to sink our teeth in.*

Ms. Adler: *Yes. And I have some information on dates from national magazine surveys. You go over your polls first. Then we can talk about my surveys.*

As these two people talked, they presented both the young men's and young women's side of the issue in a factual way without arguing about it. They did not debate the issue. They merely discussed it informally. Their discussion of the financial aspects of dating took about fifteen minutes of the total dialogue time of forty-five minutes, and it brought forth many audience questions and reactions.

The Interview

While the dialogue participants contribute equally to the discussion, the interview between two people before an audience restricts participation. One person, the interviewer, questions the other person, usually an expert in the problem area under scrutiny. The interviewer cannot be afraid to ask questions of the expert, and he or she should have some knowledge about the subject matter in order to know what to ask. In some instances the audience may respond when the interview is completed.

A common variation on the basic two-person interview is the group interview made popular by such television programs as "Meet the Press" and "Face the Nation." In such interviews, one person — usually a prominent political personality — is questioned by a number of people, usually newspaper editors or reporters.

Like the dialogue, the basic purpose of the interview is to enlighten the audience. The interviewer or interviewers serve as the audience's representatives. Their job is to get important or enlightening information from the person being interviewed. The interviewer has to be able to stay with a question until he or she is satisfied that the audience has an answer or an insight. One question should smoothly lead to another. The purpose of an interview is defeated if there is no thread which runs through the line of questions and responses.

Summary

In this chapter we described the principal types of small group interaction, placing emphasis on learning groups and problem-solving groups but covering other types as well. Because the learning and the problem-solving types are the most common, we explained both the processes involved in their use and the formats for organizing learning and problem-solving discussions.

The other types of discussion were categorized as being useful either in private discussions or in public discussions. Private discussions include those types of small group interaction which are held without the presence of outsiders and do not involve participation on the part of non-members. The ones described were the standard agenda — performance system, brain-storming, the problem census, and role playing. Public discussions include those types which take place before an audience and in some way engage participation from the audience who may or may not be members of the group. The buzz group, panel discussion, symposium, dialogue and interview were the types covered under the public category. The buzz group we recognized as a discussion type which could prove useful for both public and private discussions, especially for private groups with a large number of members.

Questions:

1. What are the three principal types of learning groups? How do they differ?
2. What are the three types of problems? How do they differ?
3. List some topics that you would find interesting for symposia.
4. With what small group units are you presently involved? What techniques do you find most useful for solving problems in the respective groups? How does the nature of each group effect the methods of problem solving?

*One of the clearest explanations for beginning
speakers is presented by Paul Soper in his text on
public speaking. Dr. Soper presents a plan for
developing the speech topic, preparing and
presenting the speech as well as a discussion of
four types of speech preparation.*

The Beginning Speeches

Paul L. Soper

Booker T. Washington, the eminent Negro teacher and speaker of
two generations ago, told the following story, which has point for the
beginning speaker:

> A ship lost at sea for many days suddenly sighted a friendly vessel.
> From the mast of the unfortunate vessel was seen the signal: 'Water,
> water; we die of thirst!' The answer from the friendly vessel at once
> came back: 'Cast down your bucket where you are.' A second time the
> signal, 'Water, water; send us water!' ran up from the distressed ves-
> sel, and was answered: 'Cast down your bucket where you are!' And a
> third and fourth signal for water was answered: 'Cast down your
> bucket where you are.' The captain of the distressed vessel, at last
> heeding the injuction, cast down his bucket, and it came up full of
> fresh, sparkling water from the mouth of the Amazon River.

You are to be a public speaker. The task seems complex and for-
bidding. How to begin? What to say? How to act? The answer is:
begin where you are. Begin with what you are and what you already
know.

Franklin Delano Roosevelt's advice to his son James on how to make
a public speech was, 'Be sincere, be brief, be seated.' This was an
oversimplification. Nevertheless, one of the best speeches the author of
this book ever heard was the brief opening speech of a student in a
beginning course in speech. The talk lasted three and a half minutes. It
seemed not half that long. But everyone in the room completely lost

From the book *Basic Public Speaking*, third Edition by Paul L. Soper. Published by Oxford
University Press, 1963. Reprinted by permission of the author.

himself in that speech, and for days afterward relived what had been said. The speaker described an act of heroism of a friend of his during a battle of World War II. He did not "orate." He did not use elaborate phrasing or flowery language. He was simply sincere. He let the quiet bravery of his friend speak for itself. The details of the event were real and vivid. They were concise. He described a small grove of trees in a ravine between two hills in western Germany; a bleak late afternoon in December; two American soldiers waiting for darkness to fall, so that they could get back to their own lines—one (the speaker) lying on his back beneath a bush with a bullet in his chest, the other crouched beside him. The speaker described the look of exhaustion on his friend's face; the feelings of fear as footsteps on dry leaves became louder, and then, after an eternity, receded. He described how, after night had fallen, his friend half dragged and half carried him two miles, through underbrush and across roads guarded by German sentries, and finally, how, nearly dead from weariness, they were surprised, almost shot, and then carried to safety by a scouting party from their own company.

This was genuine communication. It held the audience, partly because of the interest of the subject matter, but also because the speaker had (1) a subject about which he could speak sincerely, (2) a real urge to communicate it, (3) the self-confidence that goes with solid preparation, and (4) a friendly and modest manner.

To get off to a good start as a speaker, do not clutter your mind with many rules and methods, which will only worry you if taken 'at one gulp." Instead, find a stimulating subject, work on it until it comes to life, and keep it alive as you impart it to your listeners. The following suggestions on developing, rehearsing, and presenting the speech will be the only directions necessary for your first appearance before your class audience.

A. Developing the Speech

1. Selecting the Subject

Select a subject connected with your own experience, and on which, if necessary, you can get further information in the library or elsewhere. The subject should, when properly developed, be interesting both to you and to your audience. It should not be broad or complex. Most subjects are too general; almost never is one too specific or narrow. Examples of suitable subjects for short beginning talks are listed at the end of this chapter.

2. Deciding What You Are to Accomplish with Your Subject

Do you want only to explain, describe, or narrate something? Or do you want to change your listeners' opinions or persuade them to do something? To make sure you know what you are setting out to do, write out your purpose in the form of a complete sentence. If your subject were "Mountain Climbing," you might state your purpose as follows: "I am going to show you how to scale mountain peaks." This would be mainly an expository or informative purpose rather than a persuasive one. But if your purpose were to show that your audience should not attempt difficult mountain climbing without training, your purpose would be persuasive, for your intention would be to influence the action of your audience. Most beginning speeches are informative rather than persuasive.

3. Gathering the Materials

Unless your talk is based entirely on your own experience — and it seldom can be — find materials from more than one outside source. Read not one but several magazine articles, or get information from more than one book. Get various writers' points of view and compare them. Go to *The Reader's Guide to Periodical Literature* in the reference room of the library and find out what magazine articles are listed under your subject or a related heading. For information in books, go to the card catalogue. Talk over your subject with other people, and take notes on ideas that occur to you and on facts that you read.

4. Introducing the Speech

You should prepare a few opening remarks that will arouse interest and state and clarify your purpose. For example:

> Do you have good reasons for buying the things you buy? Or are you, like millions of other consumers, an unknowing victim of perhaps the most cleverly influential and insidious force in modern life — advertising?
>
> What is advertising? It is propaganda. I shall demonstrate wherein advertisers employ ingenious propaganda devices to entice you and other prospective buyers.

The last sentence, above, is the statement of the specific purpose of your talk. It projects and limits its development, and you will be ready to build the body of the speech only after this purpose is clearly fixed in your mind.

5. Developing the Body of the Speech

In building the body of your talk, do everything possible to make the organization and supporting materials interesting and clear. Organize the main ideas into as simple, concrete, and orderly a plan as you can. Discard everything that is not relevant to your purpose. Define unfamiliar terms; use as many concrete examples as possible; present the testimony of experts whenever needed for support of assertions; and ask questions to point up transitions from one thought to another.

Outline the body of the speech according to a system of main heads and subheads. Make sure that the main heads directly support the specific purpose, and that the subheads support the main heads. If your instructor prefers, use what is called a topical, or key-phrase, outline.

I. The testimonial
   A. Forms of
      1. That of expert
      2. That of prominent person
      3. That of "the man in the street"
   B. Examples of
      1. Expert on golf clubs
      2. Prominent person on Blue Cross
      3. "Man in the street" on health studio
II. The band-wagon technique
   A. Definition
   B. Examples of
      1. Ford
      2. Pontiac
      3. Royal Globe Insurance
III. The association technique
   A. Things we like
      1. Glamourous women
      2. Gay times
   B. Things we dislike
      1. Auto accidents
      2. Bad luck in fishing

As set forth in a sentence outline, the same material would be developed more explicity and completely, as follows:

I. The testimonial is an important propaganda device.
   A. It takes three leading forms.
      1. It may be testimony by an expert.
      2. It may be testimony by a prominent person.
      3. It may be testimony by "the man in the street."
   B. These forms of testimony appear in many advertisements.
      1. A case of expert testimony is Sam Snead's support of Strata-Bloc golf clubs.
      2. The prominent industrialist, F.C. Foy, testifies that Blue Cross "really works!"

      3. "The man in the street"—Hugh Watts, a bookkeeper—says he developed a perfect physique at Cosmopolitan Health Studio.

II. The band-wagon technique is particularly effective.

    A. It implies, "Everybody does it. Why not you?"

    B. Examples of this technique are:

      1. "Watch the Fords go by."

      2. "Haven't you been a Pontiac spectator long enough?"

      3. "Wherever you go Royal Globe is there."

III. The association technique is also frequently used.

    A. Things we like are associated with a product.

      1. Pictures of glamorous women using Palmolive soap exemplify this sort of appeal.

      2. A picture of a group of people having a gay time drinking Taylor wine illustrates this technique.

    B. Things we dislike are associated with not buying a product.

      1. Auto accidents are associated with not using Goodrich tires.

      2. Bad luck in outboard fishing is associated with not using an Evinrude outboard motor.

6. Concluding the Speech

Conclude your talk with a brief summary of the main heads, and perhaps also a quotation or illustration that will support your purpose.

> Numerous hard-to-detect propaganda devices are being used on us every day. Three of the most important and insidious are the testimonial, the band-wagon, and the association techniques.
>
> According to the Institute for Propaganda Analysis, we are fooled by these propaganda techniques because "They appeal to our emotions rather than to our reason." This may be fun for us and profitable for advertisers. But it is more fun, and more profitable for us, to know how these techniques work.

B. Rehearsing the Speech

Everybody remarks the ease of professional actors on the stage. When this is true, as it should be, of amateur actors as well, people often say that so-and-so "just acted naturally." But they did not see him in the first rehearsal. Actors practice every movement and every line probably thirty times, some of the movements and lines sixty or a hundred times. Many public speeches are merely first rehearsals, which is one reason why plays are generally preferred to speeches.

You will perhaps be ready for an oral rehearsal of your speech when you have organized it as suggested in Section A above. Your instructor may want you to write it out word for word and memorize it. But, as is explained in the last section of this chapter, most speeches for training are neither written nor memorized. Find a time when you may use some room without being disturbed, and, standing as if you were addressing your audience, go through the entire speech. You may need to use fairly detailed notes the first time. Then go through the speech again, with the aid of only a few key words or phrases to mark the main divisions of thought.

After you have tried out the speech as a whole, practice those parts of it that give you the most trouble. At this stage, be very experimental. It would be helpful to rehearse at least parts of the speech before a mirror. Do you appear to be sincerely communicating ideas? Is your posture erect? Do you have ease and freedom of movement? If you feel constricted, take limbering-up exercises.

Then listen to your voice. Do you pause as often as you need to, to get a new supply of breath, to relieve tension, and to think? Do you stress important words and yet avoid an unrelieved hammering out of ideas? When all the parts of the speech are well in mind, again rehearse it as a whole, practicing to develop a sense of real communication with your listeners. You may at this stage get a roommate or classmate to serve as a practice audience. In any case, try to imagine the audience and occasion of the actual presentation.

c. Presenting the Speech

When you are called upon to speak, walk calmly to the speaker's position, address the chairman, and then turn toward your listeners and address them in appropriate words such as "Ladies and Gentlemen" or "Fellow Students." Establish eye contact with your audience at once, and maintain it throughout the entire speech. Do not ignore any of your listeners. If you take a position beside or behind the speaker's stand, avoid leaning on it. If you feel that you cannot get along without notes, you may, with your instructor's permission, have a few key words written large on a sheet of paper that you place on the speaker's stand, or on a small card that you hold in your hand. But do not look at your notes excpet when necessary. Speak louder than you feel you should. The chances are that then your volume of voice will be about right. But do not worry about how you sound, look, or feel. Keep your mind on the business of getting your ideas across to your audience.

d. Developing Self-Confidence

When going before an audience, you have "nothing to fear but fear itself." Self-consciousness is by no means uncommon among beginning speakers. But few college students are seriously troubled with stage fright. In general, they are less frightened of an audience than are older people. And probably not more than one student in a thousand is unable to overcome stage fright.

Speakers, no less than athletes and race horses, need to be keyed up. Many famous speakers and actors confess that they are always nervous or frightened just before "going on." Apparently their fear does them no harm. Once your initial nervousness is over, your mind and body will be "toned up" to do a better job than if you had at first been relaxed.

The best remedy for fear and self-consciousness is persistent practice in speaking. But the following suggestions may help:

1. Apply reason to the cause of your fear.

Nobody will hurt you. Your listeners are friendly and want you to succeed. They will understand your difficulties, especially in a speech class, where everybody is "in the same boat."

2. Come before your audience fully prepared.

You have reason to be afraid if, at the last possible moment, you have hurriedly read over or "thought up" some ideas, and then scribbled some random notes about them on a piece of paper. Being prepared means knowing your subject so well, through study and oral practice, that when you stand before your audience you will not have to worry about ideas or words.

3. Assume a confidence you may not feel.

An appearance of confidence is contagious. If you give your audience a chance to feel confidence in you, you will begin to feel it in yourself. If necessary, take a few relaxing breaths before you get up to speak. Be especially deliberative in your opening remarks. If you obey your first impulse—to hurry—you will only aggravate your nervousness. Pause as often as you need to. Do not feel embarrassed if some of your words fail to come out as you had hoped they would. Your listeners won't worry about it if you don't.

4. Overcome fear through action.

The football player gets over his opening-gun jitters by energetic movement. You must do likewise. Don't be afraid to "let yourself go." You will only increase tenseness by holding yourself in. Besides, you will learn through trial and error. Although you may not feel like doing so, utter vigorously the confident phrases you prepared in the privacy of your own room. Your audience will be well impressed by them. Everybody who has acquired skill in speech, or in anything else, has been willing to try and to try hard. You must do the same. You will never break down the barriers to vigorous speech and action without a courageous exercise of will.

e. Types of Preparation and Delivery

The material of this section need not particularly concern you in the preparation of your first speeches. But before you have proceeded very far in the course, you should know the four types of speech preparation and delivery and the advantages and disadvantages of each.

Speeches may be (1) written out in full and *memorized*; (2) written out in full and read from *manuscript*; (3) *impromptu*; or (4) *extemporaneous*. The memorized speech is most often used as a lecture or sermon or on special occasions of formal oratory. But it may be used for any occasion, provided the speaker has time for memorizing. The manuscript speech is most frequently used to present subject matter requiring precise wording, as in many research papers and reports. The impromptu talk is one that is presented without any special preparation, usually on a moment's notice, at informal gatherings, group discussions, and committee meetings.

The extemporaneous speech, which is the type most often used for speech training, is prepared but neither written out nor memorized. The speaker's objectives are worked out, however; his materials and the way he is to present them are planned; and the structure of the speech is organized in detail and outlined. The extemporaneous speech may also — and ordinarily should — be rehearsed orally.

The distinctions drawn between these four types of speeches are, of course, somewhat academic. An impromptu speech might be better prepared than an extemporaneous or memorized speech if the person speaking impromptu has had years of experience in the field of his speech subject. There are also many speeches that, although supposedly prepared, are in fact no more than impromptu. Many extemporaneous speeches may, through repeated presentations, become almost wholly memorized. Follow the advice of your instructor regarding which type of speech to use. He may want you to have experience in all four types. You should, however understand the advantages and disadvantages of each.

1. *Advantages and Disadvantages of the Memorized Speech*

The memorized speech and the manuscript speech are often the most advisable kinds to use in political speaking and in all situations in which inadvertences of wording may be very costly to the speaker. The memorized speech, like the manuscript speech, encourages careful preparation of the wording. But the written words may not be those best suited for oral presentation. Written discourse is almost always less direct, less simple, and less emphatic than oral discourse. Besides, most speakers are reluctant to alter their words, once they are 'fixed' on paper. The memorized speech is easier to rehearse than the extemporaneous speech, and its length may be accurately gauged. When perfectly memorized, it leaves the speaker's mind free for the task of communicating. But memorization is usually not perfect, so that the danger of "stalling" is greater than in the extemporaneous speech. Exact wording is harder to recall than ideas, and disruption in the flow of memorized words is especially distracting.

2. *Advantages and Disadvantages of the Manuscript Speech*

The only advantage of the manuscript speech over the memorized one is that the former puts no strain on the speaker's memory. The disadvantages of the manuscript speech are that, except when used by a person exceptionally well trained in reading, it sounds "read" rather than truly communicative; the manuscript also constitutes a barrier between the speaker and his audience, for his eyes must be upon the written words, except for intermittent, furtive glances, which may be distracting and may cause jerky reading. The main reason for avoiding the manuscript speech in a training course is that you will never acquire complete communicativeness through reading. For exercises in the use of the voice, however, or for proficiency in reading, manuscript speaking is often valuable.

3. *Advantages and Disadvantages of the Impromptu Speech*

Mark Twain implied the severe limitations of impromptu speaking when he said, "It usually takes me more than three weeks to prepare a good impromptu speech." No one, except when called on to speak without prior warning, should resort to spur-of-the-minute concoctions as a substitute for prepared speeches. It is a practice that encourages glibness as a substitute for solid content. Impromptu speaking does train students to think on their feet, however, and since most people are occasionally asked to speak impromptu, some experience of the kind aids self-assurance. Group discussion, of course, necessarily involves some impromptu speaking.

4. *Advantages and Disadvantages of the Extemporaneous Speech*

The advantages of the extemporaneous speech have already been indicated: it trains the beginning speaker to organize ideas for oral utterance, to think on his feet, to communicate, to speak conversationally, and to adapt his speech to his audience. On the other hand, it may discourage a careful use of language and encourage too great reliance upon inspiration. The extemporaneous speaker often leaves out important matter or strays from the point, and often talks overtime.

Despite its liability of misuse, the benefits of extemporaneous speaking make it the most commonly used type in the basic speech course. The results are best when the speech has been outlined in detail and rehearsed orally. Beginning speakers should have the opening and closing remarks especially well in mind, since these are the most difficult to extemporize.

Some instructors forbid the use of any notes. Certainly you should do without them if you can. But if you do use notes, they should consist, as has already been suggested, of only key words or phrases, written large enough so that they can be easily read.

Questions:

1. What are the advantages and disadvantages of the four types of speech preparation and delivery? Which do you find most useful?

2. Which type of preparation would you use to prepare for a symposium speech? Why?

3. What is stage fright? Is it ever beneficial to have stage fright? How does one overcome it?

4. Do you remember the last time you prepared a speech? Which was more difficult—the preparation or the delivery? Was the experience pleasant or painful?

5. Should every college student be required to have a course in public speaking? Why or why not?

*Marcus Fabius Quintilian (c.A.D. 35 - 95) was the
first teacher of rhetoric in Rome to receive an official salary. His last years were spent in writing*
Institutes of Oratory *in which appears this famous
description of the ideal speaker.*

The Ideal Orator

Quintilian

Let the orator, then, whom I propose to form, be such a one as is
characterized by the definition of Marcus Cato, *a good man skilled in
speaking.*

But the requisite which Cato has placed first in this definition, that
an orator should be *a good man,* is naturally of more estimation and importance than the other. It is of importance than an orator should be
good, because, should the power of speaking be a support to evil,
nothing would be more pernicious than eloquence alike to public
concerns and private, and I myself, who, as far as in my power, strive
to contribute something to the faculty of the orator, should deserve
very ill of the world, since I should furnish arms, not for soldiers, but
for robbers. May I not draw an argument from the condition of mankind? Nature herself, in bestowing on man that which she seems to
have granted him preeminently, and by which she seems to have distinguished us from all other animals, would have acted, not as a
parent, but as a step-mother, if she had designed the faculty of speech
to be the promoter of crime, the oppressor of innocence, and the enemy
of truth; for it would have been better for us to have been born dumb,
and to have been left destitute of reasoning powers, than to have received endowments from providence only to turn them to the destruction of one another.

From *Institutes of Oratory: or, Education of an Orator,* trans. John Selby Watson,
Bohn's Classical Library (London: Bell, 1891), Vol. II, Book XII, pp. 391-392, 402.

My judgment carries me still further; for I not only say that he who would answer my idea of an orator, must be a good man, but that no man, unless he be good, can ever be an orator.

Questions

1. Do you agree with Quintilian's last statement that unless a man be good, he can never be an orator? Give examples of speakers to support your position.
2. List the ideal orators you have either heard or heard of.
3. Find the meanings of the terms *ethos* and *source credibility*.

The following three speeches represent different purposes, occasions and attitudes:

Kennedy's Inaugural Address

Advice to Youth

"Cooperation — An Opportunity and a Challenge"

Inaugural Address

John F. Kennedy

(Delivered at Washington, D.C., 20 January 1961.)

Vice President Johnson, Mr. Speaker, Mr. Chief Justice, President Eisenhower, Vice President Nixon, President Truman, reverend clergy, fellow citizens: We observe today not a victory of party but a celebration of freedom-symbolizing an end as well as a beginning—signifying renewal as well as change. For I have sworn before you and Almighty God the same solemn oath our forebears prescribed nearly a century and three-quarters ago.

The world is very different now. For man holds in his mortal hands the power to abolish all forms of human poverty and all forms of human life. And yet the same revolutionary beliefs for which our forebears fought are still at issue around the globe—the belief that the rights of man come not from the generosity of the state but from the hand of God.

We dare not forget today that we are the heirs of that first revolution. Let the word go forth from this time and place, to friend and foe alike, that the torch has been passed to a new generation of Americans —born in this century, tempered by war, disciplined by a hard and bitter peace, proud of our ancient heritage—and unwilling to witness or permit the slow undoing of those human rights to which this nation has always been committed, and to which we are committed today at home and around the world.

Let every nation know, whether it wishes us well or ill, that we shall pay any price, bear any burden, meet any hardship, support any friend, oppose any foe to assure the survival and the success of liberty.

This much we pledge—and more.

To those old allies whose cultural and spiritual origins we share, we pledge the loyalty of faithful friends. United, there is little we cannot do in a host of new cooperative ventures. Divided, there is little we can do —for we dare not meet a powerful challenge at odds and split asunder.

To those new states whom we welcome to the ranks of the free, we pledge our word that one form of colonial control shall not have passed away merely to be replaced by a far more iron tyranny. We shall not always expect to find them supporting our view. But we shall always hope to find them strongly supporting their own freedom—and to remember that, in the past, those who foolishly sought power by riding the back of the tiger ended up inside.

To those people in the huts and villages of half the globe struggling to break the bonds of mass misery, we pledge our best efforts to help them help themselves, for whatever .period is required—not because the Communists may be doing it, not because we seek their votes, but because it is right. If a free society cannot help the many who are poor, it cannot save the few who are rich.

To our sister republics south of our border, we offer a special pledge —to convert our good words into good deeds—in a new alliance for progress—to assist free men and free governments in casting off the chains of poverty. But this peaceful revolution of hope cannot become the prey of hostile powers. Let all our neighbors know that we shall join with them to oppose aggression or subversion anywhere in the Americas. And let every other power know that this hemisphere intends to remain the master of its own house.

To that world assembly of sovereign states, the United Nations, our last best hope in an age where the instruments of war have far outpaced the instruments of peace, we renew our pledge of support—to prevent it from becoming merely a forum for invective—to strengthen its shield of the new and the weak—and to enlarge the area in which its writ may run.

Finally, to those nations who would make themselves our adversary, we offer not a pledge but a request: that both sides begin anew the quest for peace, before the dark powers of destruction unleashed by science engulf all humanity in planned or accidental self-destruction.

We dare not tempt them with weakness. For only when our arms are sufficient beyond doubt can we be certain beyond doubt that they will never be employed.

But neither can two great and powerful groups of nations take comfort from our present course—both sides overburdened by the cost of modern weapons, both rightly alarmed by the steady spread of the deadly atom, yet both racing to alter that uncertain balance of terror that stays the hand of mankind's final war.

So let us begin anew—remembering on both sides that civility is not a sign of weakness, and sincerity is always subject to proof. Let us never negotiate out of fear. But let us never fear to negotiate.

Let both sides explore what problems unite us instead of belaboring those problems which divide us.

Let both sides, for the first time, formulate serious and precise proposals for the inspection and control of arms — and bring the absolute power to destroy other nations under the absolute control of all nations.

Let both sides seek to invoke the wonders of science instead of its terrors. Together let us explore the stars, conquer the deserts, eradicate disease, tap the ocean depths and encourage the arts and commerce.

Let both sides unite to heed in all corners of the earth the command of Isaiah — to "undo the heavy burdens...(and) let the oppressed go free."

And if a beach-head of co-operation may push back the jungles of suspicion, let both sides join in creating a new endeavor not a new balance of power, but a new world of law, where the strong are just and the weak secure and the peace preserved.

All this will not be finished in the first 100 days. Nor will it be finished in the first 1,000 days, nor in the life of this Administration, nor ever perpaps in our lifetime on this planet. But let us begin.

In your hands, my fellow citizens, more than mine, will rest the final success or failure of our course. Since this country was founded, each generation of Americans has been summoned to give testimony to its national loyalty. The graves of young Americans who answered the call to service surround the globe.

Now the trumpet summons us again — not as a call to bear arms, though arms we need — not as a call to battle, though embattled we are — but a call to bear the burden of a long twilight stuggle year in and year out "rejoicing in hope, patient in tribulation" — a struggle against the common enemies of man: tyranny, poverty, disease, and war itself.

Can we forge against these enemies a grand and global alliance, north and south, east and west, that can assure a more fruitful life for all mankind? Will you join in that historic effort?

In the long history of the world, only a few generations have been granted the role of defending freedom in its hour of maximum danger. I do not shrink from this responsibility — I welcome it. I do not believe that any of us would exchange places with any other people or any other generation. The energy, the faith, the devotion which we bring to this endeavor will light our country and all who serve it — and the glow from that fire can truly light the world.

And so, my fellow Americans: ask not what your country can do for you — ask what you can do for your country.

My fellow citizens of the world: ask not what America will do for you, but what together we can do for the freedom of man.

Finally, whether you are citizens of America or citizens of the world, ask of us here the same high standards of strength and sacrifice which we ask of you. With a good conscience our only sure reward, with history the final judge of our deeds, let us go forth to lead the land we love, asking His blessing and His help, but knowing that here on earth God's work must truly be our own.

Advice to Youth

Mark Twain

(Saturday Morning Club, Boston, April 15, 1882)

Being told I would be expected to talk here, I inquired what sort of a talk I ought to make. They said it should be something suitable to youth — something didactic, instructive; or something in the nature of good advice. Very well; I have a few things in my mind which I have often longed to say for the instruction of the young; for it is in one's tender early years that such things will best take root and be most enduring and most valuable. First, then, I will say to you, my young friends — and say it beseechingly, urgingly —.

Always obey your parents, when they are present. This is the best policy in the long run; because if you don't, they will make you. Most parents think they know better than you do; and you can generally make more by humoring that superstition than you can by acting on your own better judgment.

Be respectful to your superiors, if you have any; also to strangers, and sometimes to others. If a person offends you, and you are in doubt as to whether it was intentional or not, do not resort to extreme measures; simply watch your chance and hit him with a brick. That will be sufficient. If you shall find that he had not intended any offense, come out frankly and confess yourself in the wrong when you struck him; acknowledge it like a man, and say you didn't mean to. Yes, always avoid violence; in this age of charity and kindness, the time has gone by for such things. Leave dynamite to the low and unrefined.

Go to bed early, get up early — this is wise. Some authorities say get up with one thing, some with another. But a lark is really the best thing to get up with. It gives you a splendid reputation with everybody to know that you get up with the lark; and if you get the right kind of a lark, and work at him right, you can easily train him to get up at half-past nine, every time — it is no trick at all.

Now as to the matter of lying. You want to be very careful about lying; otherwise you are nearly sure to get caught. Once caught, you can never again be, in the eyes of the good and the pure, what you were before. Many a young person has injured himself permanently through a single clumsy and ill-finished lie, the result of carelessness born of incomplete training. Some authorities hold that the young ought not to lie at all. That, of course, is putting it rather stronger than necessary; still, while I cannot go quite so far as that, I do maintain, and I believe I am right, that the young ought to be temperate in the use of this great art until practice and experience shall give them that confidence, elegance and precision which alone can make the accomplishment graceful and

211

profitable. Patience, diligence, painstaking attention to detail — these are the requirements; these, in time, will make the student perfect; upon these, and upon these only, may he rely as the sure foundation for future eminence. Think what tedious years of study, thought, practice, experience, went to the equipment of that peerless old master who was able to impose upon the whole world the lofty and sounding maxim that "Truth is mighty and will prevail" — the most majestic compound fracture of fact which any of woman born has yet achieved. For the history of our race, and each individual's experience, are sown thick with evidences that a truth is not hard to kill, and that a lie well told is immortal. There in Boston is a monument to the who discovered anesthesia; many people are aware, in these latter days, that that man didn't discover it at all, but stole the discovery from another man. Is this truth mighty, and will it prevail? Ah, no, my hearers, the monument is made of hardy material, but the lie it tells will outlast it a million years. An awkward, feeble, leaky lie is a thing which you ought to make it your unceasing study to avoid; such a lie as that has no more real permanence than an average truth. Why, you might as well tell the truth at once and be done with it. A feeble, stupid, preposterous lie will not live two years — except it be a slander upon somebody. It is indestructible, then, of course, but that is no merit of yours. A final word: begin your practice of this gracious and beautiful art early — begin now. If I had begun earlier, I could have learned how.

Never handle firearms carelessly. The sorrow and suffering that have been caused through the innocent but heedless handling of firearms by the young! Only four days ago, right in the next farmhouse to the one where I am spending the summer, a mother, old and gray and sweet, one of the loveliest spirits in the land, was sitting at her work, when her young son crept in and got down an old, battered, rusty gun which had not been touched for many years, and was supposed not to be loaded, and pointed it at her, laughing and threatening to shoot. In her fright she ran screaming and pleading toward the door on the other side of the room; but as she passed him he placed the gun almost against her very breast and pulled the trigger! He had supposed it was not loaded. And he was right: it wasn't. So there wasn't any harm done. It is the only case of the kind I ever heard of. Therefore, just the same, don't you meddle with old unloaded firearms; they are the most deadly and unerring things that have ever been created by man. You don't have to take any pains at all, with them; you don't have to have a rest, you don't have to have any sights on the gun, you don't have to take aim, even. No, you just pick out a relative and bang away, and you are sure to get him. A youth who can't hit a cathedral at thirty yards with a Gatling gun in three-quarters of an hour, can take up an old empty musket and bag his mother every time, at a hundred. Think what Waterloo would have been if one of the armies had been boys armed with old rusty muskets supposed not to be loaded, and the other army had been composed of their female relations. The very thought of it makes me shudder.

There are many sorts of books; but good ones are the sort for the young to read. Remember that. They are a great, an inestimable, an unspeakable means of improvement. Therefore be careful in your selection, my young friends; be very careful; confine yourself exclusively to Roberson's *Sermons*, Baxter's *Saint's Rest*, *The Innocents Abroad*, and works of that kind.

But I have said enough. I hope you will treasure the instructions which I have given you, and make them a guide to your feet and a light to your understanding. Build your character thoughtfully and painstakingly upon these precepts; and by and by, when you have got it built, you will be surprised and gratified to see how nicely and sharply it resembles everybody else's.

Cooperation

An Opportunity and a Challenge

An Address

It is a pleasure and a privilege to be here with you today. These great annual meetings are always an inspiration to me, and double so today. After that glowing introduction by our toastmaster I must confess, however, that I'd like to turn the tables and tell a little story on Chuck. When I say it's about the nineteenth hole and a certain gentleman whose baritone was cracked, those of you who were at the Atlanta conference last year will know what I mean. But I won't tell it. Chuck Forbes is too good a friend of mine and seriously, I know full well we all realize what a tower of strength his yeoman service has been to the association in these trying years.

Yes, gentlemen, trying times. So you'll pardon me if I cast aside the glib reverberations of glittering generalties and the soothing syrup of sugar-coated platitudes and put it to you the only way I can, straight English.

We're losing the battle!!

From every corner the people are being weaned away from the doctrine of the Founding Fathers. They are being detoured from the high-speed highways of progress by the utopian highwaymen.

Now, the man on the street is a pretty savvy fellow. Don't sell him short. Joe Doakes may be fooled for a while, but in the end he wants no part of the mumbo jumbo the global sabateurs are trying to sell him. After all, he is an American.

But he has to be told.

And we're not telling him!

Now let me say that I do not wish to turn the clock back. None of us do. All forward-looking businessmen see themselves as partners in a team in which the worker is a full-fledged member. I regard our employees as our greatest business asset, and I am sure, mindful as I am of the towering potentials of purposeful energy in this group of clear-sighted leaders, that, in the final analysis, it is the rock foundation of your policies, too.

But the team can't put the ball across for a first down just by pushing it. The guards and the tackles can't do their job if the quarter-back doesn't let them in on the play. And we, the quarter-backs, are muffing the ball.

Reprinted from "The Language of Business," *Fortune*, Vol. 42, No. 5 (November 1950), p. 114.

How are we to go over for a touchdown? My friends, this is the $64 question. I don't know the answers. I am just a plain spoken business-man. I am not a soothsayer. I have no secret crystal ball. But I do know one thing: before we round the curve into the home-stretch we have a job to do. It will not be easy. I offer no panaceas or nostrums. Instead I would like to suggest that the real key to our problem lies in the appli-cation of the three E's. What are the three E's? **Enterprise! Endeavor! Effort!**

Each and every one of us must appoint himself a salesman—yes, a missionary, if you will—and get out and do some real grass roots selling. And when we hit the dirt, let's not forget the customers—the greatest asset any business has.

Now, much has been done already. But let's not fool ourselves: the surface, as our chairman has so wisely said, has hardly been scratched. The program is still in its infancy. So let me give it to you straight from the shoulder. The full implication, gentlemen, depends on us.

So let's get on the beam! In the cracker-barrel fashion, let's get down to earth. In good plain talk the man on the street can understand, let's remind Joe Doakes that the best helping hand he will ever find is the one at the end of his own shirt sleeve.

We have the know-how.

With sights set high, let's go over the top!

(The speech is not a parody. It is a loose compilation based on a syste-matic count of the expression and constructions most commonly used in current U.S. business speeches. Included are the sixty principle clichés of reverse gobbledegook.)

Questions:
1. Someone has said that a memorable quote can ruin a good speech. Explain this statement. Does it apply to the Kennedy speech? Is this a good example of speechmaking? Why or why not?
2. On what occasion would the Twain speech be appropriate?
3. Have you ever heard a speech similar to "Cooperation—An Oppor-tunity and a Challenge"? If you have, do you remember your initial reactions at the time of presentation?
4. What is the specific purpose of each speech? To what degree do you think each speech achieved its purpose?
5. Have someone read these speeches aloud to you. How does your reaction differ when hearing a speech and when reading a speech?

Speech

Carl Sandburg

There was
What we call "words",
a lot of language,
syllables
each syllable made of air.

Then there was
silence,
no talk at all,
no more syllables
shaped by living tongues
out of wandering air.

Thus all tongues
slowly talk themselves
into silence.

From *Honey and Salt,* © 1963 by Carl Sandburg. Reprinted by permission of Harcourt Brace Jovanovich, Inc.